WITHDRAWN

HARVARD LIBRARY

WITHDRAWN

SAVING FAITH

SAVING FAITH

Making Religious Pluralism
an American Value at the
Dawn of the Secular Age

David Mislin

CORNELL UNIVERSITY PRESS   ITHACA AND LONDON

Copyright © 2015 by Cornell University

All rights reserved. Except for brief quotations in a review, this book, or parts thereof, must not be reproduced in any form without permission in writing from the publisher. For information, address Cornell University Press, Sage House, 512 East State Street, Ithaca, New York 14850.

First published 2015 by Cornell University Press

Printed in the United States of America

Library of Congress Cataloging-in-Publication Data

Mislin, David, author.
 Saving faith : making religious pluralism an American value at the dawn of the secular age / David Mislin.
   pages cm
 Includes bibliographical references and index.
 ISBN 978-0-8014-5394-6 (cloth : alk. paper)
 1. Religious pluralism—United States—History. 2. Protestantism—United States—History. 3. Liberalism (Religion) —Protestant churches—History. 4. Christianity and other religions—United States—History. 5. United States—Church history—19th century. 6. United States—Church history—20th century I. Title.

BL2525.M57 2015
277.3'08—dc23
                                                                    2015012100

Cornell University Press strives to use environmentally responsible suppliers and materials to the fullest extent possible in the publishing of its books. Such materials include vegetable-based, low-VOC inks and acid-free papers that are recycled, totally chlorine-free, or partly composed of nonwood fibers. For further information, visit our website at www.cornellpress.cornell.edu.

Cloth printing   10 9 8 7 6 5 4 3 2 1

Contents

Introduction: The Gilded Age Crisis of Faith and the
Reevaluation of Religious Pluralism ... 1

1. Twilight Faith: The Embrace of Doubt as the Embrace
of Diversity ... 14

2. Correcting Elijah's Mistake: The Liberal Protestant
Embrace of Comparative Religion ... 40

3. An Expansive Kingdom of God: The Articulation of
Protestant-Catholic-Jewish Commonality ... 63

4. Drawing Together: The Cooperative Impulse in Liberal
Religious Thought ... 90

5. A Larger Vision: The Quest for Christian Unity ... 119

6. Proclaiming Common Ground: The Goodwill Movement
and the Shaping of a Jewish-Christian America ... 140

Epilogue: Making Religious Pluralism an American Value ... 163

Notes ... 167
Selected Bibliography ... 199
Acknowledgments ... 209
Index ... 211

SAVING FAITH

Introduction

THE GILDED AGE CRISIS OF FAITH AND THE REEVALUATION OF RELIGIOUS PLURALISM

One Sunday in the spring of 1897, the Congregationalist minister Lyman Abbott received new members into his congregation at the highbrow Plymouth Church in Brooklyn. In that morning's sermon, Abbott extolled the virtues of his congregation and suggested that the new congregants had chosen well in electing to join Plymouth. Yet strikingly absent from his message was any suggestion that people gained some great spiritual advantage through their affiliation with the church. Indeed, Abbott forcefully proclaimed the opposite, declaring that neither his church, nor his denomination, nor even Christianity could claim to be the only place where one might learn religious truth. "In entering into Plymouth Church you are not entering into a fellowship which teaches you to look upon all other churches as inferior," Abbott remarked. Those hearing the sermon quickly understood just how broad the clergyman's definition of a "church" was. "All religions—Jewish and Christian, Roman Catholic and Protestant, Pagan and Biblical—*all* religions involve aspirations after God which God has stirred in the human heart."[1] Essential religious lessons, Abbott observed, could be learned in other Protestant churches and denominations, as well as in Catholic, Jewish, and even nonmonotheistic communities.

Few Protestant ministers of the late nineteenth century enjoyed Lyman Abbott's prestige and influence. There were, of course, more famous clergymen, such as the evangelist Dwight Moody, who frequently attracted crowds numbering in the thousands at his revival meetings throughout the nation. But when it came to the respectable, educated middle-class members of major Protestant denominations in the United States, Abbott held enormous sway. Having begun his career as a Congregationalist minister, he shifted for a time to literary pursuits, working for *Harper's* before joining Henry Ward Beecher's *Christian Union*. When Beecher—himself perhaps the most prominent American minister during the 1860s and 1870s—retired from his pastorate at Plymouth Church, he appointed Abbott as his successor. Abbott thus returned to ministry in one of the nation's most celebrated pulpits. Abbott also became editor of the *Christian Union*, which—renamed the *Outlook*—became a leading source of general interest and religious news. By the end of the nineteenth century, it boasted a nationwide readership of nearly a hundred thousand people. As a major player in the political and cultural worlds as well as in the religious sphere, Abbott enjoyed close personal connections with numerous public figures—including Theodore Roosevelt, who for a time served as a contributing editor at the *Outlook*.[2]

Lyman Abbott used his enormous influence to spread his message of liberal Protestant thought. He was a staunch proponent of both evolutionary theory and rigorous biblical scholarship. Even more significant, perhaps, was his inclusive view of religious difference. He believed that Protestant Christianity could not claim the exclusive possession of religious truth. The same sentiments that he expressed to the new members at Plymouth Church recurred in his rhetoric time and again. In 1912, when he delivered the commencement address at Clark College, Abbott proclaimed an essential commonality among Protestants, Catholics, Jews, and even certain skeptics. "We are all aiming for the same place," he declared. "We are seeking the same end, if we only know it."[3]

In his affirmations of commonality among belief systems and his acknowledgment that non-Protestant traditions contained valuable messages, Lyman Abbott offered a crucial endorsement of the religious pluralism of the late nineteenth- and early twentieth-century United States.[4] Nor was he alone in doing so. In the decades between 1870 and 1930, dozens of other liberal Protestant ministers and theologians similarly embraced and affirmed the diversity of faiths in the nation. These prominent liberals set aside exclusivist claims to the sole possession of truth and instead began to cast Catholics, Jews, Hindus, Buddhists, Muslims, and even doubters as adherents of valid systems of belief and important partners in the project of securing a future for religious commitment in the United States.[5]

The changing views of Abbott and his fellow Protestant liberals had their roots in a seismic cultural shift that began in the decade after the Civil War and presented unprecedented challenges to what historians have labeled America's "Protestant establishment."[6] During the early decades of the nation's history, Protestant churches had enjoyed nearly unquestioned control over the nation's religious life. Even after the disestablishment of the last remaining state church in 1833,

Protestant communities and their leaders exerted enormous influence on government and public institutions. Much to the chagrin of the growing Roman Catholic population, the curricula in many of the newly founded public school systems featured readings from the Protestant King James Bible and lessons that valorized Protestants' role in history while depicting the Catholic Church as backward and corrupt.[7] Nowhere was Protestantism's wider influence more apparent than during the Civil War, when the humanitarian work of the army was essentially outsourced to Protestant reform organizations. During the conflict, numerous clergymen enjoyed even greater access to political power as they received appointments to government commissions. "In God We Trust" made its appearance on currency, and some religious leaders grew so convinced of the diminishing separation between Protestant institutions and the federal government that they advocated amending the Constitution to include references to "Almighty God as the source of all authority and power in civil government" and to "Jesus Christ as the Ruler among nations."[8]

If the Civil War represented the heyday of Protestant America, what followed proved to be anything but. Not only did the much-promoted "Sovereignty of God" amendment fail to win passage, but by the mid-1870s, members of the Protestant establishment felt besieged on all sides. In a sermon commemorating the nation's centenary, the Congregationalist minister Newman Smyth (who, like Lyman Abbott, would fervently espouse his appreciation of religious pluralism) insisted that the nation had reached a critical turning point. Although its first century had witnessed the "expansive vigor of Protestant institutions," those very institutions now faced a grave challenge from the forces of "secularism." Smyth was hardly optimistic about the state of religion in the United States. "Have we not already drifted far enough toward a civil life divorced from all sanctions of religion, and a liberty as empty and brazen as marked the French Revolution?" he asked.[9]

The mere mention of France conjured up all sorts of dire images in the minds of nineteenth-century Americans, including what in Smyth's time was the recent memory of the anticlericalism of the Paris Commune, during which rebels had executed the city's archbishop and more than thirty priests. Both the French Revolution and the Paris Commune were ingrained in the American conscience as examples of liberty run amok and religion paying the price. Now, Smyth warned, these same secular forces were loose in the United States. They threatened to "emasculate our school system of moral vigor," rid all traces of God "from the halls of legislation and the courts of jurisprudence," and put an end to the sacredness of the Sabbath by making "all days of the week alike before the law."[10]

Smyth was hardly alone in offering such a grave assessment about the future of American faith. "There are wide indications that religion is at low tide in this country," declared a Presbyterian minister in western Pennsylvania.[11] A New England Congregationalist observed that "the church is void of children," while "the act of worship" had come to be viewed as "of small importance for any." Unless things changed, the next generation would come of age in "a state properly described as atheistic."[12] These concerns found their way onto the pages of widely read periodicals. "Among our advanced thinkers," declared an author of an essay in the popular *North American Review*, "all the old religions, including Christianity . . . must soon die," while another writer predicted that a "settled state of unbelief" would soon take hold.[13] In the *Outlook*, Lyman Abbott invoked the biblical tale of a scorned prophet to emphasize the declining stature of the clergy. "In the olden times every boy bowed reverently," he declared. "Now the minister gets along very well if the boy does not cry out, 'Go up, thou baldhead.'"[14]

These dire warnings seem quite puzzling because, on the surface, they hardly comported with reality. An ever-growing number of Americans attended church during the late nineteenth century. Indeed, the years between 1870 and 1926 witnessed an enormous increase in the percentage of the population that belonged to a church. Monetary contributions also rose significantly.[15] Nor, indeed, was there anything particularly new in these melodramatic pronouncements about declining religiosity. The Puritans had barely stepped off their boats before they began issuing jeremiads lamenting the moribund state of faith in colonial New England. In the succeeding two and a half centuries, there was hardly a moment when—at least to hear clergy tell it—American faith was secure.[16]

Yet there was a difference in the religious anxiety of the late nineteenth century. In part, as several scholars have noted, the force of these Protestants' protestations reflected their own sense of personal failing. Ministers like Abbott came of age at the height of the Second Great Awakening, when powerful conversion narratives and claims of firm commitment to one's religious belief were commonplace. Abbott and his cohort, however, never attained the same sense of assurance that had seemingly come easily to their parents. Moreover, these Protestant leaders entered their careers amid the religious fervor of the Civil War. But war is by definition a liminal experience, and the intensity of faith commitments demonstrated at the height of combat proved impossible to sustain in the normality of peacetime.[17] Unattainable expectations, however, do not sufficiently explain the anxious rhetoric of liberal Protestants during the Gilded Age. Something occurred that caused these Protestants to look past their growing congregations and expanding coffers and to question the future of religious faith in the United States.[18]

That something was the encounter of American culture with strange and unfamiliar aspects of modern life, which radically altered the nature of anxieties about religious commitment in three important ways. First, challenges to religion morphed beyond critiques of specific Christian doctrines into assaults on the very foundations of faith. "Today the very life of Christianity, nay, the very being of God is vociferously called into question," noted one observer.[19] Protestant leaders employed a variety of terms—including "irreligion," "skepticism," "materialism," "infidelity," "unbelief," and "indifference"—to describe the antireligious currents of the day. But beneath these varied (and not entirely synonymous terms) lay the shared conviction that secular forces challenged not merely Christian tenets but the foundation of all religious belief.

To many observers, these forces had their origin in new scientific and philosophical theories that sought to define existence strictly in terms of natural forces. Foremost among these was the evolutionary philosophy that followed in the wake of Darwinian theory and seemed to many to leave little room for belief in the soul or human free will. According to the theories advanced by the British thinker Herbert Spencer and his American disciples, God was nothing more than an "unknowable" force that would forever elude description. So, too, advances in biblical scholarship undermined many inherited verities about scripture. Many Americans believed that this knowledge rendered all traditional forms of belief outmoded. As one Protestant observer noted with contempt, these people had concluded that traditional religious values were "superfluous, or even obstructive," and abandoned them in favor of new "systems of individual ethics."[20]

The extent to which it appeared that essential aspects of religious belief and not just peculiar doctrines of Protestantism were under assault was further revealed by the fact that Catholics and Jews offered the same grim outlook as liberal Protestants did. One Roman Catholic bishop lamented that "the spirit of secularism is in the air," and "the great body even of nominal Christians live as though their religion were a dream or an untruth."[21] Meanwhile, the editors of the widely read *Catholic World* warned their readers that "the tempest of irreligion blows strident and strong," and nothing short of the "weal" or "woe" of "the generations to come" was at stake.[22]

Jewish observers were no less worried about declining levels of religious commitment. A Reform rabbi decried the "notorious fact" that a growing number of Jews showed little interest in joining a synagogue. Their absence, he insisted, represented a symptom of "sheer indifferentism."[23] Another observer noted that "the spirit of indifference which has been prominent in the Christian Church has appeared among the Jews," in part because "religious training is no longer what it was in the Jewish home."[24]

The second element of late nineteenth-century American life that explains liberal Protestants' anxieties was the increased cosmopolitanism—at least in the major urban areas in which these liberals lived and worked. The spike in immigration during the final third of the century greatly augmented an already visible and influential population of Roman Catholics and Jews. Moreover, the combination of heightened interest in Asia and a growing population of Chinese and Japanese immigrants brought increased awareness of Hinduism and Buddhism. Similar opportunities for travel also introduced Americans to Islam, or, in the parlance of the day, Mohammedanism.

Beyond merely expanding what scholars have labeled the American "religious marketplace," this increased visibility of non-Protestant faiths led many Protestants to question their beliefs. For some, the apparent similarities between Christianity and other religions confirmed their suspicion that all faith traditions were of human origin and none contained any timeless truths. For others, Hinduism, Islam, and Buddhism offered a spiritual fulfillment that they found lacking in Protestant Christianity.

The final development that explains liberal Protestants' anxieties was the emergence of a distinctly modern culture in the United States. As ever-growing numbers of Americans abandoned the rural areas of their childhoods for the nation's burgeoning metropolises, they found plenty of activities to occupy their time. To the great annoyance of Protestant leaders, few of these activities had anything to do with religion or churchgoing. Membership statistics notwithstanding, it seemed that American churches were losing their hold over a generation of young, successful urbanites. These people had not become "opposed to religion" in the same way that adherents of Spencer's philosophy had, but they had nevertheless, one minister observed, ceased to be "interested in what the church has to say."[25] Protestant churches could not compete with the enchantments of the modern city and a growing "preference for diversion to worship."[26]

This confluence of factors—novel scientific and philosophical theories, the increased visibility of other religions, and competition from popular cultural institutions and leisure activities—contributed to the widespread perception that, in the words of one minister, "Christianity is doomed."[27] Given the numerical and financial strength of their institutions, it seems highly improbable that many Protestant leaders actually thought that their entire belief system was truly on the verge of complete collapse. Yet it seems equally impossible to doubt their conviction that they faced grave challenges.

In responding to these challenges, American Protestants had two options. The first was to retrench to orthodox belief and refuse to make any accommodation to modern thought. This was the approach adopted by many influential Protestants, especially (though certainly not exclusively) in rural parts of the United States. As the nineteenth century drew to a close, calls increased for strict adherence to biblical teaching and an avoidance of mainstream modern culture. These sentiments would, of course, underlie the rise of fundamentalism in the early twentieth century.[28]

But there was another option. While modernity dramatically altered the nature of the challenges to Protestants' religiosity, it also provided critical new tools by which liberal leaders could work to save American faith. Approaches that previous generations had viewed as akin to selling out now represented acceptable means of accommodating Protestant Christianity to modern life. It was thus possible to sustain one's beliefs without rejecting scientific theories, philosophical ideas, and cultural values that had enormous appeal. Liberal Protestants employed three particular strategies to prove that modern thought and culture need not prove inimical to religious faith.

Scholars of American religion have thoroughly documented two of these three strategies. In the first approach, clergy and theologians who were particularly concerned about the perceived conflict between religion and science formulated what became known as the New Theology. These Protestant intellectuals encouraged the free use of reason and the acceptance of modern thought, insisting that God intended faith and knowledge to be complementary. At the same time, liberal Protestants sought to bring their churches and institutions into closer alignment with the cultural values around them. This second method, exemplified by the Social Gospel movement, was marked by efforts by ministers to address topics of popular concern and to play an active role in political and social reform movements. The effort to link religion and popular culture also inspired churches to make better use of the nascent advertising industry and growing mass media.[29]

There was a third and perhaps more significant strategy that liberal Protestants employed in their effort to reconcile faith with modern culture. Unlike the New Theology and the Social Gospel, however, this final method has been largely overlooked. Amid the clamor of arguments that science had undermined the foundations of religion, that other faith traditions disproved the uniqueness of Christianity, and that religious practice was incompatible with a sophisticated modern life, these liberals began to expand their conception of belief. They proclaimed that one could maintain religious faith while harboring significant doubts. They affirmed that Buddhism, Hinduism, and Islam were valid religions that offered valuable teachings. Perhaps most significantly, they emphasized their many points of commonality with Catholics and Jews. They abandoned centuries of anti-Catholicism and anti-Semitism and looked to their Catholic and Jewish neighbors as critical partners in their campaign to ensure a future for religion in American life.

The cumulative effect of this shift in liberal Protestants' attitudes was profound. By the early twentieth century, some of the nation's most prominent clergymen had entirely rejected the long-standing claim that Protestantism—or, indeed, particular Protestant denominations—had a monopoly on true religion. Instead, these influential liberals began to celebrate the religious diversity of the United States. For the first time, it became possible for respectable, middle-class mainline Protestants not merely to tolerate America's religious pluralism but to fully and wholeheartedly embrace it.

There were crucial limits to this new understanding of pluralism, many of which help to explain why this transformation in Protestant thought has largely escaped the attention of historians. First, although many liberal Protestants became enthusiastic about diversity, they were by no means the relativists that many of their intellectual descendants would become. Even as they affirmed the beliefs and practices of Catholics, Jews, doubters, and, albeit to a lesser extent, Hindus, Buddhists, and Muslims, none of the religious leaders considered here thought that all religions were equally valid. Indeed, they saw relativistic claims as a symptom of the decline of traditional religious commitments. Yet the absence of relativism does not negate the significance of this shift in liberal Protestant thought. It is entirely possible to celebrate the diversity of beliefs in society while still holding a preference for one's own convictions or holding that one's religious perspective is superior. It was precisely this distinction that led Lyman Abbott to urge his congregants "who live in the latter glory of the kingdom of God . . . to look with respect upon all dimmer revelations as true utterances of him, imperfect . . . but real."[30] The same view came to be widely articulated by liberal clergy and theologians during the late nineteenth and early twentieth centuries.

A second important limit that has tended to obscure the extent of liberal Protestants' embrace of religious pluralism was their inability to appreciate the full implications of their ideas and rhetoric. They notably did not extend their newfound appreciation of religious difference into the realms of racial and ethnic diversity. Indeed, many of the staunchest voices in support of religious pluralism—once again Lyman Abbott provides an instructive example—were also the loudest champions of Anglo-Saxonism. This highly racialized worldview situated white, Anglo-Saxon civilization as the apex of human development. The insistence on preserving such sharp distinctions between religion and other forms of difference is all the more striking given that—especially in the case of Jews—it is difficult to clearly delineate between religious and cultural identity. Yet liberal Protestants like Abbott held fast to this distinction. They no longer required non-Protestants to convert, but they still insisted that immigrants acculturate and adopt the standards of white, middle-class Americans. Moreover, these liberals largely ignored African Americans and their religious commitments in their pronouncements on the beneficial nature of pluralism.

From a twenty-first-century perspective, it is difficult to understand how these Protestant leaders could become so inclusive in their views of religious difference without more seriously questioning their presumption of racial and cultural superiority. To be sure, some did slowly and tentatively question their assumptions about human difference. For the most part, though, it was not until the 1920s that discussions of religious pluralism began to inspire deeper reflection and broader conversations about race, culture, and ethnicity. Nevertheless, however incongruous this mental state might seem to the modern reader, the inconsistency in liberal Protestants' thought should not obscure the very real transformation in their understanding of religious pluralism.

Saving Faith traces the process by which anxieties about declining religious commitments prompted two generations of liberal Protestant leaders to affirm the diversity of beliefs and practices around them. Chapter 1 explores the origins of this process, as the seemingly rampant skepticism of the Gilded Age led many Protestants to reexamine the nature of doubt. Drawing on two theological ideas—the "person of Jesus" as the essential element of Christianity and the progressive nature of revelation—these liberals effectively created the category of the Christian doubter. This strategy provided the theological template for liberals' reconsiderations of other forms of religious diversity.

Chapter 2 examines the flip side of doubt, namely, the growing popularity of spiritual exploration and religious comparison that flourished in the late nineteenth century. By once again employing the model of revelation as a gradual, unfolding process, liberal Protestants not only affirmed non-Christian traditions as valid religions, but they also recast these belief systems as evidence of the superior truth found in Christian teaching. This new outlook fostered widespread interest in comparative religious study, a phenomenon enacted on a massive scale at the 1893 World's Parliament of Religions.

The remaining four chapters consider how liberal Protestants' newfound enthusiasm for pluralism affected their relationships with one another and with Roman Catholics and Jews, the two religious groups with whom they interacted most frequently. Chapter 3 chronicles the emergence of a sense of commonality among liberal Protestants, Jews, and Catholics as they faced the shared challenges of secular critique and conservative backlash. Chapter 4 examines the practical manifestations of these changed attitudes, as liberal Protestants sought to unite in efforts to restore their influence and combat the impression that churches did little besides squabble. Some of these cooperative endeavors led to the establishment of institutions that included Catholics and Jews. Even when they did not, members of the three faith traditions found ample opportunities to cooperate in support of political and social causes.

Chapter 5 explores an unsuccessful campaign in the early twentieth century to reunite Protestantism and Catholicism into a single Christian church. While this effort was limited to a small cohort of intellectuals and was almost certainly doomed from the start, it is highly instructive of both the aspirations and limits of new views on diversity. Chapter 6 assesses the goodwill movement of the 1920s, which sought to create national institutions to foster greater sympathy among Protestants, Catholics, and Jews. It was this movement that began to expand discussions of pluralism beyond the realm of the religious and into areas of race and ethnicity.

There are some important limits to this study, and they seem worth acknowledging at the outset. First and foremost, this is a study of an elite cohort of Protestant clergy, theologians, and highly educated laity who all adopted the core tenets of theological liberalism and who belonged to one of the larger, more established denominations (primarily Congregationalists, Episcopalians, and Presbyterians, with a smaller number of Baptists, Methodists, and Disciples of Christ). In their support for religious pluralism, these liberals certainly did not represent all of American Protestantism. Conservative exclusivism remained widespread in churches throughout the United States. For every minister who affirmed doubt or who sought closer ties with Catholics and Jews, there were many others who unabashedly expressed anti-Catholic and anti-Semitic rhetoric while demanding absolute conviction from their congregations.

Nor is there compelling evidence that the inclusive views espoused by liberal ministers widely filtered down to local churches. As I have shown when evidence allows, there are some indications that at least a few congregations followed their respected and charismatic ministers in adopting the liberal outlook on diversity. But these instances seem to have been limited to major urban areas, such as New York and Boston. In other parts of the country, liberal ministers struggled to lead congregations whose members were far more conservative than they were.

Indeed, region and geography present another important limit on this study. For the most part, the transformation in liberal Protestants' views on religious pluralism occurred in places where religious pluralism mattered. Reevaluations of diversity resulted from direct encounters with committed believers of other faiths. Contrary to popular belief, this did not exclusively mean urban areas. Residents of small towns, especially those that were home to industries that employed immigrant labor, could find themselves face to face with religious difference. By and large, though, the clergy and theologians who embraced pluralism were situated in the cities and larger towns of New England, the mid-Atlantic, and the developed sections of the upper Midwest (roughly a large swath stretching from Pittsburgh through northern Ohio to Chicago and upward to the Twin Cities). The lack of modernization in the post-Reconstruction South, coupled with the inability of theological liberalism to gain significant traction in the region until well into the twentieth century, explains why southern voices are absent from this study.[31]

These disclaimers should not minimize the significance of this study. While liberal clergy and theologians did not speak for all (or perhaps even the majority) of American Protestantism, they nevertheless exerted an outsized influence within their denominations and in the culture at large. The years between 1870 and 1930 witnessed liberals' gradual takeover of the nation's major denominations. These ministers enjoyed friendships with cultural luminaries and access to political power. Liberals like Lyman Abbott, Newman Smyth, Washington Gladden, and countless others who appear in this study guided mainline Protestantism at a historical moment when its institutions had the power to sway public opinion. The values they helped to foster among Protestant elites would ultimately gain a wider hearing as mainline leaders exerted an even greater influence on American culture at large during the middle decades of the twentieth century.[32]

Ultimately, as numerous scholars have noted, it would take several more decades before the idealization of religious pluralism took root in American society at large. The force of decades of anti-Semitism, anti-Catholicism, and outright ignorance and disdain for non-Western traditions would take considerable time to overcome. Widespread acceptance of the "tri-faith" ideal and the emergence of the conception of "Protestant-Catholic-Jew" America did not occur until after World War II.[33]

Yet the enthusiasm for religious pluralism expressed by this limited group of liberal Protestant clergy provided a crucial precedent for the shift in attitudes that occurred at midcentury. The two generations of liberal leaders who guided Protestantism from the 1870s through the 1930s made it respectable for American churchgoers to affirm the beliefs and practices of non-Protestants. They made it possible to conceive of religious diversity as something that made the United States a better place rather than something that kept it from reaching its full potential.

More significantly, these liberals created both the language and the institutions that provided the foundation for the broader acceptance of religious pluralism. The rhetoric of "brotherhood," which emerged as the central metaphor of efforts to cultivate interfaith sympathy among Protestants, Catholics, and Jews during the 1930s and 1940s, appeared time and again in spoken and written output of liberal Protestants during the late nineteenth and early twentieth centuries. More significantly, many of the organizations created by the earlier generations of liberal Protestant leaders—notably the Federal Council of Churches and the various "goodwill" groups of the 1920s—were instrumental in spurring the broader culture to adopt the liberal perspective on religious diversity. In a few cases, particularly those of liberals in the Federal Council of Churches who became involved in the National Conference of Christians and Jews, we can trace a direct intellectual and institutional lineage from affirmations of pluralism in the early 1900s through the efforts to popularize the vision of a Judeo-Christian America at mid-century.

Saving Faith thus chronicles the often-overlooked prologue to the more familiar story of the embrace of pluralism and multiculturalism in the United States during the second half of the twentieth century.[34] The well-documented shift that occurred around World War II represented the culmination of a project begun by a vanguard of liberals a half-century earlier.

But this is also an important story in its own right. The significance of this study is not limited to its revision of our understanding of the historical processes and timeline by and on which liberal Protestants reevaluated their views about religious pluralism. An examination of the period between 1870 and 1930 offers enormous insight into numerous facets of Protestant liberalism and the relationship between these Protestant liberals and the rest of American society.

Most critically, it is clear that we must view the embrace of religious pluralism as a core tenet of liberal theology, not an ancillary element of it. Acknowledging this reality is all the more important because the late nineteenth and early twentieth centuries marked a critical period in the development of American religious liberalism. These decades witnessed the movement of liberal theology from the periphery to the center of major denominations. By the early 1900s, liberals constituted the majority of elite clergy and theologians who controlled the nation's largest and most influential Protestant denominations. Thus the movement of liberal theology to the mainstream of American Protestantism coincided with the emergence of liberals' new outlook on pluralism. Enthusiasm for diversity would thus be firmly ensconced in the liberal platform for decades to come.

Equally important is the role that an acceptance of doubt played in the evolution of views on pluralism. Doubt is central to discussions of faith in the modern world, yet few scholars have traced the connection between views on doubt and views on diversity. Those who have done so have adopted the view that religious diversity breeds doubt by exposing religious believers to competing faith traditions. But at this crucial moment in the development of American religious liberalism, the relationship ran in the other direction. Liberal Protestants affirmed questioning and uncertainty as normal, healthy elements of a religious life, and they accepted the possibility that many believers would never escape their doubts. By the end of the nineteenth century, liberals considered doubt to be completely compatible with faith. This acceptance of uncertainly led liberal Protestants to acknowledge the ambiguity of all religious conviction, which made it possible for them to hold their own claims in abeyance while they considered the teachings of Catholicism, Judaism, and other faith traditions. Not only did the years between

1870 and 1930 mark the time when liberal Protestants made peace with doubt (which in its own right is a lasting legacy of this period, given that this view of doubt has been championed by generations of liberal voices ever since), but the acceptance of religious uncertainty also provided the major impetus for reevaluations of pluralism.

For contemporary readers, this study offers a reminder of an obvious but important point. Throughout much of American history, the nation's religious establishment was liberal. In the contemporary United States, we have grown accustomed to thinking of the most influential religious institutions as being conservative and using their influence to advance a braking force against social progress in a range of areas. Moreover, we have grown accustomed to interfaith alliances in support of conservative causes. But it has not always been so. For the better part of a century, the most powerful religious institutions and their leaders were liberals—and, in fact, were more liberal than the average American. With a few exceptions, these early interfaith efforts did not seek to enforce a traditionalist conservatism. Rather, they sought to push American society toward their founders' progressive idealism.

The stories told here provide a needed reminder of a rich history of activism in support of liberal causes that brought Protestants together with their neighbors of other faith traditions. This phenomenon began in the late nineteenth century and shaped American life for much of the twentieth—ultimately making possible transformative movements like the civil rights campaigns of the 1950s and 1960s.

At its core, this is the history of two generations of Protestant leaders who perceived that the old ways of believing had become obsolete. Much like their counterparts in the political sphere, the mugwump and Progressive reformers, these liberal Protestants found the best method of preserving their cultural authority to be extending that authority to others.[35] Thus, in their effort to preserve American religion, they greatly expanded their conception of those believers who could rightly be termed religious. These Protestants were thus critical actors in proactively shaping the future values of the United States. They were not, as a long-standing scholarly stereotype has suggested, mere sellouts to the values of a modern, consumerist culture.[36] Rather, I argue, this generation of liberal leaders was marked by its commitment to thoughtful, intentional theological innovation.

As liberal Protestants reflected on the diversity of faiths and beliefs around them, they expressed an ideal that would ultimately redefine how ordinary American believers understood the nation's religious landscape. In 1897, it was a novelty for Lyman Abbott to tell his congregants that all religions contained important truths. Fifty years later, because of the precedent established by Abbott and his generation, such sentiments would become pervasive.

1

TWILIGHT FAITH
The Embrace of Doubt as the Embrace of Diversity

"There is a large class of honest inquirers," noted the Congregationalist minister Washington Gladden, "who are troubled, more or less by certain aspects of revelation, but who are trying to find their way into the light." At face value, this was hardly a remarkable observation. Protestant ministers and theologians had long stressed the importance of overcoming doubt and working from ambiguity to certainty in one's religious convictions. But Gladden was not sure that believers would always find their way into the light and overcome their doubts. He thus thought it crucial that his congregants know how to sustain their faith commitments even amid profound spiritual uncertainty. The key, said Gladden, was for Protestant churchgoers to be—in Alfred Lord Tennyson's famous distinction—"honest doubters" rather than cynical nonbelievers.

Gladden assured his congregants that doubt did not necessarily signal the beginning of an inevitable slide into unbelief. Questioning conducted in the right spirit would not prove detrimental to faith. Those who were "ready to welcome any ray that breaks into their darkness" and who retained a commitment to faith despite their uncertainty met with Gladden's approval. Those "whose unbelief is willful or passionate or sullen" did not. The God Gladden worshipped welcomed doubt. The "honest scrutiny of the foundations of faith is far more pleasing to God than the blind and bigoted credulousness of many an orthodox confessor," he declared.[1]

Washington Gladden is best known to history for his writings on labor and class issues, and for his role in popularizing the ideas that formed the core of the Social Gospel. But his influence went far beyond his leadership on social and economic concerns. Gladden was the voice of an entire generation of theologically liberal Protestants in the United States, and his musings about faith and doubt spoke to the experience of many other religious Americans. Those musings also reflected his personal religious journey. Gladden followed what was literally and figuratively an unorthodox path to ministry. He earned his degree from Williams College, and with the exception of a few courses at Union Theological Seminary, he had little in the way of formal theological education. Gladden also entered the ministry with relatively few commitments to any specific denomination or set of doctrines, the result of a childhood upbringing that took him from Methodism to Presbyterianism and finally to Congregationalism.[2]

As he approached his mid-forties, Gladden experienced considerable uncertainty about whether or not he had entered the right profession. After leaving his first pastorate in the wake of a nervous breakdown ("a more foolhardy undertaking it would have been difficult to imagine," he later recalled of this job, noting that his naïveté was second only to the "fatuity of the people" who hired him), he bounced between work as a minister and as a writer.[3] As he questioned his own career choices, he began to reflect openly on questions of faith and doubt. In one sermon, he affirmed the "the lack of absoluteness and finality in religious attainment and experience." Christians, Gladden declared, should not "expect to get to the end of their thinking" about religious matters "in this world or in any world." His solution was for Christians to "stand with their faces toward God" rather than "away from God." In other words, Gladden insisted, doubt could never be overcome. But it could be tempered by a desire for faith. "We all believe somewhat and doubt somewhat. There is no doubter who has not his beliefs; there is no believer who has not his doubts," he told his congregation, adding that the difference between the two rested in "which of these mental states predominates."[4]

Shortly after he preached these sermons, Gladden became pastor of the First Congregational Church of Columbus, a move that inspired a greater sense of confidence. Gladden spent the rest of his career in Ohio and by all accounts found a greater sense of purpose in his ministry there. He routinely counseled younger clergy who sought his advice on how to convey contemporary religious ideas to their congregations, and the ideas he expressed—including those about doubt—gained popularity in the wider circles of the Protestant community. Theological liberals like Gladden came to represent the public face of Protestantism in the United States at the precise moment that large numbers of Americans experienced a profound crisis of faith.[5]

During the closing decades of the nineteenth century, a strident critique of religion rapidly gained popularity in the United States. Prominent skeptics drew on deep-seated cultural anxieties that resulted from the Civil War and the massive structural changes to American society during the Gilded Age, and they exploited popular scientific and philosophical ideas to attack the foundations of theistic religion. These critics did not merely assail specific Christian doctrines such as the divinity of Christ or the existence of the Trinity. Rather, they challenged the fundamental tenets of belief, including the existence of a divine being and the presence of a moral order in creation.

Astute Protestant observers quickly perceived that it would prove impossible to discredit skepticism. But if uncertainty could not be eliminated, it might be co-opted. During the late nineteenth century, liberal Protestants in the United States found a way to baptize skepticism and reinterpret doubt and uncertainty as normal elements of a healthy spiritual life. Christianity, they argued, did not resist doubt. It welcomed it.

In revising their perspective on faith, these Protestants transformed Americans' understandings of the nature of religious community and the role of the clergy. Liberals abandoned their conception of the church as an exclusive club whose teachings prospective members needed to accept in order to join. Rather, they recast it as a community of faithful doubters, who worked through their questions and anxieties under the guidance of ministers who neither judged nor condemned uncertainty. Liberal Protestants buttressed these views with evidence from the emerging field of the psychology of religion, as university psychologists provided apparent scientific proof that religious commitments were rarely free of ambiguity.

This shift in attitudes about doubt marked the crucial first step in the process by which liberal American Protestants came to embrace religious diversity in the late nineteenth-century United States. Their willingness to countenance a permanent state of uncertainty signaled a newfound acceptance of people who held views about religion that diverged from the teachings of orthodox Christianity. It was the acceptance of doubt that prepared Protestants to find value in the beliefs of Catholics, Jews, Buddhists, Hindus, and Muslims.

In particular, two theological strategies that Protestant liberals adopted to support their newfound view of doubt—their emphasis on the "person of Jesus" as the central doctrine of Christian teaching and their assertion of the progressive nature of revelation—provided concrete methods by which they would later reinterpret their relationship with other faith traditions. Ultimately, an acceptance of doubters set many American Protestants on a course toward the affirmation of pluralism.

When late nineteenth-century Protestants proclaimed the permanence of doubt, they did so in response to the crisis of faith that pervaded society in the decades following the Civil War. Indeed, this widespread questioning of long-standing belief had its origin in the bloody conflict of the early 1860s. As recent scholars have observed, death was the defining feature of the war. In its wake, six hundred thousand young men who had served in uniform were dead, as were approximately fifty thousand civilians. Beyond the sheer magnitude of the loss of life, the Civil War abolished long-standing cultural assumptions about death. The conflict rendered obsolete the assumption that death would typically occur in the home—the bastion of Victorian piety—and in the presence of loved ones. Weapons of previously unknown power destroyed human bodies and shattered expectations about burial.[6]

Most Americans sought to make sense of the war's human toll by imbuing the conflict with religious meaning. They insisted that the war either represented a righteous campaign against an unrighteous enemy (an argument employed by both sides for different reasons) or, in the case of the North, that it represented an opportunity for the nation to atone for the sin of slavery. But unpleasant recollections of the war persisted, and not just in the writings of the conflict's few harsh critics. Among those troubled by the war was Hamilton Wright Mabie, a writer and purveyor of thoroughly respectable, middle-class opinion. Having participated in the college's theological society while a student at Williams, Mabie remained devoted to the Episcopal Church for his entire life (so much so that the bishop of New York once reportedly remarked, "Mabie, if I ever catch you out after dark, I will ordain you right then and there").[7] In the late 1870s, Mabie joined Henry Ward Beecher and Lyman Abbott on the editorial staff of the *Christian Union,* a position that granted him enormous power to shape the religious views of the journal's Protestant readership. He remained with the *Christian Union* (and later the *Outlook*) for the rest of his career, even as he published his own collections of stories and essays. One twentieth-century historian somewhat justifiably dismissed Mabie as "a dealer in the most saccharine morality and the most standard textbook opinions." Yet for all his Victorian sentimentality, Mabie could not rationalize away the gruesomeness of the Civil War. Nearly four decades after the conflict, he wrote of it as a "storm of sorrow" in which "there were no homes which sorrow might not enter, no firesides where care and anxiety did not find a place."[8]

For Hamilton Mabie and others, the fundamental change wrought by the war was that it made the realities of human suffering unavoidable. During the early nineteenth century, middle-class Americans had developed an increasingly humanitarian outlook and had grown more attuned to the dismal conditions in which many of their fellow citizens lived. Those people who did manage to maintain their obliviousness of human suffering before the conflict found it impossible to sustain in its aftermath. The late nineteenth century forced Americans to face discomforting questions about the nature of the world and the conditions of life. "Men have never been blind to the tragic facts of life; but they never before have known them so widely, so intimately; and out of this knowledge there has come, as was inevitable, a great depression," Mabie observed. He surmised that increasing communication around the globe had made Americans more aware than ever before about suffering in foreign lands. In the face of ever-growing knowledge, he mused, "something like despair has overtaken many of the most sensitive men and women; and they cry out passionately, not against their own fates, but against the fate of the race."[9]

In his diagnosis of the "despair" that characterized his fellow citizens, Hamilton Mabie acknowledged the depth of the perceived crisis in the nation's life. It was not merely that people were troubled because they saw others suffering around them; huge numbers of Americans were themselves enduring considerable hardship. The final decades of the nineteenth century were, in the words of one historian, a "period of trauma." The United States endured a series of severe economic recessions between 1873 and 1897; between 20 and 30 percent of Americans found themselves without work at some point during each year. Economic desperation led in turn to social dislocation, as people took up their roots in an often-fruitless search for better opportunities. Perhaps unsurprisingly, this sense of gloom found an outlet in the nation's cultural output. Writing in the 1890s, Mabie bemoaned the "wave of intense depression" that had characterized literature and art for the previous two decades. It sometimes appeared, he wrote, "as if all the old sanctions had lost their authority, the old aspirations spent their force, and the old hopes dissolved in a mist of sadness."[10] That the religious commitments of the American people could survive intact in such a culture might have been too much to hope. And, indeed, they did not.

Into this breach stepped Robert Green Ingersoll, who became the primary spokesperson for the sharpening critique of Christianity and of theistic religion more broadly. Ingersoll had served in the Civil War and witnessed its horrors firsthand, and as a lawyer with a large network of correspondents, he received many accounts of the suffering that Americans endured during the economic hardship of the decades that followed. Shortly after the economy crashed in the Panic of 1893, Ingersoll received a desperate letter from his own niece, who reported that her family had lost its business to creditors just as they had taken in a twenty-four-year-old relative who was near death from consumption. She reported being "utterly without a resource," lacking any hope of finding any, and unable to muster the means to relocate. "I am not well my self, so tired in mind and body," she confessed to her "Uncle Robert," and she admitted to feeling that "death would seem sweet relief."[11]

Ingersoll channeled his anger at the ubiquity of suffering in the world into an attack on the benevolent deity of Christianity. "How do you account for the fact that the world has been filled with pain, and grief, and tears?" he asked. "Is it easy to account for famine, for pestilence and plague if there be above us all a Ruler infinitely good, powerful and wise?" The Civil War colonel pulled no punches in his campaign to discredit Christian belief, declaring, "It is a religion that I am going to do what little I can while I live to destroy."[12]

Yet Ingersoll did not articulate a nihilistic view of nature or of human potential that Americans might find difficult to palate. He was, by all accounts, a compassionate man whose generosity of spirit charmed even his critics. One acquaintance observed that "his conception of life's meaning was that of love in action," while another described him as a "sunbeam" and observed to Ingersoll that "whenever you have entered my house, either in person or by printed word you have always brought light and warmth."[13] Ingersoll affirmed that humans possessed free will and insisted that conscience developed through education, and his rhetoric had a strong humanitarian bent. "There is enough to do in this world. There are plenty needing help here," Ingersoll observed, suggesting that the proper response to the religious impulse was to "do each other good." With regard to divine figures, Ingersoll insisted, "they do not need us, and we do not need them."[14]

Robert Ingersoll's benevolent humanism terrified Protestant leaders. Their fears were well founded. As the colonel barnstormed his way across the United States giving lectures and interviews to anyone who would listen, denominational periodicals printed reports of good Christians, "hearty in their devotion" and "noted for their readiness to work for Christ," who were "overcome by the torrent of his eloquence" and "turned in favor of his untruth."[15] Two sisters in an "orthodox" midwestern town were so enchanted by his message that they begged him for a handwritten note offering some words of wisdom.[16] A professor at Lombard University in Illinois, who described the Universalist institution as "distinctly theistic," nevertheless reported that students and faculty from its College of Liberal Arts and Divinity were "delighted" by Ingersoll's lecture there.[17] Even Henry Ward Beecher, arguably the most famous Protestant minister in America, declared to a friend his view that Ingersoll represented "one of the intellectual giants of the century" and possessed "a heart as big as an ox."[18]

While his personality and optimistic assessment of human nature were crucial to his popularity, the potency of Ingersoll's message was enhanced by its alignment with the late nineteenth-century critique of Christianity and, indeed, of theistic religion more widely. While Charles Darwin's *Origin of Species* itself did little to shake the faith of Christian Americans, ideas promulgated by British disciples of Darwin proved more vexing. Thomas Huxley, known as the Bulldog for his bellicose defense of Darwin's theory, insisted that evolutionary science provided all the needed explanation for the development of the natural world. It was impossible for humans to know what, if anything, existed beyond the material world, and he urged people to stop clinging to religious belief systems that claimed to provide such answers. This conviction led Huxley to disavow both atheism and Christianity. He coined the term "agnosticism" to reflect his view of the impossibility of human knowledge about the divine.[19]

While Huxley was responsible for the term "agnosticism," it was Herbert Spencer who popularized the concept in Britain and the United States. Spencer did not reject the possibility of religion. In fact, he considered the near-universality of religious belief in human history to be compelling evidence that it reflected a deeper truth. When the matter was evaluated with an impartial mind, Spencer wrote, the only sustainable conclusion was that "the diverse forms of religious belief which have existed and which still exist, have all a basis in some ultimate fact."[20] The issue for Spencer was the "untenable" nature of "any or all the existing religious creeds," among which he included Christianity, with the "absurdities associated with them" and the "irrational" character of "the arguments set forth in their defence."[21] The problem with existing religious systems was that they attempted to offer concrete explanations for things which humans could not possibly understand. Just because people had a sense that an "unknown and unknowable God" existed, it did not follow that they possessed certainty of religious truth. Because "positive knowledge does not, and never can, fill the whole region of possible thought," Spencer wrote, it remained necessary to maintain an agnostic outlook and to refrain from accepting Christianity and similar belief systems that claimed to explain the unexplainable.[22]

Although Spencer's views were generally unpopular in the United States, they did win the favor of a number of influential American intellectuals. Two pioneers in the field of sociology, William Graham Sumner and Lester Frank Ward, drew heavily on his work in their campaign to secularize the emerging academic social sciences. For much of the nineteenth century (and for centuries before), leadership in the American academy had overlapped considerably with Protestant churches. But Sumner, Ward, and others of their generation sought to enhance the authority of new research universities and other scientific endeavors by cutting the ties with Protestant institutions. These intellectuals were all too happy to invoke the arguments made against religion by Spencer and others.[23] Spencer's claims also gained broader publicity in the pages of Edward Youmans's *Popular Science Monthly*, and his critiques seemed to lend scientific credence to the view advanced by Ingersoll that Christian faith had become intellectually unsustainable.[24]

Evolutionary theory proved so useful in supporting the claims of skeptics and agnostics because of its apparent ability to account for ostensible marks of design in the natural world without recourse to a divine Designer. Ever since the eighteenth century, when science began to explain more and more of the world, defenders of Christianity had staked their claims in the realm of natural theology. Christian thinkers insisted that the apparent order of nature, such as the way in which plants and animals seemed designed for their habitats or the way in which their physiology served their needs, provided the best evidence for the existence of a benevolent creator. Evolution provided a naturalistic explanation for such phenomena. To intellectuals already inclined to an agnostic outlook, the theory's apparent demolition of natural theology provided yet more evidence of how untenable Christianity was in the face of modern thought.[25]

For Ingersoll and a generation of Americans surrounded by intense suffering, this particular effect of evolutionary theory was a welcome occurrence. In the aftermath of the Civil War's carnage and the dislocation and upheaval of the late nineteenth century, the belief that the world was ordered according to a divine plan seemed intellectually and morally bankrupt. "These religious people see nothing but design everywhere," Ingersoll charged. "They point us to the sunshine, to the flowers, to the April rain, and to all there is of beauty and of use in the world. Did it ever occur to them that a cancer is as beautiful in its development as is the reddest rose?"[26] As scientists and popular public figures proclaimed that suffering was a normal part of existence that did not serve a larger purpose and could not be overcome, a religious message that imbued everything with a beneficent divine purpose seemed increasingly quixotic.

Nor was the challenge of evolutionary science the only problem that Christian Americans faced. As the Congregationalist theologian George Harris lamented in the early 1890s, no sooner were religious thinkers "bravely over our fright from evolution"—a reference to Protestants' reasonably successful efforts to reconcile the theory with Christian belief by insisting that such a phenomenon needed a guiding force and arguing that Spencer's "Unknowable" bore considerable resemblance to the Christian God—when a new problem arose. "Before we are fairly rested," he lamented, "we are taking new alarm from Biblical criticism."[27] As the United States became increasingly integrated into the nexus of European ideas after 1850, large numbers of American students traveled to German universities, the hub of new methods of scriptural study. Critical scholarship of the Bible was not a novelty in and of itself, but through the efforts of German academics, its nature changed significantly. "Higher Criticism" sought to place biblical texts in their historical and intellectual contexts. Much about the Bible that had been taken for granted, such as the chronology of history in the Old Testament, the Gospel narratives of the resurrection of Jesus, and even the very identity of the authors of biblical books, now seemed dubious or even false. When it came to sustaining religious faith in the face of modern knowledge, Harris despaired, "there is no peace to the righteous."[28]

New scholarship rattled Protestants with particular force. Since the Reformation, Protestant theologians had argued that the "plain sense" reading of scripture constituted the basis of religious knowledge. They rejected the Roman Catholic view that the Bible contained layers of metaphor and allegory and instead insisted that the most obvious interpretation of scriptural texts was the correct one. But if the biblical narrative was not what it seemed, skeptics could justifiably question the very source of Protestant belief. Among the most significant consequences of the Higher Criticism was its dating of the origin of the Gospels to several decades *after* Jesus's death, specifically to the final decades of the first century CE. Christians had long cited Gospel accounts of Jesus's prediction of the destruction of the Jerusalem Temple, which occurred in 70 CE (decades after his death), as definitive proof of his divinity. But now it appeared that subsequent authors had inserted the reference into Jesus's mouth. Modern scholarship had seemingly discredited the principal argument for scriptural authority.[29]

Because theologically liberal Protestants had never subscribed to a literal interpretation of scripture, many of them were able to sidestep the challenge of biblical criticism. They focused on what they identified as the broad spirit of the texts and insisted that there was no need to question one's faith just because a text had a different author or was written at a different time than previously thought. But not everyone found this approach satisfactory. As Americans learned more about biblical criticism, Protestant ministers noted a "common perplexity" in their churches. Their congregants struggled because they did not want "to give up the Bible," yet they found themselves "absolutely incapable of holding to an irrational faith" in the wake of modern knowledge.[30] The theologically liberal minister of a Congregational church in a well-to-do suburb of New York City encapsulated the challenge posed by critical readings of scripture. "Words do not always mean the same to different men when other books are read," he observed, and it made little sense to assume it was possible to have a single, indisputable reading of the Bible. To make "salvation depend upon our use, or upon anybody's use" of things such as "the pointing of a vowel, or the placing of a preposition" constituted "a poor foundation for faith."[31]

The obvious problem was that the Bible had always been *the* foundation of faith for Protestants. Critics like Ingersoll looked on with glee as sophisticated academics mustered more and more evidence that the Bible was seemingly "simply and purely of human invention."[32] The public face of American agnosticism did not dismiss scripture as entirely without value—"the bible was written by men not altogether good, nor altogether bad"—but Ingersoll found it entirely implausible to accept "the inspiration of every so called sacred book," including that of Christians.[33] Increasingly, scripture simply did not seem to align with the contemporary understandings about the origins of its claims. In an era that valorized science, it was easy for skeptics to muster ample evidence to suggest that religious faith—and particularly Protestant Christianity—could not be reconciled with modern knowledge.

Liberal Protestants addressed the problem of skepticism by embracing a religious version of it. In some respects, they were tapping into a longer tradition. The expectation that doubt would exist within a religious life had deep roots in both Judaism and Christianity. The Hebrew Bible books of Job and Ecclesiastes both raised the disquieting suggestion that the universe was not designed in such a way that divine purpose was readily apparent and did not necessarily correspond with human expectations. The so-called Doubting Thomas of John's Gospel, while ultimately convinced by the physical evidence of Jesus's wounds, nevertheless epitomized the intellectual difficulties that tenets like the Resurrection might prompt. The fourth-century theologian Augustine admitted in his *Confessions* that his belief in God "was sometimes strong, sometimes weak," and that Christianity "demanded that certain things should be believed even though they could not be proved."[34]

Doubt had an equally rich heritage in American religious culture. The formulaic conversion narrative expected of those who sought to gain membership in colonial New England's Puritan churches required the prospective member to express uncertainty about his or her state of salvation. One convert recalled a period in which she, having encountered Jesus's promise of blessing in the Gospel, "doubted whether that promise belonged to me." Another, believing that God had sent "a measure of comfort" in a time of trial, expressed that he "doubted whether these comforts were right." Too much assuredness of one's faith was, in fact, the surest way to fail to gain admittance to the covenanted community.[35]

The United States also boasted a bolder tradition of outright skepticism. The critique of traditional authority that underlay the American Revolution had inspired questioning of the Christian religion. In some cases, this manifested itself in quibbling with theological tenets, such as the Unitarian critique of the divinity of Jesus that gained traction in the urbane towns of eastern New England at the end of the eighteenth century, or the Universalist revision of Calvinist predestination that became popular in the region's rural districts during the same era.[36]

Some skeptical critiques went further. Thomas Paine, who during the 1770s and 1780s was nothing short of a national hero for his revolution-inspiring *Common Sense*, assailed the Bible as an immoral document in his treatise *The Age of Reason*. He claimed that the God presented in scripture was ruthless and cavalier, and God's behavior could in no way be reconciled with that of a moral deity. Paine attacked the long-standing Christian assertion that the Bible constituted a divine revelation. *The Age of Reason* enjoyed a wide audience in the United States, not only among well-read college men who might be expected to enjoy such an iconoclastic volume, but also among poorer Americans who found themselves badly constrained by economic circumstance in the early republic and who attacked political, social, and religious institutions that they associated with elites.[37]

Pervasive as skepticism might have been in the United States at the close of the eighteenth century, it differed in distinct ways from the deep crisis of faith that began in the 1870s. First, few skeptics of the late 1700s questioned the ultimate foundations of religious teaching: the reality of a benevolent God and the existence of a moral order and purpose to creation. Paine's criticism of biblical revelation centered on what he perceived to be the impossibility that a moral deity would inspire scriptures that made heroes out of men like Moses, whose character was "the most horrid that can be imagined," and that, in the case of several instances in the Hebrew scriptures, seemed to condone the rape and murder of innocent people.[38] But while Paine was unrelenting in his attack on scripture, he never denied the existence of God as nineteenth-century skeptics like Ingersoll and Spencer did. On the contrary, the basis of his attack on the claim that the Bible was a divine revelation was the seeming incongruence of much of its context with the idea of a God who cared for humanity. Second, as many scholars have noted, eighteenth-century critics of Christianity did not possess an alternative intellectual framework that accounted for the natural world as simply and elegantly as Christian doctrine did. While some major components of this framework were in place by the time of Paine's writing, it was not until Ingersoll's generation that a fully formed naturalistic alternative to Christian belief existed.[39]

These two factors help to explain the third characteristic that distinguished the skepticism of the 1790s from that which arose eight decades later: the former was short-lived. In response to the upheaval of the 1790s, both in the United States and in revolutionary France, Protestant Americans initiated a campaign to strengthen their churches. The new forms of evangelical Christianity that spread in the wake of the religious revivals that began around 1800, especially in the rapidly growing Baptist and Methodist denominations and in Congregationalism and Presbyterianism, which were reinvigorated following their alliance in 1805, linked skepticism about Christianity with immoral behavior. Indeed, a key feature of revivals was preaching that emphasized the sinfulness of skepticism.

In this context, Paine's stature rapidly diminished. Despite the popularity with which *The Age of Reason* was initially greeted, both Paine and his work were assailed with increasing vehemence, and by the time of his death in 1809 he was nearly universally reviled. Subsequent generations of Americans successfully rewrote the religious history of the 1790s and downplayed the popularity Paine had enjoyed not only among college men, but also among the disempowered classes.

By 1880, a Congregationalist minister observed that it had been entirely possible for ministers to prevent church members from reading "Tom Paine, Voltaire, and the blatant infidels of the eighteenth century."[40] The ghost of the skeptic had been expunged, and for much of the early nineteenth century questioning reverted to what it had been for the Puritans. Its existence was an expected part of a healthy religious life, but it was also something that true Christians would overcome in time.[41] Even religious intellectuals like the early nineteenth-century Unitarian leader William Ellery Channing, whose own faith commitments were heavily shaped by the questioning spirit of the late 1700s, rejected both skepticism about the existence of God and claims that scripture did not represent divine revelation.[42]

By contrast, the skepticism that emerged during the late nineteenth century called the very foundations of faith into question. It also proved far more resilient. Popular literature suggested that skepticism was inevitable. One Boston clergyman bemoaned that when it came to Mary Ward's *Robert Elsmere*, the tale of a Church of England cleric who loses his faith in the face of modern scientific and philosophical ideas, his church could be divided into only two groups: those who had already read the book and "those who are going to read it." And when American audiences had finished reading Ward's story of belief lost, they turned to Harold Frederic's tale of Theron Ware's journey through the same process. After encountering contemporary theories of scientific naturalism, Ware, an idealistic young Methodist minister, becomes so uncertain about his beliefs that he leaves the ministry. Given the state of American belief by the 1890s, it is hardly surprising that *The Damnation of Theron Ware* was among the most widely read books when it was published.[43]

Historically, the American Protestant approach to doubts about religion had been to suggest that they should be overcome. New England Puritans had stressed that individual Christians should maintain some level of uncertainty about their own state of salvation—put in the simplest terms, whether they were going to heaven or hell—but doubt about Christian belief was thought of as something to be overcome. This view persisted despite the changes in the nation's religious culture during the nineteenth century as the number of denominations grew rapidly and a culture of revivalism emerged. Some of the foremost Protestant luminaries of the mid-nineteenth century offered variants of this perspective. Henry Ward Beecher, arguably the most prominent American cleric of the Civil War era, dismissed "honest skepticism" as the result of faults within "human notions of religion." He insisted that it "might be relieved" simply by presenting doubters with "the Scripture in precisely the light in which the Scripture presents itself."[44]

Beecher's contemporary and fellow Congregationalist, Horace Bushnell, likewise presented an easy solution to skepticism. "God manages," he declared, "to gain back infidels and doubters" by causing them to "doubt their doubts" and by tempering their "conceit" through "the sobering effect of years and sorrow."[45] Bushnell, a Connecticut minister who was largely responsible for setting American Protestantism on its course toward the dominance of liberal theology, preached with certainty that doubts could be "dissolved in all their degrees and combinations."[46] Such views were carried to a wider audience in Elizabeth Prentiss's *Stepping Heavenward*, one of the most popular religious novels of the mid-nineteenth century, which depicts the prolonged but ultimately successful struggle of a young Protestant woman to commit to faith and to reject inclinations toward uncertainty.[47]

As skepticism grew rampant in American culture, such optimistic views about the ease with which doubt could be overcome became unsustainable. Suffering was not, as Bushnell had suggested, a force that was bringing Americans back to Christianity from a state of doubt. It was driving them headlong into uncertainty. When Washington Gladden preached his sermons on belief and doubt during 1880 and 1881, his message exemplified a broader turn within American Protestantism toward the acceptance of doubt as a permanent aspect of the religious life. This shift in outlook would in turn produce a religious culture that was vastly more inclusive and accepting of diversity of belief and practice.

Three elements formed the basis of liberal Protestants' newfound inclusiveness toward doubters. The first was a belief that people could approach doubt in different ways. They could either adopt a cynical outlook, using uncertainty as an excuse to abandon religion, or they could maintain their commitment to Christian truths despite their uncertainty. The latter approach came to be seen as entirely compatible with Christian faith. Second, Protestants insisted that nothing in the Christian tradition opposed doubt, and they mustered considerable evidence to support a spirit of questioning. Finally, a consensus emerged that doubters were better off inside churches than outside. These strategies were employed not only by those religious leaders like Washington Gladden and Lyman Abbott who enjoyed the height of their popularity amid the rampant skepticism of the 1880s and 1890s. They also became central in the outlooks of people like Francis McConnell and Leighton Parks, who came of age during those decades and who enjoyed their greatest success during the early twentieth century.

The emphasis on a distinction between the cynical doubt of agnostics and the hopeful doubt of those who kept their "faces toward God" permeated the rhetoric of many mainstream Protestants. The Presbyterian clergyman and theologian James Henry Snowden lamented the old view by which "doubt has been closely connected with damnation as though it were leading us straight to hell."

Snowden held considerable sway over clergy and laity alike in his roles as a professor of theology at Western Theological Seminary in Washington, Pennsylvania, and as the editor of the *Presbyterian Banner*, a weekly periodical for Pennsylvania churchgoers. Like many of his contemporaries, he also wrote a number of books that endorsed theological liberalism. For Snowden, doubt was simply "uncertain belief," a "twilight between light and darkness" that was "inherent in the constitution" of the human mind. It was up to each individual whether he or she chose "the morning twilight in which a doubtful trust or hope or speculation is growing into positive knowledge" or "the evening twilight in which an accepted truth is withering into error and passing away."[48]

Other observers drew similar contrasts. One writer offered a distinction between the "volatile, uneasy, and restless spirits" who were frequently guilty of "defection and revolt from Christianity" and "souls restless, troubled, anxious, earnest, truthful, sincere, that long unspeakably for light, clearness, and rest, amid the enigmas of the universe." While the former would never have interest in Christianity, the second did retain a desire for religious conviction and found "the charges of irreverence or insincerity" to be unjust.[49] Another commentator insisted that everyone believed in some sort of "Infinite Soul." The difference between belief and unbelief rested in what people did with that belief. Even if one harbored doubts about specific "theological definitions of this Infinite Soul," he or she could still remain in the Christian tradition. The true problem was the skeptics who denied the existence of "any power not ourselves that makes for righteousness."[50]

Leighton Parks, an Episcopal priest, emphasized the problem of sustaining belief in miracles as he argued that the rejection of specific theological doctrines did not necessitate the abandonment of religious commitment. He chided those who equated the "denial of the miraculous" with a secular view of the universe as the "ceaseless grinding of this great machine." Rather, Parks suggested that doubts about miracles and other Christian tenets that strained modern credulity actually reflected a longing for deeper religious experience.[51] Parks was in good company. James Henry Snowden proclaimed that "faith in Christ" did not require Christians "to settle every hard point in theology or to be sure about every question concerning him."[52] Indeed, the Methodist bishop Francis McConnell went so far as to co-opt the language of outright skeptics like Huxley and Spencer in his affirmation of the "spirit of agnosticism which is at bottom faith." Such faith was characterized by a "willingness to leave some problems unsolved." He insisted that such a view constituted "a sincere and reverent and Christian agnosticism," which he called "agnosticism of faith and not of doubt." But McConnell did in fact affirm that Christians could maintain their doubts, provided they also retained a commitment to their faith.[53]

The second major shift in liberal Protestants' attitude to doubters was reflected in the frequent assertion that nothing in Christian tradition opposed uncertainty and questioning. Contrary to the older perspective advanced in the mid-nineteenth century by the likes of Henry Ward Beecher and Horace Bushnell, by century's end many liberals argued that Christianity actually encouraged people to question their beliefs. The Episcopal bishop Charles Brent counseled readers that religious belief was about friendship with God, and all friendships required testing "in order to be solidly set."[54] Doubt provided the critical foundation for a deeper spiritual life. "Unquestioning faith is not a Christian grace," advised Lyman Abbott and Hamilton Mabie at the *Outlook*. They told their readers that "credulity" constituted "a greater foe to Christ and his cause than skepticism." Difficulty only arose when people misunderstood the difference between *faith* and *belief*. "Faith is not belief," they declared; "it is the will to believe." While the Bible denounced "unfaith," it nowhere rejected "unbelief."[55] As long as Protestants maintained a willingness to have faith through their doubts, they remained in line with the spirit of Christianity.

Indeed, liberal Protestants considered doubt to be far less deleterious than blind obedience to biblical teaching. Francis McConnell insisted on the place "in Christian experience for legitimate suspension of judgment," thereby affirming his tradition's acceptance of uncertainty. Like the editorial writers of the *Outlook*, he considered overly "extensive claims to knowledge" far more detrimental to religious commitment than doubt.[56] So, too, the Congregationalist Amory Bradford told his congregation that people who spoke of their religious conviction "with easy confidence" had "only skimmed the surface of things." While Bradford expressed hope that believers would find light after their "long night of mental darkness," he denied that it would come easily. "A child learns the material world by coming in contact and being hurt by it," he told his congregants. "Not more easily are spiritual things learned."[57] Certain faith was something people would develop very slowly, and some might never develop it at all.

The third and final characteristic of Protestants' changing attitudes concerned the way in which they expected their churches to treat doubters. Bradford told his congregants not to waste their time worrying about aspects of Christian teaching they had difficulty understanding or accepting. "You may have no clear conception of God or the future life?" he asked in one sermon; "very well! Stop thinking about those things."[58] In his treatise on Christian ethics, Newman Smyth likewise called it a "fatal blunder" for churches to withhold membership from "any doubter" who was uncertain about belief. He denied the charge that by including such people churches might find themselves "filled with unregenerate souls." Instead, Smyth insisted, "the surest and safest way" for churches to thrive was for them "to welcome with helpful and hopeful charity those who would seek to do the truth of Christ."[59] McConnell instructed his fellow clergy to "proceed very carefully" in their interaction with doubters. He admonished them to restrain themselves from expressing judgments that might alienate people who were questioning aspects of their faith. He urged clergy to recognize the value of doubt for Christian experience in order to "keep some from leaving the Church because of supposed agnosticism."[60]

The belief that doubters belonged in churches inspired new calls for a broadminded, inclusive spirit among Protestant communities and their ministers. For the liberals who championed this new outlook, the mission of churches was no longer to prescribe belief. Rather, churches were to offer guidance and support to Christians who wrestled with their own questions and uncertainties. In his advice column in the *Outlook*, Lyman Abbott counseled readers on the importance of not trying "to be the spiritual director of our neighbor." American Protestants could no longer presume to judge one another's religious experience. Abbott insisted that clergy, too, needed to shift their expectations amid increasing doubt. "The minister will do better who succeeds in inducing his people to call upon him with their spiritual problems and their intellectual doubts," Abbott wrote, "than he who goes after them and demands their confidence." As churches became safe havens for questioners, the minister evolved from the adherence-demanding guardian of belief to the friendly, nonjudgmental source of guidance to those in doubt.[61]

These three strategies for countering skepticism by affirming the religious commitment of doubters themselves rested on two larger shifts in Protestant thought, both of which gained widespread acceptance and became core tenets of theological liberalism in the late nineteenth-century United States. The first was the conviction that the essence of Christianity lay solely in the "person of Jesus"—a somewhat vague term by which liberal Protestants meant Jesus's life, teaching, and self-understanding as communicated in the Gospels—rather than in the doctrines that had developed during the intervening millennia. The second change was the belief that revelation constituted an ongoing, progressive process. In other words, divine truth had not been revealed in its entirety centuries earlier. Rather, as humans grew in their knowledge of the world, they received new revelations of the divine. Both of these theological shifts created space for doubt in Christian life. These two theological innovations not only provided an intellectual basis for the acceptance of doubt, but, more significantly, they ultimately provided the foundation for the affirmation of other forms of pluralism as well.

Beginning in the late nineteenth century, liberal Protestants began to emphasize the *person* of Jesus as the defining characteristic of Christianity. Early articulations of this view appeared at midcentury in the writings of Horace Bushnell, who suggested that the solution to moral dilemmas was "the sacred bliss of love to Christ's person."[62] But these ideas grew in refinement during the final three decades of the century. Beginning in the 1870s, Lyman Abbott suggested that it was Jesus's very life and character that separated Christianity from all other religions. Non-Christian traditions, he mused, "have no person to awake enthusiasm of love."[63] Similarly, Newman Smyth suggested that the person of Jesus offered access to the divine on a personal level in a way that transcended the seemingly mechanistic natural world. "In and through Jesus Christ," he told his congregation, God dealt with humans neither "rigidly at the end of a long law" nor "unsympathetically from far off," but rather "directly, and personally, on the plane of personality."[64] To make his case, Smyth drew on ideas he had presented several years earlier in his treatise *Christian Ethics*. Christianity was distinct from other religions and philosophical traditions because of its foundation in "the warmth of personality whose life is to be realized in love" rather than in "abstract generality" or "cold legality."[65] Such ideas were given voice by Protestant laity as well. Hamilton Mabie considered the "recognition of the normal human life of Christ" to be "one of the great gains of modern religious thought," and he affirmed the benefit of reclaiming it from beneath centuries of doctrine.[66]

This conception of the person of Jesus as the fundamental tenet of Christianity gained a stronger intellectual foundation in the theology of Albrecht Ritschl, especially as popularized by Adolf von Harnack, a professor with whom many American religious thinkers studied at the University of Berlin. Harnack argued that Christianity in its first centuries had accommodated its beliefs to the Greek intellectual culture that dominated the eastern Mediterranean region at the time. In so doing, the early Christian church strayed from the original teachings of Jesus. But Harnack was hopeful that Higher Criticism of the Bible could retrieve the true message of Jesus by cutting through superfluous additions to scripture. He believed that the original biblical texts revealed that Jesus's significance lay not in the religious precepts he issued but rather in his very existence as divine love placed directly into human history. The Presbyterian theologian William Adams Brown, one of Harnack's students and a leading champion of his ideas in the United States, explained the significance of this view. Noting the unparalleled "moral greatness" of Jesus, Brown wrote that Jesus "could speak of God as He did because He had had experience of God in His own soul" and "He had learned in His own life that the things which are unseen are eternal."[67]

By defining Christian experience as the direct encounter with God through the person of Jesus, liberal Protestants gained the freedom to question, challenge, and reject nearly all other aspects of Christian teaching. This obviously created ample space for doubt. Lyman Abbott chastised earlier generations of Protestants for allowing "conviction of the truth" to become "the precursor and producer of conversion of the life," and for treating "sound theology" as the "mother of a true religion."[68] James Henry Snowden insisted that faith by its very nature required a person as its object. Faith "is a knowledge that rests in relation to a person," he wrote, as opposed to "knowledge that rests in sense perception or in logical demonstration." Because "Christianity is Christ" and it consisted of little more "besides his personality," the Presbyterian theologian believed that "it does not take great faith, untroubled faith, perfect faith to enter the Christian life."[69]

Washington Gladden recognized the potential of this perspective to win the commitment of "worthy and honorable people who are not members of our churches." Whatever uncertainties they might harbor, they still belonged in Christian communities, provided those communities emphasized the proper aspects of Christian belief. This large group of people "may not care very much for Christianity," by which he meant "the religion that gilds and glorifies the ecclesiastical machine." Nor did they "accept a good deal of the dogmatic baggage with which the church sometimes suffers itself to be encumbered." But they did "believe in the Christianity of Christ," and that was what mattered.[70] His fellow Congregationalist Amory Bradford went a step further, claiming the person of Jesus as the crucial weapon against unbelief. "Infidelity attacks the Bible and the Church," he proclaimed in a thinly veiled reference to the likes of Robert Ingersoll, "but bows with uncovered head before our Master."[71]

If the emphasis on the person of Jesus was one half of the theological foundation for the acceptance of doubt, new ideas about the progressive nature of revelation provided the other half. By the end of the nineteenth century, many religious Americans held that all aspects of life existed in "perpetual flux" and that "movement" represented "the law of all living things and of substance in the material universe."[72] Hamilton Mabie expressed a common view in ascribing the impulse to "constant movement" not merely to the "material" realm but to the "intellectual and spiritual spheres" as well.[73] In this vein, Newman Smyth outlined a systematic theology of progressive thought. He divided human history into three religious eras, the "primitive," the "legal," and the "Christian." Each stage had witnessed the emergence of more sophisticated ideas of the divine and increasingly mature systems of morals and ethics.[74]

This insistence that Christian revelation had not been given in its entirety nearly two thousand years earlier was what separated liberal Protestants of this generation from earlier Christian thinkers. There existed, Smyth wrote, a "general law of Christian progress" that meant that theological understanding was "not to be regarded as a closed science." Rather, growth and development were manifested in a better understanding of scriptural teaching as Christians gained "clearer insight into their nature." This view of history raised the tantalizing prospect of entirely new revelations in the future. "It is at least conceivable that God may have given a positive revelation of some truths, and left other truths to be brought out in the processes of Christian life after the close of the more immediate or supernatural revelation of his will," Smyth wrote.[75]

Hamilton Mabie likewise affirmed "a progressive revelation" of God "in knowledge and experience," and he signaled how this view informed his understanding of doubt. "The enduring element in this changing life is to be found in the quest of the soul, not in the permanence of its habitations," he declared.[76] In other words, religious belief must always remain impermanent, and if convictions are subject to change, some state of doubt and questioning is to be expected. Mabie's colleague Lyman Abbott described how progressive religious development would manifest itself in a person's religious life. "Some things which I once doubted are no longer doubtful: some things which were once traditional beliefs I have cast off as errors," he wrote, "but perhaps a still greater number of opinions have changed their form, retaining their substances, and have become in their new aspect profitable and vital convictions."[77] What was true for the individual would ultimately be true for all of humanity.

In some respects, this characterization of religious growth as a progressive development signaled the degree to which the dominant scientific worldview of the day shaped liberal Protestant theology. The notion that knowledge of the divine grew as human capacity for knowledge increased was reminiscent of the theory of cosmic evolution popularized by Herbert Spencer. Moreover, the suggestion that the individual underwent a process of development hinted at the idea of social recapitulation theory, which held considerable currency in the United States during the late nineteenth century. This theory posited that every individual, in the course of development from infancy to adulthood, retraced the evolutionary path of the entire race.[78]

Yet this was not simply a case of liberal Protestants blindly modifying their theology to match dominant cultural values. The belief in progressive revelation served to buttress Christianity against the claims of unbelievers by creating a new defense of uncertainty. If knowledge of God constantly changed throughout history, many Protestants suggested, doubt was perfectly justified. Indeed, because it left Christians receptive to future divine revelations, it was to be encouraged. Claims of religious certainty did nothing except foreclose the possibility of new knowledge of God. Washington Gladden fervently believed that the major source of Americans' alienation from Christianity was their erroneous expectation that they could attain absolute certainty in all matters of faith. It was the lack of "this positive and final treatment" that drove "scientific men" away from religion. And they were right to be suspicious of claims of certainty. Absolute knowledge was unattainable in the religious sphere. Doubt was thus unavoidable.[79]

While innovative ideas of liberal theology underlay the increasingly widespread embrace of doubt within mainline Protestant churches, this new outlook drew additional strength from the work of pioneers in the academic field of psychology. These men provided a scientific explanation for the diversity of religious belief and practice. Interest in psychology had long existed in the United States. Like much of the rest of the academy in the United States, though, the discipline transformed in the late nineteenth century from an amorphous field that explored issues of consciousness to a professionalized academic discipline that was influenced by German scholarship and characterized by empiric methodologies. The psychologists who dominated the American academy at the end of the century were deeply interested in the mental processes of religious experience.[80]

Studies of the psychology of religion rested on the premise that religious belief constituted an intrinsic part of human experience and developed according to set formulae. Three early psychologists stood at the forefront of the field: William James, Edwin Diller Starbuck, and George Albert Coe. In Starbuck's words, he and his cohort of social scientists sought "to bring together a systematized body of evidence" by which they would attain a deeper understanding of "the spiritual life of man" and "read old dogmas in larger and fresher terms."[81]

This quest for a deeper understanding of faith aligned perfectly with liberal Protestants' conception of progressive revelation, which explains why many religious thinkers embraced the new discipline with great enthusiasm. "All the problems of human conduct involve theories of the will," Newman Smyth wrote, "and cannot be solved without some inquiry into moral motives,—that is, without the aid of psychology." Because one element of Christian theology was the place of ethics in human life, he noted, "Christian ethics cannot claim freedom from subjection to the processes and tests of modern psychology." Smyth did not cede authority entirely to the developing academic field. He reserved a crucial role for Christianity in bringing about the "regenerated consciousness," a feat that psychology could not accomplish on its own.[82] While Smyth remained vague as to the precise role of psychologists, it was clear that he envisioned them playing a preeminent role alongside ministers and theologians as experts on religious experience.

Liberal Protestants' willingness to grant academics such leeway stemmed from the apparent ability of psychologists to offer scientific justification for the new conception of doubt that promised to protect Christianity from the claims of skeptics. William James, who during the 1880s and 1890s moved between the departments of philosophy and psychology at Harvard University, was at the forefront of the scientific study of religion. In "The Will to Believe," a widely read 1896 lecture, James offered a philosophical defense for maintaining religious commitment despite a lack of absolute certainty. There was a personal element to this enterprise. Like many educated Americans of his generation, James struggled with the meaning of religious faith in the wake of new scientific understanding.[83]

In "The Will to Believe" James argued that absolute knowledge of truth was unattainable, despite the human inclination to seek it. The desire to identify absolute truth constituted "a weakness of our nature from which we must free ourselves," he contended. In language that closely paralleled the claims of liberal ministers and theologians, James insisted that absolute certainty in matters of religion would forever remain elusive. But, he argued, the absence of definitive proof was not an excuse to hold faith in abeyance until clarity emerged. Agnosticism was intellectually tantamount to atheism. "We cannot escape the issue by remaining sceptical and waiting for more light, because, although we do avoid error in that way *if religion be untrue*, we lose the good, *if it be true*, just as certainly as if we positively chose to disbelieve," he insisted. Moreover, James argued that the demand for faith was a necessary part of religious experience. Humans needed to respond to the religious impulse with "active good-will, as if evidence might be forever withheld from us unless we met the hypothesis half-way." In other words, he said, faith necessarily preceded certainty, and the feeling of certainty could never be absolute.[84]

The depiction of faith and unbelief in "The Will to Believe" mirrored discussions taking place in Protestant churches. The denial of absolute certainty paralleled assertions made by many Protestants about the absence of finality in the quest for religious truth. Moreover, James's insistence that people must either accept or reject religion despite their lack of certainty closely resembled Protestants' emerging views on "good" and "bad" doubt. The idea of maintaining faith without absolute knowledge echoed Washington Gladden's notion of doubting while keeping one's face directed at God. Themes of faith and doubt recurred in James's masterwork on the psychology of religion, *The Varieties of Religious Experience*, in which he explicitly declared his view that doubt represented a normal part of a healthy religious life. "Nothing is more common in the pages of religious biography," he wrote, "than the way in which seasons of lively and of difficult faith are descried as alternating."[85]

While William James blended psychology and philosophy, many of his contemporaries who helped to develop the field of academic psychology focused on concrete issues amenable to empirical investigation. Early psychologists of religion were especially interested in the nature of conversion. And because Protestants had long viewed conversion as wrestling with and overcoming doubt, psychologists were keen to examine the role of skepticism in the conversion process.

In his study *The Psychology of Religion*, conducted during the mid-1890s, Edwin Diller Starbuck, a Harvard graduate student and future professor at Stanford University, analyzed the self-reported conversion narratives of 192 people. The respondents' statements offer significant insight into how they viewed religious doubt. "I had two years of doubts and questionings," one subject reported. "It was my disposition to look at everything intellectually. I found I must give myself up into Christ's hands."[86]

While some of his subjects steadfastly retained the traditional view of doubt as a failure of faith, Starbuck himself offered a new assessment. He situated doubt as a normal part of religious development as people grew through adolescence into adulthood, and he noted that it was especially common in young men. "Doubt is a process of mental clarification; it is a step in the process of self-mastery," Starbuck wrote. His analysis reflects the broader evolution of doubt. On the one hand, Starbuck signaled a commitment to the long-standing belief that uncertainty was something to be overcome with his linking of doubt to the transitional period of adolescence. On the other hand, though, he situated doubt as a normal, healthy part of life. Starbuck also conceded that many people retained a "certain mixture of faith and doubt" in their mature religious lives, thus giving scientific approval to liberals' assertion of a permanent state of doubt.[87]

Of these three pioneers of the academic study of religion, it was George Albert Coe who had the most to say on the matter of faith and doubt. He, like Starbuck, focused on the religious experience of adolescents and the nature of conversion, though there was a more personal relevance to the work. Coe had grown up in a traditional Methodist home where his minister father had instilled in him the belief in a rapid, sudden religious transformation that would bring with it a feeling of certainty. But Coe never underwent such a conversion experience. His uncertainty about the nature of faith—exacerbated, unsurprisingly, by his studies at the University of Berlin—turned Coe away from his initial plan to study theology and kindled his interest in psychology. After completing a PhD at Boston University, Coe joined the faculty of Northwestern University, where he remained until his 1909 appointment as professor of practical theology at Union Theological Seminary in New York. His curiosity about the religious experience of adolescents propelled him into the field of education, and he spent his career exploring the intersection of religion, education, and psychology.[88]

Coe was a frequent public speaker and a prolific writer. Though he published widely in scholarly journals, he also contributed articles to periodicals that targeted general audiences, including Lyman Abbott's *Outlook*, the *Sunday School Times*, and his own denomination's *Methodist Review*. This commitment to sharing ideas with a broad audience explains why Coe's work consistently received the endorsement of university professors and ordinary Protestant ministers alike. It also suggests that, at least initially, Coe's views on the psychology of religion reached a broader cross section of American society than the more academic works of Edwin Starbuck and William James.[89]

Like other liberal Protestants, Coe recognized that something had caused Christianity to lose its privileged place in national life and its authority over the American people. He noted "the alienation from the Church of whole classes of the population," as well as "the apparent powerlessness of organized religion to suppress or seriously check the great organized vices and injustices of society," and "the failure of the Sunday school to make the people or even its own pupils familiar with the contents of the Bible." But he remained convinced that a solution was possible. Coe believed that data from psychology studies would allow Protestants to adapt their message and reach people who had fallen away. "Experience seems to show that we cannot hope to win them back by either wailing or scolding or arguing or coddling," Coe wrote (in a statement that was perhaps more autobiographical than he intended). But psychology offered a vehicle by which to do so.[90]

The close connections between Coe's views on faith and doubt and those of leading Protestant ministers stemmed in part from a shared worldview. Despite his decision not to pursue ordination, Coe nevertheless received an excellent theological education and was heavily influenced in his religious thought by Horace Bushnell, who had set mainline American Protestantism on its course toward theological liberalism, as well as by the same cohort of German theologians who shaped the views of Newman Smyth and other prominent clergy.[91]

Coe thus saw the person of Jesus as the core of Christian belief. "Jesus was less a teacher of dogma than a renewer of life," he declared, in words that might have easily come from a preacher in the pulpit of a liberal Protestant church. "Christian faith is not faith in any *it*, but faith in *him*." Coe conceded the necessity of some elements of doctrine to satisfy what he identified as an inherent human desire for an intellectual component of religious experience. But he agreed with other liberal Protestants that a focus on the person of Jesus rendered doubts about most doctrines irrelevant. Coe likewise accepted prevalent notions about the progressive nature of revelation. In part, this resulted from his adoption of the late nineteenth-century evolutionary worldview that saw all human experience in a progressive framework. Coe endorsed a Lamarckian understanding of human development, noting the "accumulating evidence that the development of the human individual runs parallel, in a general way, to the history of his race." Similarly, he insisted, religion grew more powerful and more sophisticated as the human race progressed.[92]

While he shared the philosophical and theological outlooks of his contemporaries, Coe proved more methodical in his consideration of the relationship of faith and doubt. For him, the primary issue was whether humans possessed the ability to gain absolute, certain knowledge about any subject. He thought not. "The ultimates of knowledge," he wrote, "are simply acts of self-realization." Certain, objective knowledge would always prove unattainable because "at the foundation, knowledge is simply self-assertion." This understanding of knowledge posed an obvious problem for religion. If knowledge represented nothing more than self-assertion, it scarcely differed from faith. And once faith and knowledge became identical, Coe insisted, the former lost "all its supposed immunities," and religious people could "hold as true only such propositions as evidence renders at least probable."[93]

In taking this position, Coe might have sounded a bit like the social scientists who sought to dismiss religion as an outmoded remnant of earlier stages of human development. But for all his own struggles with belief, Coe was not cast in the mold of William Graham Sumner or Lester Ward. Rather, he belonged to the second generation of American social scientists who came of age in the 1880s and 1890s and retained some level of commitment to Christian tradition. He did not wish for people to abandon Christianity by convincing them that faith could not withstand the scrutiny of modern knowledge. He simply wanted them to acknowledge the impossibility of attaining certainty. In so doing, a person might "find a way to be religious while being noncommittal concerning questions of fact or truth which he has not yet rationally adjusted."[94] Just like contemporary clergy, Coe hoped American Protestants would learn to develop a faith that coexisted with their valid doubts.

This perspective, which Coe popularized in countless speeches and articles, represented the endorsement by a respected social scientist of an idea nearly identical to Gladden's suggestions that Christians keep their "faces toward God" while they wrestled with religious uncertainty. He stridently criticized the culture of Protestant revivals, with their claim that true faith was confirmed through emotional conversion experiences. For Coe, faith became a disposition toward belief rather than assuredness about truth. "Faith, as distinguished from knowledge," he insisted, "is not assertiveness concerning facts or truths, but is the living as though we knew that which we confess to ourselves we do not know."[95] This concept of faith as a choice to believe despite absolute certainty recurred in Coe's thought. He told a group of theology students in 1906 that faith employed not only the intellect but also "the imagination, the feelings, and the moral will," and, he added, "it contains uncertainty."[96]

Coe emphasized doubt in his research because he believed that uncertainty needed to be accepted for faith to flourish. Like his colleague Edwin Starbuck, he viewed doubt primarily as a phenomenon that emerged during adolescence as men and women gained a deeper knowledge of the natural world. But Coe was more convinced than Starbuck that doubt persisted even in the mature religious life. He criticized orthodox Christians who denounced uncertainty "as a departure or threatened departure from pure religion itself" and lauded those liberals "who take the more favorable view of doubts." Christians made a grave error when they pressured doubting adolescents to ascribe to detailed confessions of faith. "The greatest thing we can do for the doubting youth is to induce him to give free exercise to the religious instinct," Coe insisted. "Let him not say what he does not actually believe; let him not compromise himself in any way." The reason: "it is always certain that he still believes, feels, and aspires enough to give him a place among religious people."[97] Coe's argument reinforced the growing tendency to welcome questioners into churches. He gave scientific affirmation to the increasingly accepted belief that doubt need not be combated, and he affirmed that doubters still deserved a place in religious communities.

The backing of psychologists, combined with the theological foundation provided by progressive revelation and a new focus on the person of Jesus, allowed liberal Protestants' inclusive perspective of doubt as a form of religious expression to flourish. When the Episcopal priest Leighton Parks proclaimed in a 1913 sermon that the time had come for churches "to forgive . . . the sin of doubt," he was hardly making a novel claim.[98] Indeed, many American Protestants had ceased to consider doubt to be a sin at all. They had come to identify ambiguity as a normal part of the religious life.

During the 1870s and 1880s, the challenge to Christianity from skepticism had appeared grave. But by the 1890s and especially after the dawn of the twentieth century, Protestant Americans had reason for optimism. A middle ground now existed between an unquestioning belief that took no account of contemporary ideas and a skeptical agnosticism that abandoned faith because of them. Protestants had found a way to live with their doubts, and it was now possible for Americans to affiliate with a church even if they harbored misgivings about aspects of its belief and practice.

There was an even more significant consequence of this effort to imbue doubt with religious value. It marked the first instance in which liberal Protestants affirmed a more inclusive understanding of religion as a means to forge a middle path between long-standing conceptions of Christian belief and competing secular worldviews. In so doing, however, these prominent Protestant leaders conceded that there might exist multiple forms of spiritual experience and a variety of paths to religious truth. It would not be long before they applied this same logic not just to doubt but to Catholicism and Judaism as well.

Initially, though, Protestants faced another problem. Curiosity about other belief systems posed as much of a difficulty as had skepticism. Yet, as they quickly discovered, their response to doubt would provide a ready-made template for responding to this challenge.

2

CORRECTING ELIJAH'S MISTAKE

The Liberal Protestant Embrace
of Comparative Religion

Late nineteenth-century Americans loved a good spectacle, and in the summer of 1893, the United States played host to the largest, most grandiose spectacle ever put forth of global religious diversity. The World's Parliament of Religions, held in conjunction with the massive Columbian Exposition in Chicago, attracted nationwide attention. It marked the first recorded attempt to bring together representatives from all of the world's major religious traditions. For seventeen days, thousands of attendees learned about one another's beliefs and practices through lectures, question-and-answer sessions, and informal social events. Guests from as far away as China, Japan, India, and the Middle East traveled to Chicago, where they joined a wide range of Americans, among them "ministers of the Gospel of various sects and orders, both Catholic and Protestant."[1]

Interpretations of the Parliament's lessons were nearly as diverse as were the participants. To some attendees, like the Ceylonese Buddhist monk Anagarika Dharmapala, the event was an opportunity to demonstrate to the predominantly American audience the superiority of their particular belief system. Dharmapala presented Buddhism as a "comprehensive system of ethics" and a "transcendental metaphysic embracing a sublime psychology" that appealed to the "simple-minded" and the "earnest student" equally well. He suggested that his tradition was ideally suited to the needs of the modern world. Since Buddhists had little use for alcohol or violence, their belief system was well suited for a society where "the dangers of modern life originate chiefly from drink and brutality."[2] Similarly, the American convert to Islam Mohammed Webb suggested that his adopted faith was best fitted to a modern, democratic society. He noted that its emphasis on "individual responsibility" aligned with the spirit of the age, and suggested that the absence of a "priesthood" and "ministry" in Islam increased its appeal in the Western societies that valorized freedom of thought and personal liberty (Webb depicted the imam as a lay prayer leader rather than as a member of a separate clerical order). Among Muslims, Webb declared, there was no doubt that "ultimately Islam will be the universal faith."[3]

In contrast to participants like Webb and Dharmapala who sought to convince attendees that their particular religion was to be the universal faith of the future, another group of speakers at the Parliament proclaimed an overarching similarity among all of the major world religions. India's Swami Vivekananda typified this perspective in his claim that "the Brahma of the Hindus, the Ahura Mazda of the Zoroastrians, the Buddha of the Buddhists, the Jehovah of the Jews, the Father in Heaven of the Christians" were in reality all the same person.[4] Vivekananda believed that this similarity made it possible for individuals to "assimilate" elements of various religions and integrate them into a personal spiritual life that developed "according to its own law of growth."[5]

For their part, however, the American organizers of the Parliament of Religions had little interest in advancing either view. Their words and actions belied any conviction that non-Christian religions were better suited to modern life or that people were free to pick and choose elements from all the world's faith traditions. Indeed, the night before the Parliament began, the chairman of its General Committee and one of Chicago's most popular preachers, John Henry Barrows, baptized three "Chinese converts" in his First Presbyterian Church. He also invited "the Buddhist delegation" to hear a "sermon on 'Christ the Wonderful.'"[6] Barrows was far from a religious conservative. Though he had trained at Andover Seminary, one of the bastions of nineteenth-century Protestant orthodoxy, he had by the time of the Parliament come to embrace many tenets of liberalism, including the conviction that the theory of evolution posed no challenge to Christian faith.[7]

Barrows was not alone, however. Language and symbols of Christian superiority pervaded the entire Parliament. Its first formal event was purported to be "an act of common worship," yet the organizers clearly sought to appeal to Christians. The worship service commenced with a hymn containing metaphors for God that would have seemed foreign to all attendees from nonmonotheistic traditions. But many attendees did not sing even such marginally inclusive words. The tune selected for the hymn was the same one used for the doxology commonly sung in Protestant worship, and much of the crowd spontaneously sang that instead of the intended text. The world's first major interfaith gathering thus began with the incongruous sight of people bellowing "Praise Father, Son, and Holy Ghost!"[8]

More than two weeks of discussion and social interaction among people of various religious traditions did little to dampen the underlying spirit of Christian superiority—and, indeed, of Protestant superiority—manifested by the Parliament's organizers. At one of the final sessions, Barrows read a poem written especially for the occasion by an evangelical author. Although Moses would "still be reverenced," "Buddha fill his worshipers with awe," and "Mohammed from his people claim a sober life and conduct," the poet professed, "over all the creeds the face of Christ glows with white glory on the face of man."[9] Indeed, this poem perfectly encapsulated the view of Parliament organizers. There was nothing wrong with the adherents of other religions maintaining their commitments, provided that they also acknowledged the superiority of both the Christian faith and Christian civilization. The Parliament itself, planned as it was primarily by Christian Americans, seemed to confirm this latter point about civilization for organizers. Committee chairman John Henry Barrows noted that this "first school of comparative religions" had come about almost exclusively through the efforts of "representatives of that Christian faith which we believe . . . is fitted to the needs of all men."[10] Washington Gladden, who attended the Parliament and presented a lecture on the relationship of religion and economic issues, echoed this view after his return from Chicago. He reported to his Ohio congregation that no matter what one thought of other religions, "no such practical manifestation of universal sympathy and fraternity would ever have occurred to their devotees."[11]

The seeming jumble of messages from participants has led many scholars to interpret the Parliament of Religions as a confused effort that reflected broader cultural uncertainty about religious pluralism. But while the message was perhaps jumbled, the intent of the organizers was quite unambiguous. "No attempt is here made to treat all religions as of equal merit," proclaimed Chicago attorney Charles Carroll Bonney, who served as president of the Parliament. For Bonney, the event constituted a forum for putting Christianity "to the knowledge of all men."[12] It thus resembled in spirit the Columbian Exposition, the larger event of which it was a part. The entire exposition illustrated the pervasive cultural assumption of Anglo-Saxon superiority, with its White City celebrating the achievements of American and European science and technology juxtaposed with the spectacle of "primitive" peoples on the Midway Plaisance. So too, the gathering of religious leaders offered a message about the superiority of Christianity, especially in its Protestant form. As John Henry Barrows explained a few years later, the Parliament of Religions was understood by its organizers to be "a great Christian demonstration with a non-Christian section which added color and picturesque effect."[13]

Despite the unambiguous chauvinism of their views about Christian superiority, Parliament organizers nevertheless reflected liberal Protestants' evolving views on religious pluralism. In their acknowledgment that representatives of non-Christian traditions deserved a place at the event, these Protestants decisively rejected the view that Hinduism, Buddhism, and Islam were not legitimate religions. However imperfect or inferior these traditions may have seemed, they *were* religions. For prominent liberals from the nation's major denominations, the Parliament provided a venue for affirming the value of non-Christian traditions in order to promote religious faith, and preferably their own faith. In this regard, the seventeen days in Chicago were far from unique. They represented just one instance—albeit a particularly grandiose instance—of a more widespread reevaluation of the relationship between Protestantism and non-Christian faiths.

This reevaluation resulted from the same profound shift in the religious culture of the United States that had already produced new interpretations of doubt and uncertainty. As Americans increasingly questioned their inherited faith commitments, they simultaneously began to explore other avenues of spiritual fulfillment. This desire for more meaningful religious feeling coincided with a growing awareness of Hinduism, Buddhism, and Islam in the United States, a reality that vexed many Protestants. The more curious Americans learned about these religions, the more these alternative faiths seemed to challenge commonly held assumptions about the uniqueness of Christian teaching.

Therein lay the crux of the problem. Most liberal Protestants were ultimately less concerned with the actual claims of other religions than with the idea that all religions were equally true and thus interchangeable. The view became increasingly common that individuals could have, in the words of one participant at the Parliament of Religions, "not only one of these vast faiths, but all of them at his side."[14] Christianity, in other words, no longer seemed unique. And if Christianity was not unique, the cultural authority of American Protestant institutions seemed to rest on very shaky ground.

Liberal Protestants proved as determined to fight this "temper of indifferentism" toward what they perceived to be the specific truths of Christianity as they were to combat the "materialistic philosophy of the universe" advocated by skeptics like Robert Ingersoll.[15] Yet with prominent artists and intellectuals valorizing spiritual curiosity and with new evidence seeming to undercut long-standing claims of Christian uniqueness, liberal clergy and theologians realized that they could no longer dismiss other religions as entirely false.

Instead, many Protestants embarked on a new strategy. They sought to identify as many similarities as possible between Christianity and other traditions and then invoke the parallels as evidence for Christian superiority. The primacy of their own faith would thus be assured over the claims of relativists, but at the same time the truths of other sets of belief and practice would be affirmed. This was precisely what John Henry Barrows and his fellow organizers sought to accomplish at the Parliament of Religions, but they were far from alone in doing so. During the 1880s and 1890s, the very same strategy of emphasizing similarity to buttress Protestantism was expressed in theological schools, churches, and periodicals throughout the nation.

This approach to America's increasingly visible religious diversity had profound consequences. Most obviously, it resulted in far greater knowledge and acceptance of religions that were almost entirely unknown a few decades earlier. Moreover, the Parliament forced Protestant Americans to situate their growing enthusiasm for religious pluralism in the context of their intractable commitment to a highly racialized worldview. Finally, this strategy also had the unintended consequence of narrowing the gulf that had separated Protestants from their Catholic and Jewish neighbors. The more liberal Protestants learned about Hinduism, Buddhism, and Islam, the less strange Catholicism and Judaism began to appear.

As educated Americans of the late nineteenth century questioned their long-standing beliefs and found traditional Protestant Christianity less fulfilling, it was foreseeable that they would look for alternatives. And look they did. This newfound curiosity about alternative forms of religious expression and its concomitant desire for new sources of spiritual meaning had many outlets, some of which bore little resemblance to any recognized form of religion.

The desire for deeper spiritual fulfillment first manifested itself in efforts to imbue traditionally secular phenomena with religious meaning. In the nation's burgeoning metropolises, new activities and institutions assumed many of the roles that churches had previously served. The late nineteenth century witnessed the development of urban cultural institutions, such as symphony orchestras, which were established during the 1870s in major cities including Boston and Chicago. In New York, which by century's end had secured its status as the nation's leading city, new cultural opportunities abounded, including the symphony, libraries, the Metropolitan Museum of Art, and the Museum of Natural History. Urban residents imbued these institutions with enormous purpose. This period witnessed what one historian has labeled the "sacralization" of American cultural institutions. Elites increasingly looked on museums and orchestras not merely as sources of entertainment, but as sites for self-growth and personal fulfillment. The sense of participation in something larger and greater than oneself, which Americans had long sought to achieve through religion, came to be provided by urban cultural institutions. The result, as Protestant observers noted, was that many educated city dwellers came to believe that "they can get on and prosper without the personal acceptance or formal acknowledgment of Christianity."[16]

While Protestants generally tolerated the challenge to religious practice from new cultural institutions, they grew increasingly anxious about another source Americans looked to for spiritual fulfillment: non-Christian religions. Part of their concern stemmed from the increasing accessibility of these very religions. After the Civil War, as the cost of transatlantic travel fell, the European tour that had once been a special privilege reserved for the highest elites became more common and lost its luster. Young men who longed for rugged adventure began to look to Asia as an alternative to the seemingly sedate, feminine European travel experience. Transpacific expeditions benefited from the launch of a steamship line between San Francisco and Japan in 1867 and the completion of the transcontinental railroad two years later.[17]

As they traveled to Asia, Americans came into close contact with Hinduism, Buddhism, and, in the case of those sojourners who undertook the increasingly popular round-the-world tour, Islam (known in the parlance of the day as Mohammedanism). For a generation of Americans struggling with skepticism about the tenets of Protestant Christianity, many of whom were artists and intellectuals and already doubted the cultural superiority of the United States, it seemed that the religions they encountered in India, China, and Japan might provide a meaningful alternative.[18]

When these travelers—historian Henry Adams, artist John LaFarge, physician William Sturgis Bigelow, and writer Alexander Russell Webb among the most noteworthy—returned to the United States, they brought with them new knowledge about Hinduism, Buddhism, and Islam, which they often continued to practice. Given the prominence of such men in intellectual and cultural circles, these religions gained greater attention in the United States. While the hundreds of thousands of Asian immigrants who arrived in the late nineteenth century certainly heightened the visibility of Hinduism and Buddhism, it was through the efforts of these intellectuals that the religions gained respectability. The heated rhetoric of nativists notwithstanding, immigrants tended to keep their religious views private, and most had more immediate, practical concerns than proselytization. The few who actively sought to win converts met with little success. As Lyman Abbott and the *Outlook's* editors assured their readers, "neither Buddhism nor Hinduism" was "attracting large numbers who are willing to acknowledge their conversion." The real problem for Protestants was that both traditions (and Islam as well) were "being studied in some form or other by so many" that it made "careful attention to the subject of comparative religion of the greatest importance" to concerned Christians.[19]

Many of the people engaging in comparative study were religiously disaffected Americans who sought more fulfilling avenues of belief and practice in these newly visible religious traditions. Abbott's assistant editor, Hamilton Mabie, acknowledged the appeal of other religions in the way they spoke to deep aspects of human nature. In certain moods, he declared, "one easily comprehends the charm of Oriental mysticism; the charm of unbroken silence in which one pursues and at last overtakes himself" and ultimately "is alone with himself, and within the invisible horizons of his own thought all mysteries are hidden and revealed."[20] With his firm commitment to Christianity, it is highly unlikely that Mabie would ever have given himself to "Oriental mysticism." But the journalist's invocation of a non-Christian tradition typified the extent to which alternative conceptions of religiosity had gained cultural currency in late nineteenth-century America.

Just as skeptics drew strength from natural science and biblical scholarship, Americans who were serious about exploring alternative religious options found support in the developing academic field of comparative religious study. The project of rigorously evaluating religions alongside one another began in Europe in the early nineteenth century as an effort to elucidate the precise relationship between Christianity and other traditions with which it came into contact. Starting at midcentury, though, comparative religion reached the United States. Like many other aspects of religious and biblical study, it swiftly became the domain of highly educated specialists. These scholars brought greater sophistication and a spirit of genuine curiosity to religious study, and they intentionally sought to eliminate overt apologetics for Christianity from their work.

One of the earliest of such endeavors was the 1871 volume *Ten Great Religions*, written by the Unitarian minister James Freeman Clarke, who sought to offer a comparative treatment of theology in the same manner that natural scientists might undertake a comparative study. Clarke partly succeeded. His research was largely limited to providing a synthesis of more sophisticated works of European scholarship, but he nevertheless received credit both at home and abroad for elevating the level of religious study in the United States. This dispassionate approach to the study of faith traditions aligned well with the larger goals of the developing research universities, which became the primary sites of religious scholarship after the 1870s. In 1873, Boston University established the nation's first chair in the "comparative history of religion, comparative theology, and philosophy of religion," and Harvard and other institutions quickly followed. Soon after, the archetype of the new research university, the University of Chicago, established the nation's first major program in religious studies that was not intended primarily as a training ground for ministers.[21]

To many observers, the rigorous academic comparison of religions seemed like it might drive the final nail into the coffin of a Protestant tradition already battered by the skepticism wrought by evolutionary philosophy and biblical criticism. Indeed, the study of other belief systems posed several distinct challenges to Protestant Christianity. The first was the ease with which other religions, especially Buddhism, seemed to be reconcilable with the worldview of the very skeptics who were already assailing Christianity for its incompatibility with modern science and philosophy. American intellectuals who found it nearly impossible to reconcile Christian belief with modern thought emphasized the seeming alignment of Buddhist teaching with the positivist philosophy of Auguste Comte.[22]

A far greater source of anxiety stemmed from the claim of many academic religious scholars that close resemblances existed between Christianity and other religions. Buddhism had long posed a challenge for religious scholars who held to the superiority of the Christian tradition: of the several major world religions, Buddhism seemed to resemble Christianity most closely. It also had a large number of adherents and was clearly transnational, thus making it harder to dismiss as a regional, "ethnic" religion, as European scholars had attempted to do with Hinduism. More worryingly, Christianity and Buddhism seemed to share smaller characteristics as well. While some Protestants contemptuously suggested that any similarities proved only that earlier generations of Buddhists had stolen Christian ideas, many other critics drew precisely the opposite conclusion. They pointed to similarities between the childhood stories of Jesus and Siddhartha Gautama (the Buddha) as evidence that beloved Christian stories had been lifted from other sacred texts. The Episcopal priest Leighton Parks noted the claim "frequently urged against the religion of Christ" that numerous instances in the Gospel accounts of Jesus's life "have been borrowed from earlier Oriental religious books."[23]

Seeming parallels between religious texts further undermined the Christian claim that the Bible was a unique divine revelation. Edwin Arnold's long poem, *The Light of Asia*, was a major source of such ideas. Arnold, whose work enjoyed immense popularity among educated readers in late nineteenth-century America, not only cast Buddhism in a favorable light but also emphasized numerous similarities in the persons of Jesus and Gautama.[24]

Though less popular with American intellectuals than Buddhism was, Islam posed many of the same challenges to Christian claims of superiority. It, too, was clearly an international religion, and like Christianity and Buddhism, Islam was perceived to have a "missionary" impulse that required expansion and conversion. According to American observers like John Henry Barrows, Islam was far more successful in spreading its message than were "the disciples of the Indian sage," and, more worryingly, it had begun "winning some of the races of mankind more rapidly" than Christianity.[25] Moreover, as a result of Islam's later development, it retained many elements of Christian belief, including the concepts of prophets and apostles sent by God, the resurrection of those who died, and an ultimate, final judgment.[26] These parallels—especially in a tradition that developed centuries after Christianity—likewise undermined claims of Christian uniqueness.

American Protestants grew troubled that comparative religious study seemed only to encourage religious exploration that bred relativism or indifference to truth. If Christianity, Buddhism, and Islam already shared many common elements, there was nothing to prevent mixing and matching among them. The same would be equally true for Hinduism, Confucianism, and countless other traditions. Moreover, although they often did not want to cut all ties to Christianity, the people who indulged in such spiritual exploration believed that non-Christian practices often proved superior. They particularly enjoyed meditation, which appeared to offer a vehicle, absent from Protestant practice, for coping with the frantic pace of modern life.[27]

Such religious eclecticism found a voice among artists and intellectuals in the final decades of the nineteenth century. People like Thomas Wentworth Higginson, a longtime traveler in New England's most liberal religious circles, increasingly advocated the view that all religions represented equally inferior pieces of a larger religious truth. In 1867, Higginson joined Ralph Waldo Emerson, Lydia Maria Child (herself the author of an earlier book on comparative religion), and other like-minded spiritual explorers in establishing the Free Religious Association. The group sought to collapse the barriers that separated the world's religions and to foster a free atmosphere of spiritual exploration unhindered by traditional doctrinal systems. In his 1870 lecture "The Sympathy of Religions," Higginson insisted that all religions were in essence the same. He pointed to common elements found in each of the word's major religious traditions, including shared ethical views and common practices of identifying sacred time and space. Exemplifying the relativism that infuriated mainstream Protestants, Higginson encouraged members to draw freely from all religious texts, including the Bible, without privileging any of them. At its conferences and in its publications, the Free Religious Association proclaimed that all people had the capacity to blend different traditions' teachings together in a personal spiritual synthesis. Higginson used his speech at the Parliament of Religions to advocate just such a practice. "The humblest individual thinker may retain the essence of religion, and may moreover, have not only one of these vast faiths, but all of them at his side. Each of them alone is partial, limited, unsatisfying," he declared.[28]

Nor was the Free Religious Association unique in this enterprise. During these same years, the well-to-do New Englander Sarah Farmer, whose own religious views reflected a blend of Christian and Baha'i influences, established a retreat at Greenacre, Maine. There she offered an "entirely unsectarian" summer school for the "scientific study of various forms of philosophical and religious thought."[29] Also popular was the Theosophical Society, founded in 1875 by the enigmatic

Russian spiritualist Helena Blavatsky and the Civil War veteran Henry Steel Olcott. Building on the long-standing American fascination with spiritualism and its founders' own explorations of the occult, Theosophy borrowed heavily from Hinduism and Buddhism and incorporated ideas of Karma and reincarnation. But what made the work of Blavatsky and Olcott particularly troubling to Protestant observers was their willingness to blend traditional Christian theologies—such as the doctrine of original sin—with religious ideas they encountered in Asia.[30] Such eclectic practices also found their way into worship practices. The book of services used at the Bell Street Chapel in Providence, Rhode Island, encouraged the use of readings from the Buddha and the medieval Islamic theologian Omar Khayyam.[31]

Even for those liberal Protestants who embraced theological innovation in the face of modern thought and culture, people like Higginson, Farmer, and especially Blavatsky and Olcott went too far in their syncretistic approaches to religion. By freely blending Christian teachings with elements of other religions, these curious explorers conveyed the message that Christianity simply represented one tradition among many and lacked a unique, divine sanction. Even the most liberal of mainstream Protestants would not countenance such a claim.

Americans' curiosity about non-Christian religions and the resulting popularity of spiritual eclecticism presented Protestants with three options. The first was simply to ignore both phenomena by holding fast to the old conviction that "heathen religions are dying" and would soon cease to pose a challenge. This approach found favor even among some theological liberals who otherwise were quite broad-minded about religious pluralism. The Presbyterian minister and theologian James Henry Snowden was one of the early champions of the new outlook on doubt. But he did not extend his inclusiveness to the followers of other religions. "No words need to be wasted," he declared, "in demonstrating that [Jesus] is the right religious leader for us to follow. Buddha, Confucius, and Mohammed are not to be mentioned in his presence."[32] But while this strategy of avoidance might have worked at Snowden's church in western Pennsylvania, the prominence of those who embraced other religious traditions rendered it a less useful strategy in the nation's intellectual and cultural hubs.

The second possible option was to disavow any similarity between Christianity and other religions and to attack the scholars who claimed that there was, thereby undercutting the grounds of favorable comparison. This was the approach favored by more orthodox Protestants who generally remained leery of liberal theology and its inherent accommodation of modern thought and culture. Buddhism and Christianity "have almost nothing in common," declared one Protestant intellectual, who went on to denounce "modern scholars" who had "grown up amid the light of Christianity" only to "slur and disparage the mother that bore them, and to sound the praises of some old mother of darkness and superstition."[33] Ministers also promulgated this message to churchgoers, especially in rural areas. The pastor of the Congregational church in the small town of Waucoma, in northeastern Iowa, explained to congregants that clear differences existed "between the christian [sic] religion and the modes of worship adopted by many of the heathen nations."[34]

There was a third option, however, which became popular among the liberals who increasingly dominated the elite institutions of American Protestantism. Rather than avoiding or denouncing comparative religion, this strategy called for its wholehearted embrace. Liberal Protestants who adopted this approach affirmed the similarities among religions and then attempted to employ those similarities as proof of the superiority not only of Christianity, but also of Protestantism. But in so doing, they were forced to defend other religions as sources of considerable truth.

Liberal Protestants' initial wave of enthusiasm for comparative religion crested during the 1890s, but it rested on a foundation of theological innovations that had occurred over the course of the century. Some of these innovations had little to do with non-Christian religions. The first crucial development was the gradual moderation of liberal Protestants' views about human salvation. Beginning in the mid-eighteenth century, as discomfort with rigid Calvinism grew among the descendants of the New England Puritans, many religious thinkers rejected the once-common belief that all non-Christians faced certain damnation. The initial manifestation of shifting attitudes came in the context of children. Puritans had firmly held that only a small number of infants and children would attain salvation.

In the wake of the emphasis on personal conversion during the revivals of the Second Great Awakening, Americans began to question how children, who lacked the capacity for the self-reflection necessary to receive God's grace, could so unfairly be sentenced to an eternity of torment through little fault of their own. Moreover, society as a whole adopted a more sentimental view of childhood. As middle-class Americans became more visibly attached to their children, the notion that the nation's beloved children were damned to hell if they died at a young age seemed untenable. Horace Bushnell, the champion of liberal theology in the United States at mid-century, rejected the assumption that each child "is to grow up in sin" and only be converted after "he has come to a mature age." He argued instead that religious Americans should embrace the possibility that the children with proper education would "cleave unto what is good and right."[35] As the century progressed, other Protestants, including the theologians Charles Augustus

Briggs and James Henry Snowden, who as Presbyterians were intellectual heirs to Calvinism, came to soften their views on the religious state of children. Snowden observed that a "complete change all along the line" had occurred. Over the course of the nineteenth century, Protestantism had witnessed the "utter abandonment of the old doctrine and universal acceptance of the belief that all infants dying are saved." By the 1890s, even some of the most ardent defenders of Calvinist orthodoxy had come to view infant damnation "with a shudder as something unchristian and barbarous."[36]

Having proclaimed the salvation of children who were too young to have consciously accepted Christianity, many liberal theologians applied the same logic to those who lived in faraway lands and lacked contact with Christian teaching. Charles Briggs explicitly linked the salvation of young children and non-Christians in faraway lands. In his view, "God's electing grace saves all infants, and not a few of the heathen."[37] To make the same point, James Henry Snowden invoked the biblical prophet Elijah, who erroneously thought "there was only one saved man in Israel when there were 7000," and he suggested that so too there were "more saved souls in the world" than American Protestants had hitherto acknowledged.[38] Other influential voices agreed. It would be an "unethical conception of God" that would allow "vast multitudes of his human children to perish and to sink into hopeless perdition" without providing "the truth" needed "for their salvation," declared one author, while another cautioned readers against the assumption that all non-Christians were damned, noting that the Bible "is silent on the fate of the heathen."[39] Liberal Protestants did not claim that the religious beliefs of such people were sufficient for achieving salvation. Rather, they argued that in the case of both young children and non-Christians throughout the world, God took pity and granted salvation to deserving people who through no fault of their own had never encountered Christian teaching.

Although proponents of this new perspective on salvation did not set out to affirm the value of non-Christian religions, their new outlook nevertheless caused a shift in how liberal Protestants viewed other traditions. Though they continued to maintain that Buddhism, Hinduism, and Islam were inferior to Christianity, these Protestants now conceded that these religions shared many of the same elements of truth that Christian teaching espoused. As with his evolving views on doubt and uncertainty, the Congregationalist minister Washington Gladden offered one of the most eloquent summaries of the shift that occurred in how some Protestants viewed these other traditions. "I was taught in my youth to regard all these as false religions," he confessed to his congregation, noting the once-common view that "they originated in deceit and trickery." By the end of the nineteenth century, Gladden preached, "no teacher of reasonable intelligence uses any such language about them." Other religions were instead seen as "sincere efforts of human souls to find the unseen power behind phenomena, and to put themselves in communion with Him."[40]

Liberal Protestants' embrace of progressive revelation—a critical element in their acceptance of doubt—provided additional strength to their new outlook on non-Christian religions. Mary Abigail Dodge, one of the few women of the late nineteenth century to openly espouse the ideals of theological liberalism, was among the first to note the acceptance of the theory that non-Christian religions had merit because they seemed to represent earlier stages of religious development. Dodge, a New Englander who is perhaps best remembered as an activist for women's rights, was—under her pen name of Gail Hamilton—a prolific writer of stories, novels, and essays. She contributed to numerous publications, including the *Christian Union* and the *Outlook*, where her work found champions in Lyman Abbott and Hamilton Mabie. Dodge was also a practicing Congregationalist who delighted in the opportunity to hear theological perspectives that differed from her own. She was unafraid to announce her views on a range of subjects, and in her boldly titled 1876 collection *Sermons to the Clergy* endorsed many of the tenets of liberal Protestantism, including the reconcilability of faith with science and the free exercise of reason in religious thought and practice.[41]

During the 1880s, Dodge noted the increasingly popular view among Protestants that, in her words, "the ethnic religions, antedating Christianity in their origin, have been providential and even preparatory to Christianity."[42] Like most Protestants, she denied the existence of parity between her own faith and these earlier "ethnic" belief systems. But Dodge was quite willing to concede that belief systems like Hinduism and Buddhism were not without value. She lamented that the Hindu Vedas lacked "sufficient moral impulsion" for the sacred texts to take root in the Western world, while she ascribed to the Bible a simplicity and clarity that gave it universal value.[43]

Liberal Protestants widely accepted this view that other religions were well suited to specific cultures and specific periods but that Christianity had progressed beyond all lesser-developed forms of religious expression and had emerged as a truly global faith. Islam posed some obvious difficulties by complicating this narrative of constant progress. But Protestants solved this dilemma by noting that it had developed before the Reformation. While Islam was inferior to Protestantism, John Henry Barrows suggested, it had been an improvement on the beliefs and practices of the Roman Catholic and Eastern Orthodox churches of the Middle Ages.[44]

Thus, liberals convinced themselves that the development of various religious traditions aligned perfectly with the vision of racial development offered by social theorists, who claimed that remnants of earlier stages of development persisted in higher forms of life. The apparent similarities between Christianity and other religions were not evidence of Christianity's lack of uniqueness but rather of its superiority. The psychologist and practicing Methodist George Coe noted that the Bible contained the "remains of early religion, fragments of discarded customs and beliefs" which Christians had ultimately perfected.[45] Likewise, the Episcopal priest Leighton Parks proclaimed that Christianity exceeded other religions only in "the *degree* of its revelation," not in the content.[46] Non-Christian religions were "broken-lights of the one great central sun," in Washington Gladden's analogy, but "the Father of light" had provided "heathen" with "all the truth they could receive" in their current state.[47] And Lyman Abbott told his congregation at Brooklyn's Plymouth Church that while the Christian Bible represented God's "supreme revelation," other teachings, such as "the ethical provisions of Confucius" and "the aspirations of Brahmin and Buddhist after a nobler conception of God," were also the result of God "revealing himself" in human history.[48]

One obvious consequence of this strategy was that it forced Protestants to present a more nuanced explanation of what precisely made Christianity's revelation different from that given to other religions. When Hinduism, Buddhism, and Islam were denounced as containing nothing but falsehoods, there was little need to explicate where the differences lay. But the embrace of comparative religion necessitated explaining what made Christian belief better than the tenets of Gladden's "broken-lights."

To elucidate the points of difference, many Protestants followed the same route they had traced in their consideration of doubt: they invoked the person of Jesus as the essential difference. Indeed, even before their embrace of comparative religion, Protestants had long held that Jesus was by the nature of his self-understanding distinct from the founding figures of other traditions. Whereas Buddha and Mohammed "put the centre of their systems in some idea or external end," Jesus had grounded "all ideas and methods in devotion to Himself."[49]

With the acceptance of comparative religion, Jesus became *the* sole point of difference that separated Christianity from other religions when other aspects of teaching seemed identical. An Illinois minister affirmed that Hinduism contained "the great fundamentals of true religion" and insisted that "no *such* gulf . . . as is often supposed" separated it from Christianity. But because Hindus lacked the "magic key to unlock the human heart, found in the Cross of Christ," their beliefs lacked the "ineffable holiness of the highest Christian character."[50] So, too, in his comparison of Christianity with Islam, John Henry Barrows noted "the immeasurable superiority of the Prophet of Nazareth over the Prophet of Arabia."[51] Lyman Abbott noted that despite the fact that they conveyed "splendid ideas," other religions "have no person to awake enthusiasm of love."[52] It was this conviction of "the supreme place of Jesus" that led George Coe to declare that "we need not hesitate to compare Christianity . . . with the other religions of the world."[53]

This embrace of comparative religion became a common feature of liberal Protestant thought during the final decades of the nineteenth century. The spread of this practice into the popular press and into Protestant churches was exemplified by the Episcopal priest Leighton Parks, who spent much of a trip through India, China, and Japan during the 1880s reflecting on the beliefs of the non-Christians he encountered. Parks, the rector of a parish in Boston's tony Back Bay, was highly influenced by the liberal theology of the city's respected bishop, Phillips Brooks, and later in his career would become a leading voice of religious liberalism from his pulpit at St. Bartholomew's Church in New York.[54]

Parks found that the more he learned about other religions during his travels, the less he could accept the notion that they were devoid of value. He reflected that as he encountered the faith traditions of Asia, the more convinced he became that they were, as he wrote of historic Hinduism, "not far from the kingdom of God."[55] In Japan, he enjoyed a prolonged conversation with a monk who, Parks confessed, got the better of him in a theological debate. This encounter left him with "much to think of, for in a nation 'very superstitious' we had met a man who was 'working righteousness.'"[56] Upon returning to the United States, Parks continued his study of Hinduism and Buddhism by examining their sacred texts, which he found not to be "dead books" as he expected but rather "the staff of life to 'living, breathing, thinking men.'" As he immersed himself in these works, the priest gained a newfound sympathy for other Americans who had likewise experienced a "sudden awakening" to other religions and had realized that "the Bible is not the limit of revelation."[57]

In a series of lectures that he delivered at Boston's Lowell Institute in the winter of 1885, Leighton Parks sought to allay anxieties about non-Christian faiths by emphasizing the many similarities that all religions shared. Given the growing popularity of spiritual eclecticism among Boston's elites, Parks was addressing a very relevant topic for his audience. The clergyman adopted a novel approach to religious comparison, seeking to make "the religions of the world become the great 'Evidences of Christianity,'" a phrase that invoked William Paley's outmoded 1794 attempt to prove Christian doctrine on the grounds of natural evidence. By emphasizing commonly held beliefs, Parks thought it possible to demonstrate what many other liberal Protestants had begun to claim: that Christianity contained the highest, purest religious truths that existed in primitive forms in other religions.[58]

One element of Parks's strategy involved crediting Hinduism and Buddhism with developing concepts of the divine, the world, and humanity that were essential to Christian teaching. He reminded his Boston audience that Christians traced their conception of a personal God to the religion of ancient Israel, and consequently they privileged historic Judaism as the principal source of many Christian beliefs. But Parks insisted that Hinduism had been equally influential in providing the source of fundamental doctrines. A major characteristic of nineteenth-century liberal theology was its emphasis on divine immanence—that is, the idea that God was not aloof but rather was present in the created world. Parks believed that this notion of God's relationship to creation developed from historic Hindu teachings about the relationship between nature and the divine. Christianity was not a unique religion but rather a bringing together into one unity the separate truths taught by other traditions. "In the life of Jesus," Parks declared, "is gathered the Aryan revelation of the Immanence of God, and the Semitic revelation of the Personality of God."[59]

Both before and after the 1893 Parliament of Religions, exercises of comparative religion took place in churches, community organizations, and popular journals throughout the United States. In Columbus, Washington Gladden presented his congregation with a multiweek sermon series on the major religions of the world, which proved so popular that he preached it again several years later. He acknowledged a debt to Leighton Parks, whose Lowell Institute lectures he credited as an inspiration to attempt his own comparison of religious traditions. Like most Protestants, Gladden denied the validity of attempts to "say that one religion is as good as another" just because the believers "all are equally sincere." Yet he encouraged his congregants to learn from Hinduism, Buddhism, Confucianism, and Islam, because each contained "much precious and inspiring truth" that would be beneficial to Protestants' own religious commitment. "Our comparisons ought to clarify our own conceptions," Gladden declared, "and strengthen our hold upon the enduring realities of religion."[60]

Other instances of comparative religious study abounded. In 1894, the Suffolk South Association, a group of Congregational ministers in and around Boston, heard lectures titled "The Relation of Christianity to the Ethnic Religions" and "Points of Difference between [Christianity] and the Ethnic Religions."[61] More significant still, it was not merely clergy exploring the subject. Boston's Congregationalist Old South Church held a series of classes for members that consisted of "a general discussion of the comparative value to life of different types of religion, including Catholicism, Quakerism, Methodism, Unitarianism, Hebraism, Bushido, Stoicism, and Buddhism."[62]

One particularly instructive instance of this phenomenon occurred in Montclair, New Jersey, in 1897. A community organization comprising members of the town's Protestant churches organized a series of lectures comparing Christianity and Buddhism. The Buddhist perspective was presented by Anagarika Dharmapala, who was on a tour of the United States that had resulted from the popularity he attained when he spoke at the Parliament of Religions. He had gained particular favor with the Free Religious Association and with Sarah Farmer of the Greenacre retreat, and he had established branches of his Maha Bodhi Society in New York, Chicago, and San Francisco.[63]

It became quickly apparent that the Protestant churchgoers of Montclair were not the Greenacre's spiritual seekers. One of the event's organizers was the local Congregationalist minister, Amory Bradford, whose theological liberalism did not overcome his anxieties about the spread of other religions. Bradford had recently garnered attention with his dire (and false) claim that the number of Hindus and Buddhists in the United States had surpassed the number of Christians in Asia, and the evening seemed designed to assuage the fears of people like him.[64] The other speaker, the Harvard philosopher George H. Palmer, quickly dismissed Dharmapala's claim of parity between Christianity and Buddhism. Palmer conceded the "close kinship between Buddhism and Christianity." He noted that, among other commonalities, both religions represented "gospels of deliverance" from the trials of human life by offering a message of immortality. Palmer insisted, however, that Buddhism represented "the smaller faith." Its pessimistic view on human nature and its goal of the loss of self in nirvana were inferior, more primitive religious teachings than the optimistic message of individual potential found in Protestant Christianity.[65]

Given Montclair's proximity to New York, the debate between Palmer and Dharmapala caught the attention of Lyman Abbott, who reported on the event in the *Outlook*. Its coverage of the evening portrayed Palmer as the clear winner and, more significantly, emphasized the liberal Protestant conviction that such "friendly" comparisons of religious belief would always confirm the faith of Christians. Abbott and his fellow editors suggested—in a barely veiled reference to the Free Religious Association and similar groups—that "certain circles in Boston and elsewhere" might do well to undertake such exercises to restore their own commitment to the Christian faith.[66] The gulf between liberal Protestant views and Dharmapala's perspective became clearer when the monk sent a letter to the *Outlook* lamenting their presentation of Palmer's "one-sided view" of his "much-maligned religion" and urging the editors to give him space for a rebuttal. Though they printed Dharmapala's lengthy letter, they did not revise their assessment of the Montclair event.[67]

Abbott did, however, commission a series of articles that sought to examine non-Christian religions and their relationship to Christianity. So, too, did the editors of the more highbrow *North American Review*. Both journals featured experts on Islam, Hinduism, Buddhism, and Confucianism, who introduced readers to key tenets and practices of each tradition while also drawing comparisons and contrasts to Christian belief.[68] These experts followed the pattern of Protestant liberals and found aspects of non-Christian traditions to praise while nevertheless insisting on the primacy of Christianity. Arthur Henderson Smith, a Congregationalist minister and a missionary in China, wrote in the *Outlook* that there were "many resemblances between the teachings of Christ and those of Confucianists." Ultimately, though, he concluded that the former pushed nations "toward the morning dawn of a bright future," while the latter constituted "a spent force."[69]

Similarly, the Harvard Sanskrit professor Charles Rockwell Lanman noted that Hindu belief had parallels in Christianity that might "prove to be of value for our religious life" despite their tinge of "Indian pessimism." He enthusiastically cheered Protestants' growing interest in other religions, which he characterized as "a step in advance, clear and great." But Lanman had little patience for the smorgasbord approach to religion favored by many prominent intellectuals. "There may indeed be much unintelligent dabbling in Buddhism and sundry other 'isms' of the East," he wrote, decrying the consequent development of an "irreverent and weak and flabby eclecticism."[70] For Lanman and others, the study of other religions was not meant to inspire experimentation but rather was a vehicle to secure one's commitment to Christianity by recognizing that only it offered the height of religious truth.

Considered in light of these widespread attempts to employ comparative religious study to identify points of commonality among traditions while ultimately confirming Christian belief, the 1893 Parliament of Religions seems far from unique. Most of its Protestant participants recognized it for what the organizers intended it to be: a more grandiose instance of a relatively common phenomenon. One Methodist bishop insisted that the Parliament would offer testimony to the universality of Jesus. In "the most magnificent spectacle the Christian world has ever seen," everyone would pay tribute to Jesus, including "the Unitarians, who recognize him as a man; the Mohammedans, who recognize him as a prophet; the Jews, who recognize him as one of their teachers; and then all the classes of Christians who recognize his divinity."[71] Washington Gladden rejected the position of Thomas Wentworth Higginson and other members of the Free Religious Association that the purpose of the Parliament was to formulate "a universal religion, to supersede all the others."[72] Its true purpose was to highlight the superiority of Protestant Christianity. "The Parliament is likely to prove a blessing to many Christians by marking the time when they shall cease thinking that the verities and virtues of other religions discredit the claims of Christianity," declared John Henry Barrows. "Why should not Christians be glad to learn what God has wrought through Buddha and Zoroaster—through the sage of China, and the prophets of India and the prophet of Islam?" he asked.[73] Why not, indeed? For Barrows and his fellow Protestants, everything God had wrought in those religions had been wrought in higher, purer form through Christianity.

While its message was not unique, the size and scope of the Parliament of Religions did lend it greater significance in shaping American Protestant attitudes about religious pluralism. In many respects, the event bolstered Protestants' confidence. The conviction of the superiority of Christianity, especially the ubiquitous view that only Christians could have arranged such a gathering, made many Protestants even more firmly committed to the missionary enterprise. James Henry Snowden reaffirmed his view that while they contained many truths, other faiths were "twilight religions," and their adherents needed to receive Jesus, "the light of the world."[74]

Yet the emphasis on comparative religious study caused a shift in liberal Protestants' conception of mission work. Leighton Parks, the Episcopal priest who was among the first to articulate the value of Hinduism and Buddhism, remained adamant that "foreign missions" were an inevitable aspect of Christian practice. But the underlying motive of that work had changed. Earlier endeavors emphasized the need to save the "heathen" from their false beliefs and practices. Liberal Protestants now sought to complete the existing but imperfect religious commitments of non-Christians. The "millions in Africa, in India, in Japan," Parks declared, who were separated from Christianity were nonetheless each still a "child of God."[75] The very fact that they possessed some sense of religious truth made it all the more imperative that they receive the full truth. "If Christianity is absolute," observed the Boston Congregationalist George Gordon, "that absoluteness must be shown, in part at least, by the final divine interpretation which it puts upon the previous imperfect disciplines of the various nations to whom it is sent."[76] In other words, Christians had an obligation to put forth their superior religious message to peoples who had previously received less developed revelations.

The Presbyterian minister and Parliament of Religions organizer John Henry Barrows embodied the new confidence about Christian missions that emerged after the 1893 event. While he conceded that Christianity still remained one belief system among many, he insisted that "the comparative study of religions" revealed that Christianity was "so adapted to universal acceptance that its prevalence seems more than probable."[77] Barrows himself celebrated the success of the Parliament by departing on a tour of Asia funded by the Chicago heiress Caroline Haskell, who reported that she had "been struck with the many points of harmony between the different faiths" that were presented at the gathering. She believed that Christians might find greater success in their Asian missionary efforts by emphasizing these similarities, and she dispatched Barrows to India and Japan for that very purpose.[78]

When he returned from his two-year tour, the Protestant minister acknowledged with unusual charitableness that "America has some things to learn from India," and that "the study of Eastern Scriptures will bring into new radiance hidden beauties and treasures of our religion." But he had not become a relativist. While he thought that Protestants might gain new appreciation from examining Hinduism and Buddhism, Barrows denied the possibility that "Western Christendom" would ever receive meaningful religious insight "from the mixtures of darkness and twilight to be met with in India." Rather, he retained the same convictions that he emphasized during the Parliament. The people of India needed the full religious enlightenment that would come only through encounter with Christianity. He implored his fellow Protestant Americans to ensure that the ranks of missionaries were "largely and continuously augmented."[79]

While the sheer size of the Parliament of Religions did much to bolster the confidence of Barrows and his cohort of liberal Protestants, the event nevertheless raised some disquieting issues. First and foremost, when they conceded that other religious traditions contained elements of truth, these Protestants crossed a bridge over which they could not return. They granted immense authority to Hinduism, Buddhism, and Islam by situating them alongside Christianity. However much they continued to claim their superiority, as Lyman Abbott did in his insistence that Christianity was "the only world-religion" capable of truly transforming character, the reality was that they had helped to define their tradition as one world religion among many.[80]

The scope of the Parliament, with its attendees from Europe, Asia, and the Middle East, also forced liberal Protestants to see religious pluralism in the broader context of racial, ethnic, and cultural diversity. Visibility did not translate to acceptance of these other forms of diversity, however. The eloquent contributions of nonwhite participants from both the United States and abroad did little to shake the organizers' faith in the superiority of white, Anglo-Saxon, Protestant civilization.

In an era when liberal Protestants were generally unconcerned with racial issues, Barrows and his fellow organizers did, to their credit, recognize the importance of including African Americans. Representatives of the African Methodist Episcopal Church were welcomed to the advisory committee that planned the Parliament.[81] Yet recognition of the beliefs and practices of African Americans was barely existent during the event. The African American clergyman Benjamin Arnett was a featured speaker during the opening ceremony based on the organizers' desire, he noted, "to give color" to the festivities. Indeed, in a telling reflection of the perspectives on race and religion held by Barrows and others, Arnett was given the peculiar task of representing not only African Americans but the people of Africa as well—despite the fact that he had been born in Pennsylvania and had never left the United States. Still, he availed himself of the opportunity to use religious language to advocate for racial equality. Noting that he was the final speaker, Arnett insisted that while African Americans "come last on the program," they could not be "least in this grand assembly where the Fatherhood of God and the brotherhood of man is the watchword of us all."[82]

Despite Arnett's efforts, his attempt to persuade the Parliament's white Protestant organizers to carry their rhetoric of religious inclusion into the realm of race went nowhere. Eventually, liberal Protestants would begin to reevaluate their attitudes toward racial and ethnic difference in light of their new enthusiasm for religious pluralism. But that project would not begin in earnest until the 1920s.

Equally unchanged were commitments to the superiority of Anglo-Saxon civilization. In part, this reflected the reality that even the most broad-minded American participants in the Parliament of Religions saw little of value in Asian, African, and Middle Eastern cultures. Thomas Wentworth Higginson, despite his advocacy of an eclectic spirituality that drew on Hinduism and Buddhism, noted Western preeminence in nonreligious aspects of life. "Every Oriental that comes to us," he insisted, "concedes to us the power of organization, the power of labor, the method in actual life which they lack."[83] Indeed, the representatives of non-Christian religions who spoke at the Parliament often echoed these same sentiments. The American convert Mohammed Alexander Webb noted that other religions should not be defined by the people who practiced them in much of the world. Religious truth was not exemplified, he declared, "in the character and the acts and the thoughts of a poor, ignorant coolie."[84] Most strikingly, Protap Chunder Mozoomdar, a "liberal Hindu" who advocated an interreligious eclecticism, claimed that the Christians brought the benefits of civilization to India. "We are Hindus still and shall always be," he insisted, yet he warmly noted that "now sits Christianity on the throne of India," bringing "its gospel of peace" and "scepter of civilization." Indeed, according to Mozoomdar the "civilization" of European Christians had proved beneficial to Hinduism. In "modern India," the "religious instincts" had been "stirred."[85]

To be sure, some of the visiting dignitaries used their speeches at the Parliament to challenge American assumptions of their racial and cultural superiority. In the end, though, these voices were drowned out by the louder tributes to Anglo-Saxon, Protestant superiority. Liberal Protestants were thus able to sustain their clear delineation between religious pluralism and other forms of diversity in the aftermath of the Parliament. Not only had their sense of religious superiority seemingly been confirmed, but their feeling of cultural and racial eminence had been as well.

In other ways, though, the Parliament of Religions forced Protestants to reevaluate their assumptions, and the project of comparative religious study ultimately contributed to two major changes in the religious landscape of the United States. First, the event provided a highly visible opportunity for Catholics and Jews to stake their claim as core stakeholders in the nation's spiritual life. While contemporary accounts devoted the greatest attention to the representatives of more exotic-seeming religions such as Hinduism and Buddhism, the event attracted the participation of Jewish and Catholic Americans. Indeed, prominent Catholics enthusiastically supported the Parliament from the early days of its planning. James Gibbons, the cardinal of Baltimore and de facto leader of the American Catholic Church, hailed the event as "worthy of all encouragement and praise."[86] The bishop John Ireland served on the advisory council, while another bishop, John J. Keane, worked as a liaison with John Barrows and the coordinating committee to ensure "the proper and adequate presentation of Catholic doctrine."[87] Gibbons, Ireland, and Keane all spoke at the Parliament, as did numerous other prominent Catholics.

Jewish Americans likewise contributed to the Parliament, with several noted rabbis, including Emil Hirsch and Kaufmann Kohler, offering lectures. Despite his claim that Americans were "a Christian people," Barrows credited "devout Jews" for their cooperation in planning the event. Indeed, this joint effort had inspired a new feeling of commonality. "These friends, some of whom are willing to call themselves Old Testament Christians, as I am willing to call myself a New Testament Jew, have zealously and powerfully cooperated in this good work," he observed.[88] The experience of planning an event that brought them face to face with Hindus, Buddhists, Jains, Muslims, and Zoroastrians left liberal Protestants like Barrows feeling much closer to Catholics and Jews by comparison.

The Parliament also forced Protestants in the United States to grapple with their own denominational division. Washington Gladden observed with bemusement what happened when the "true blue sectarian . . . who has come up to worship at the shrine of their denominational idols" arrived at the Parliament. By "sectarian," Gladden referred to those Protestants who identified primarily with their particular denomination rather than with Christianity as a whole. "It is very curious," he continued, "to observe the effect which the Parliament has upon these sectarian convictions. In the face of the great fundamental realities of religion, the foolishness of emphasizing the small peculiarities on which these sects are built is evident enough."[89] The large-scale differences separating Christianity from other traditions seemed normal and natural in the aftermath of the Parliament. Divisions within Christianity, however, did not. "Sectarianism is not confined to the Christian church," Gladden told his congregation, noting that Buddhists from India, China, and Japan "are quite as much opposed to each other as are Papist and Protestant in Christendom."[90] This was, in fact, not a new realization. Nearly a decade earlier Leighton Parks had discovered that he had no leg to stand on in criticizing "Buddhism on account of its divisions."[91] But at the Parliament, Protestantism's divisions, strikingly similar to those found in seemingly inferior religions, proved highly embarrassing for liberals like Gladden. If Christianity was indeed superior, it should have long ago evolved beyond the tendency to split.

The argument that internal division constituted a major failing of Protestantism drew strength from the redoubled commitment to mission work that emerged from the comparative enterprise. John Barrows lamented that "the disciples of other religions" often became confused by the manifold "divisions of Christendom." The lack of a unified, coherent message among Christian missionaries diminished their efficacy. "Christendom must be purified, and to a much greater extent unified, before the swiftest conquests of missions are possible," he declared.[92]

In the early decades of the twentieth century, other leading Protestants offered more pointed critiques. "What does the non-Christian know or care about our ecclesiastical differences?" asked a prominent Episcopalian. "Why should the non-Christian be contaminated with inter-denominational controversies, especially in the kindergarten stage of his Christian education?"[93] Leighton Parks disagreed that the "heathen" failed to appreciate the nuance of different Protestant beliefs and practices, but he likewise believed that denominational difference impeded missionary activities. "It is our want of mutual love which shocks them," Parks observed, noting that constant squabbling among missionaries from different Protestant traditions did little to demonstrate the merits of Christianity.[94]

Among liberal Protestants, the enthusiasm for comparative religion began to wane after 1900. But the two major lessons of the Parliament remained. Having addressed the challenges of skepticism and curiosity to their satisfaction, liberal Protestants shifted their reconsiderations of religious diversity to more immediate targets. During the 1890s, and especially after 1900, leading Protestants initiated a campaign to forge closer ties among churches of various denominations. They also sought new cooperative endeavors with Catholics and Jews, whom they increasingly came to identify as important stakeholders in the nation's religious life.

3

AN EXPANSIVE KINGDOM OF GOD
The Articulation of
Protestant-Catholic-Jewish Commonality

In the winter of 1903, Charles Snedeker, the dean of the Episcopal cathedral in Cincinnati, Ohio, invited David Philipson, the rabbi of the city's largest Reform synagogue, to present a lecture on the Jewish understanding of Jesus. Philipson later recalled the "great sensation" that such an occurrence caused in the midwestern town. He remembered with pleasure that the Episcopalians responded favorably to him, despite the fact that his talk had included a "frank statement of the differences" separating his "point of view from theirs." Following the gathering, the rabbi and the priest journeyed together in the direction of their respective homes and devised a plan to develop a permanent community organization that would foster interreligious discourse. The Cosmic Club, as it became known, boasted twenty-five members, approximately half of whom were "ministers of all denominations, Catholic, Jewish, and the various Protestant sects." The rest were "men from the other learned professions."[1]

Over time, however, the nature of the group's efforts changed. Whereas Philipson's presentation to the Episcopalians had largely emphasized difference, the Cosmic Club strove to highlight the similarities shared by Jews, Catholics, and Protestants. The group contributed to the making of what the rabbi believed to be the "quite ideal" state of "inter-religious relationships" in Cincinnati, where "priest, pastor, and rabbi" all "toiled together in community."[2] Philipson called it one of the highlights of his career to participate in an interfaith club that "furnished an affirmative answer to the piercing questions of the ancient prophet of Israel, Have we not all one Father? Has not one God created us?" It was Philipson's close ties with Christian ministers in Cincinnati that shaped the conviction that the rabbi was held, in the words of one of the city's Methodist ministers, "in great esteem as scholar citizen gentleman and minister of God."[3]

This affirmation of similarities among Protestantism, Catholicism, and Judaism—the three major religious traditions in the United States—was hardly unique to Cincinnati. Throughout the nation, Americans increasingly emphasized common elements of belief and practice shared by Protestants and Catholics, by Protestants and Jews, and sometimes by all three (because Protestants tended to play a critical role in such enterprises, there were relatively few instances of Jews and Catholics stressing their own similarities without the involvement of Protestants). Affirmations of commonality often took place in the context of interfaith celebrations or worship services. In 1880, a Lutheran pastor and a Catholic priest from Washington, Pennsylvania, jointly conducted a memorial service for a young woman whose mother was Lutheran and whose father was Catholic. A nationally read Protestant periodical reacted favorably to the service, noting that elements of the two traditions could be combined in such circumstances, and that doing so caused "no harm to the dead" and would "often comfort the living."[4] In 1897, representatives of numerous Protestant churches participated in the dedication of a new synagogue in New Haven, Connecticut.[5] Three years earlier, Disciples of Christ, Presbyterian, Congregationalist, and Methodist ministers had taken part in a similar celebration in Cleveland. And during that same week in 1894, a Roman Catholic priest in Brooklyn was recognized for fifty years of ministry, and several Protestant clergymen—including Lyman Abbott—and a Jewish rabbi took part in the festivities.[6]

That Abbott would celebrate the work of a Catholic priest might well have surprised anyone who knew him as a young minister. A decade before his rise to prominence as Henry Ward Beecher's handpicked successor, Abbott had decried the presence of "Romanism" as one of the principal reasons that there was "never a time in our history when a revival [was] more needed."[7] He similarly cast Judaism as a markedly inferior religion, and even drew parallels between its historical practices and elements of Roman Catholic worship that he found most objectionable.[8]

But as his theological views moved in a liberal direction in subsequent years, so too his perspective on Catholicism and Judaism evolved. Abbott used the prominence that came with his pulpit at Brooklyn's Plymouth Church and his editor's desk at the *Outlook* to laud new expressions of interfaith commonality. In a frank acknowledgment of the anti-Semitic prejudice harbored by many Americans, Abbott and his assistant editor Hamilton Mabie admitted that "many will criticise such fraternity" as was shown at the Cleveland synagogue dedication. But they insisted that such critique was without merit. "The Jews were not untrue to themselves in inviting the Christians to participate in the service, neither were the Christians untrue in accepting the invitation," they explained, "since both Jews and Christians worship one God and work together in many ways for the coming of His Kingdom on Earth."[9]

This proclamation that Christians and Jews shared a common commitment to bringing God's kingdom to earth highlighted liberal Protestants' newfound feelings of affinity toward Roman Catholicism and Judaism, which in turn reflected their larger enthusiasm for religious pluralism. The acceptance of doubt had prepared Protestants like Abbott to concede their lack of certainty in matters of faith, a concession that paved the way for the suggestion that non-Protestant and non-Christian traditions might have religious value. The project of comparative religion had likewise impelled many Protestants to identify points of significant commonality with other belief systems.

These developments significantly shaped interactions with Catholics and Jews, who were far more prevalent in American society than Hindus, Buddhists, or even skeptics. Having abandoned their rigid exclusivism, liberal Protestants forged connections with like-minded Catholics and Jews. These relationships rested on the foundation of a common middle-class culture and drew strength from shared critiques of the secular forces that seemed to drive unbelief and of the conservative elements in each faith tradition. More importantly, they reflected a mutual commitment to social action as a fundamental aspect of religious experience.

By the dawn of the twentieth century, liberal Protestants began to view a person's position on the spectrum from secularism to theological conservatism as being of equal or greater importance than his or her religious affiliation. They increasingly recognized that they had more in common with liberal Catholics and Jews than with some of their fellow Protestants. And as they abandoned criticism of other religious systems, these Protestants began to identify some practices and beliefs of Catholicism and Judaism that seemed superior to those of their own churches. This evolution in Protestant thought resulted in a religious culture in which an exclusivist commitment to Protestantism gave way to inclusive affirmations of the faith commitments of a sizable—and rapidly growing—population of Jewish and Catholic Americans.

Liberal Protestants' enthusiastic affirmations of the beliefs of their Catholic and Jewish neighbors marked an enormous departure from their own history and from the views expressed by many of their contemporaries. Though it abated periodically (during the early republic, for example), anti-Catholicism had long been a staple of national discourse. It was particularly prevalent at several points during the nineteenth century, such as during the wave of Irish migration in the

1830s and 1840s. In these decades, anti-Catholic sentiment increasingly manifested itself in outright violence and hostility, such as the burning of the Ursuline Convent in Charlestown, Massachusetts, by a mob of Protestant nativists in 1834, and a series of anti-Catholic riots in Philadelphia in 1844 that left at least fourteen people dead and fifty injured. Nativist hostilities peaked in the early 1850s with the rise of the American ("Know-Nothing") Party, which sought to enact strict immigration restrictions. Though it briefly abated as debates about slavery and the Civil War occupied the nation's attention, anti-Catholicism again spiked amid the social and economic anxieties of the long depression of 1873 to 1897.[10]

During the closing decades of the nineteenth century, numerous public figures articulated anti-Catholic sentiments, including James Blaine, the unsuccessful Republican nominee for president in 1884, who denounced "Romanism" alongside "rum" and "rebellion" as one of the major woes plaguing society. Notable Protestant clergy, including the prominent social reformer Josiah Strong, made attacks on Roman Catholicism a central element of their religious message. In the rhetoric of the American Protective Association (APA), which boasted more than a million members at its peak around 1894, anti-Catholicism reached a fever pitch not seen since the 1850s.[11]

It is extremely difficult to disentangle nineteenth-century Americans' specific anxieties about Roman Catholicism as a system of religious belief from their broader fears about foreign immigrants. But anti-Catholic critiques typically rested on a single foundation: Roman Catholicism was seen to be incompatible with democracy because it, unlike Protestantism, curtailed individual freedom. Catholics were believed to be required to follow every whim of the Holy See (a suspicion exacerbated by nineteenth-century innovations such as the official declaration of papal infallibility in 1870). These views were firmly ingrained in American culture well into the twentieth century. When rumors circulated during the 1908 presidential election that the wife of Republican candidate William Howard Taft had Catholic family members, the claims of his unsuitability for office grew so rancorous that Theodore Roosevelt took it on himself to respond.[12] That same year, the Congregationalist minister Newman Smyth admitted that "most Protestants" found it hard "to believe that any good can come out of Rome" because they were "under the inherited conviction that between Romanism and civilization it is a fight to the death."[13]

In contrast to anti-Catholicism, anti-Semitism in the United States was subtler in its appearance and more gradual in its development. Many Americans retained the historical hostility to Jews long endemic to European Christianity. They held, among other things, that Jews had not recognized Jesus Christ as the Messiah and were responsible for his death. Stereotypes that depicted Jews as greedy, unprincipled, and unsavory businessmen were rife in cultural discourse.

Despite the widespread existence of such ideas, though, the rampant hostility to Jews that characterized much of European life never materialized in England's American colonies or in the early United States. From the time of the establishment of the first synagogue in New York around 1700, Jews had enjoyed freedom to worship relatively unhindered, developed friendships and business partnerships with Protestants, and generally (though not entirely) avoided the vitriolic assaults that Catholics endured. They also escaped the violence visited on Catholic immigrants. Jewish Americans did, however, encounter discrimination in other aspects of public life, as with the existence of laws restricting Sunday commerce that prevented Jews from conducting business on a day that was not their Sabbath.[14]

Much like anti-Catholicism, a more virulent anti-Semitism appeared at the end of the nineteenth century. Claims that Jews had killed the Christian Messiah grew more pervasive, as did caricatures of the nefarious Jewish businessman. As eastern European Jews fled to the United States to escape violence inflicted on them in Russia and elsewhere during the 1880s, these long-standing anti-Jewish sentiments coalesced with the same nativist spirit that underlay attacks on Catholic immigrants. Moreover, the increasingly common depiction of Jews—even those whose families had lived in the United States for generations—as an unassimilable "other" reflected the growing popularity of race-based categorization in the late nineteenth century. Beginning in the 1870s, these factors resulted in more overt discrimination directed toward Jewish Americans. A new resort at Coney Island proclaimed that it was not open to Jews, and the Grand Union Hotel in Saratoga Springs, New York, refused to welcome a prominent Jewish banker as a guest.[15]

Many liberal Protestants forcefully denounced the increasingly rampant anti-Catholic and anti-Semitic rhetoric. It was not that hostility toward Catholics and Jews disappeared from national discourse but rather that these prominent Protestants began to oppose rather than champion such sentiments. These leaders attacked their coreligionists who harbored intolerant views. Washington Gladden lamented it as "one of the most melancholy signs of the times" that many of his fellow Protestants continued to "believe evil and only evil" about Catholics.[16] Similarly, a minister from Minnesota decried anti-Semitic views of his fellow Protestants, who, he declared, had neglected "to study the Bible" in light of modern knowledge. What resulted was the blind acceptance of "false notions and wretched prejudices," such as the oft-repeated claim that Jews killed Jesus—a claim, the minister noted, that was about as accurate as laying the blame on "the American people" for the "assassination of Lincoln."[17] By the early twentieth century, noted liberal Protestants were among the most outspoken critics of prejudice against believers of non-Protestant faiths, reflecting their broader desire, expressed by Hamilton Mabie, to set aside prejudice and "half-knowledge."[18]

The shifting views of leading Protestants did not go unnoticed by their Catholic and Jewish neighbors. Even during the height of the APA's power during the early 1890s, Catholic observers pointed to Protestant criticism of the nativist league as evidence that it was not a Protestant body but rather an antireligious one. One Catholic writer noted that "the profession of Protestantism" by the association's members was "but a poor mask, torn off effectually by a number of prominent non-Catholic ministers, on whom in great measure has devolved this defence of our common Christianity."[19] Catholics were particularly appreciative of Washington Gladden, who employed his national renown as an asset in the battle against anti-Catholicism. He received credit for dealing "a blow which sent the A.P.A. movement reeling" during the 1890s and more broadly for "the spirit of fair play" in his "attitude toward the Catholic Church."[20]

This was not the first time that Protestant Americans were critical of overt discrimination or hostility against other traditions, or even the first occasion on which they identified common elements of other traditions.[21] But the force and conviction with which nationally prominent Protestants—and even some ordinary churchgoers—challenged prejudice and asserted the right of Catholics and Jews to live free from discrimination marked the dawn of new cultural values that would grow in popularity as the twentieth century unfolded. Such attitudes drew support from public figures as well, including Theodore Roosevelt. At the height of the APA movement, Roosevelt served on the United States Civil Service Commission and used his position to denounce the "secret society" as "base and contemptible." The future president unequivocally stated his opposition "to any discrimination against or for any man because of his creed," adding, "We demand that all citizens, Protestant and Catholic, Jew and Gentile, shall have fair treatment in every way."[22] With declarations like these, Roosevelt signaled the shift away from religious exclusivism toward a more inclusive ideal of Catholics and Jews as equal participants in society.

A critical foundation for Protestant affirmations of Catholicism and Judaism was an emerging sense of cultural commonality as growing numbers of Jewish and Catholic Americans entered the middle class. This, in turn, minimized the gulfs that separated Protestants from their non-Protestant neighbors. While specific elements of Catholicism and Judaism still seemed different or strange, the adherents of these belief systems increasingly dressed, shopped, voted, and lived like middle-class Protestant Americans.

For Catholics, the initial steps in the process of acculturation occurred during the Civil War, when large numbers of Catholic men joined the Union Army and fought and died alongside Protestant soldiers. Priests, too, volunteered for the chaplaincy corps, and with a shortage of Protestant chaplains, they offered pastoral care to young men whose understanding of Catholicism had been shaped by the fiery nativist rhetoric of the 1850s. Following the war, the children of the initial wave of Irish immigrants entered the middle class. Most American Catholics remained firmly ensconced in the working class, but an ever-growing number did achieve sufficient socioeconomic success to be able to take on the trappings of middle-class life. As a consequence of their rise in status, Catholics came into closer personal contact with Protestants in their work and leisure. Even in Washington, Pennsylvania, which was hardly the most cosmopolitan corner of the United States, the minister James Henry Snowden noted that "better and kindlier feelings are growing up between Protestants and Catholics and the reason is that they are getting better acquainted with each other."[23]

As Catholics' social status changed, their political affiliations also began to shift. Middle-class Catholic voters increasingly rejected the Democratic Party, long synonymous with urban immigrants who were perceived to be blindly loyal to corrupt bosses. They instead turned to the Republican Party, which was associated with the northern establishment class. In his 1896 presidential campaign, William McKinley nudged the party away from its previous rhetoric of nativism by actively reaching out to Roman Catholics. Catholics also grew more forceful in their expressions of respect for American political institutions. "Catholics in this country are far from desiring to see brought about any union of church and state," wrote a prominent Illinois Catholic, insisting that in reality "they would be among the first to denounce the attempt, were the attempt ever made."[24]

Catholics were not merely assimilating culturally; this generation also began to adapt its religious practices in ways that made them more closely resemble those of their new Protestant neighbors. The 1880s and 1890s witnessed the rise of the so-called Americanist Catholics—bishops like John Ireland of St. Paul, Minnesota, and John Lancaster Spalding of Peoria, Illinois, as well as Catholic University of America president John J. Keane and Cardinal James Gibbons of Baltimore. Unlike earlier Church leaders who emphasized the distinctiveness of their religious faith against American culture, these Roman Catholics insisted not only, in what became Ireland's best known phrase, that it was desirable that "church and age" should "unite," but also that the Catholic Church unite specifically with the United States of the present day.[25] Contemporary America represented, in Spalding's view, "the divinely appointed leader" in a "mighty movement toward a social life in harmony with our idea of God and the aspirations of the soul."[26]

Jewish Americans had undertaken a similar project of cultural and religious assimilation, which in many respects anticipated that of Catholics. Beginning in the 1830s, the writer and religious leader Isaac Leeser initiated efforts to make

Judaism more closely resemble American Protestant practice. He minimized the use of the traditional term *hazan* to signify the leader of worship (there were few actual rabbis in the United States before the Civil War), choosing instead the term "minister," a title that would be adopted, along with "reverend" and "pastor," by other Jewish leaders. Following the model of Protestant Christianity, Leeser placed greater emphasis on the reading and study of scripture than had been customary in Jewish practice, and he incorporated Protestant-style sermons into worship. He also developed Jewish Sunday schools to parallel the movement for Christian education that was rapidly gaining in popularity. By the middle of the nineteenth century, synagogues increasingly resembled Protestant churches in their aesthetic, and organs were installed to foster a style that marked a significant departure from traditional liturgical music in Jewish worship.[27]

Many American Jews also set aside cultural practices that separated them from their non-Jewish neighbors. Some ceased to obey the prohibition of eating shellfish (which led to a debacle in 1883 when shrimp, crab, and clams were served at a banquet celebrating the ordination of the first four rabbis to graduate from Hebrew Union College). A number of synagogues moved Sabbath observances to Sunday, and many of those that did not nevertheless adopted the practice of holding religious lectures on the day of Christian religious activity. To be sure, even some Reform Jewish leaders did not advocate such significant departures from tradition. But they did accept the view of Kaufmann Kohler that Judaism needed a "living creed" rather than one that remained stagnant.[28]

Protestants lavished praise on acculturated Jews and Catholics. Theodore Roosevelt insisted that "the Americans in whom I believe include Jews and Catholics and Protestants."[29] For Roosevelt, a member of the Dutch Reformed Church, religious affiliation did not matter so long as one subscribed to middle-class American values, and this generation had proved that non-Protestants were fully capable of showing their Americanness. He was far from alone. An organizer of a Catholic summer school in New London, Connecticut, noted the "cordial welcome extended to the school by the descendants of the Puritans," including the state's former governor, who wrote that Catholics should not "*build a fence* round your Summer-School, because if you do *that fence* will keep us out, and we want to be in—*we want to be in with you.*"[30] Lyman Abbott and the editors of the *Outlook* singled out Ireland, Keane, and Spalding for having "proved their loyalty both to the Church and to the rising power of democracy"—a critical rejection of the widespread assumption that Catholicism and democracy were incompatible—and lauded their efforts to advance "moral and spiritual brotherhood among Christians."[31] This emerging language of brotherhood would become the guiding metaphor for interfaith efforts throughout the twentieth century.

Of the prominent Americanist Catholics, John Ireland boasted the most boisterous personality (the Minnesota bishop was dubbed the "consecrated blizzard of the northwest") and enjoyed the greatest public stature. He also did more than any other individual Catholic to change the views of Protestants about his faith tradition. Theodore Roosevelt proclaimed that "there is not a man in the county . . . who renders better service to the whole people" than Ireland, and he counted his friendship with the bishop as "one of the great benefits I have derived from being in Washington."[32] Indeed, it was not merely Protestant elites who admired Ireland. Ordinary churchgoers likewise confessed that the archbishop from Minnesota had inspired them to adjust their views about Roman Catholicism. One correspondent reported that a group of Republicans had arisen "to their feet" when a Methodist minister read one of Ireland's speeches and had raised "such rousing cheers as had not been vouchsafed even to [William] McKinley."[33] Another writer confessed to Ireland that in his youth he "came to despise everything Catholic," but one of the bishop's articles had so changed his feelings "that hereafter instead of apathy or tolerance I hope to show friendliness and respect to my catholic neighbors, their friends and religion."[34] Protestants were not merely tolerating their Catholic neighbors; rather, it was the case that "increasingly Roman Catholics are glad that there are Protestants in this country" and "increasingly Protestants are glad that there are Roman Catholics in this country."[35]

Though no late nineteenth-century Jewish leader attained the near-celebrity stature of John Ireland, Protestants still credited prominent Jews with prompting a change in their views. Protestant observers heralded Jews for "the intelligence and the culture and the charity" they demonstrated. The emphasis on these traits signaled a new acceptance by Protestants of Jews who had attained the trappings of middle-class respectability, and it inspired them "to forget many of our differences" rather than dwelling on them. Despite the anti-Catholicism and anti-Semitism that remained present in much of American society, the visibility of acculturated Catholics and Jews pushed many liberal Protestants to abandon such sentiments.[36]

While a growing sense of shared cultural identity provided the initial basis of Protestant affirmations of the religious beliefs and practices of Roman Catholics and Jews, a more important ingredient was the perception held by members of all three traditions that religious commitment was under assault from contemporary intellectual and cultural forces. Among Catholic and Jewish Americans, the specter of secularism and its component elements, indifference, irreligion, and unbelief, loomed large, just as it had for Protestants. The sense that religion was in decline in the United States challenged fundamental assumptions about the nature of the religious differences separating Protestants, Catholics, and Jews.

For Roman Catholics, anxieties about declining religious commitment were nothing new. Throughout the nineteenth century they had lamented the seemingly secular tendencies of modern thought; what changed was how they conceived of Protestants' role relative to contemporary ideas. Catholics initially assumed that Protestantism could not withstand the intellectual challenge it faced. Without the intervening authority of a church hierarchy that could explain and negotiate what seemed to be an ever-expanding chasm between contemporary scientific and philosophical thought and biblical teaching, American Catholics expected Protestants to be unable to cope. Protestant communities would either continue splintering into different denominations as they fought with one another, or they would spiral into skepticism. As late as the early 1880s, the liberal Catholic bishop John Spalding observed that "the characteristic feature of our age is indifference to God and soul" and insisted that the division of Protestantism into countless sects represented the fundamental cause of this reality. Protestants lacked any system of authority to maintain religious truth, and amid the intellectual challenge of modern thought, people were left to "drift away into indifference."[37] John Ireland, perhaps American Protestants' favorite Roman Catholic, had likewise declared that only his church possessed "the mighty power to resist vice and unbelief."[38]

In the middle of the 1880s, though, Catholics' attitudes slowly began to shift. For a time, Catholics had gleefully contrasted declining attendance in Protestant churches with the robustness of participation in their own. "It is well known," boasted one observer during the 1870s, "that while in most Protestant churches many seats are usually unoccupied during religious service, in the Catholic churches the same seat is frequently filled by three, four, or even five different persons, who take it in succession at the various Masses."[39] It was not long, however, before Catholics perceived that they were not immune to the problem of decreased religious commitment. Despite it being an "age of culture, progress, and enlightenment," one observer lamented, "church-going, outside of certain circles, is purely optional, and when indulged in at all, the material side, personal display, curiosity, and sensational sermonizing are the magnets which fill the pews."[40] By 1894, one priest lamented a developing "indifference of Catholics" characterizing both those who were "entirely unmindful of the duty they owe to God and to his Church" and those who "seem alive to certain commandments" but had "lost sight of the rest."[41] In a time when traditional religious experience was ever more debased by many intellectual and cultural leaders, many Catholics ceased to view Protestants as an irrelevant factor in the battle between religion and secularism.

Instead, they began to consider them to be a crucial ally. But doing so first meant abandoning long-standing rhetoric that claimed that Protestantism represented "the work of Satan."[42]

Critical to this reorientation in Catholic thought was the belief that the conflicting truth claims of Catholics and Protestants did little but sour Americans on religion. Mary Catherine Chase, who herself had converted to Catholicism, forcefully advanced this view. "Heretofore each exponent of his creed has hedged himself behind his own barrier, calling upon life's wayfarers to come to this or that fold and 'see how sweet the Lord is,'" she wrote. The end result, though, was not that people found themselves firmly convinced of the truth. Rather, "the poor soul, bewildered by so many voices crying out from every direction, knew not which way to turn," and instead found "the whole matter as a fraud and a delusion."[43]

Increasingly, Catholics emphasized their similarities to Protestants and situated their common Christianity against the claims of unbelievers. "I am catholic, of course, to the tiniest fibre of my being," John Ireland declared in an 1890 speech. But, he added, "God forbid that I should see in America the ground which Protestantism now occupies swept away by the devastating blast of unbelief."[44] Augustine Hewit, a Catholic convert who edited the widely read *Catholic World*, insisted that Protestants and Catholics shared a view of Christianity as "a supernatural, revealed religion" and that both groups affirmed "the Divinity of Christ, and the Inspiration of the Scriptures." These points of agreement far outweighed differences. "The old disputes between us are nearly obsolete, and the great contention now, is for Christianity against an un-Christian and even anti-Christian philosophy of naturalism, secularism, revived paganism."[45] John Spalding concurred, arguing that skeptics' attacks on the Bible rendered earlier squabbles between the two branches of Christianity less relevant. "The old controversy between Catholics and Protestants has, to a large extent, lost its meaning," he declared, "because problems of a more radical import have forced themselves on our attention."[46]

These Catholics had not abandoned their conviction of their own superiority (indeed, Hewit believed that the implication of commonality was that Protestants could easily return to Rome), just as Protestants who affirmed interreligious commonality retained the belief that they possessed the highest form of religious truth. What was novel, though, was the perception shared by members of both traditions that their similarities were more significant than their differences. Many Catholics who adopted this outlook saw little reason to persist in centuries-old attacks on Protestant belief. William C. Robinson, a judge on the Connecticut Supreme Court who had converted from Protestantism to Catholicism and who participated in several interreligious discussions in New Haven, declared that "the day is passed when attacks on so-called 'Protestant errors' can serve any useful purpose."[47]

For their part, Protestants welcomed these Catholic declarations of accord in the face of the claims of skeptics, and they responded in kind. Lyman Abbott, who never missed an opportunity to use the *Outlook* as a clarion by which to blast a message of interreligious understanding, insisted that it was not only better to be a Roman Catholic than a "materialist," but it was also superior to being "a poor Protestant."[48] It became a matter of common faith among liberally oriented Protestants that Catholicism had much of value and deserved recognition as a force for advancing the message of Christianity in the United States. Washington Gladden insisted that Catholics and Protestants were "Christian brethren" who agreed far more often than they disagreed and that it was "better to emphasize our agreements and rejoice in them."[49] Likewise, the Boston minister George Gordon insisted that "all forms of the Christian church have room to work in this land," because both Catholic and Protestant churches constituted "regiments in the institutional army of the Lord Jesus Christ."[50]

While Protestants and Catholics shared a common Christian identity which lent itself to the rhetoric of belonging to an "army" for Jesus against the forces of a secular culture, the Protestant encounter with agnosticism and skepticism more closely resembled that of Reform Jews than that of Catholics. Protestants who had for years worried about the corrosive effect of unbelief found a recognizable ally in Kaufmann Kohler, who in the 1890s was rabbi of Temple Beth-El in New York and was arguably the most prominent Reform rabbi in America. Kohler lamented that "agnosticism has become the disease of the century."[51] Jews, whose tradition relied heavily on written scripture, faced the same problems with biblical criticism that had created so many difficulties in Protestant churches. One Protestant theologian called attention to the fact that members of both traditions found themselves in the same boat as new theories of the Bible brought "increasing uncertainty as to the original facts of both the Hebrew and the Christian religions."[52]

Even more importantly, liberal Protestants and Reform Jews had a parallel experience in contending with breakaway systems that offered a secular alternative to traditional belief. Within Protestantism, more radical forms of Unitarianism and Universalism served as a way station for a complete departure from Christianity. Despite their rejection of core Christian doctrines, early nineteenth-century Unitarian leaders like William Ellery Channing and Andrews Norton had insisted on remaining within the Christian tradition. They stressed their belief in a personal God, emphasized the importance of Jesus's moral and ethical teachings, and proclaimed the verity of divine revelation in both scripture and the natural world. As the century progressed, however, growing numbers of

Unitarians cut ties with their Christian roots in favor of a more experimental religiosity unconstrained by the tenets of any one tradition. Indeed, many of the foremost advocates of the spiritual forays into Hinduism and Buddhism that so irked mainstream Protestants—people like Thomas Wentworth Higginson and his cohort in the Free Religious Association—were former Unitarians.[53]

The most liberal forms of Protestantism appeared to offer a jumping-off point not merely to spiritual exploration but to outright unbelief. This was as true for ordinary Americans as it was for intellectuals, as suggested by a thirty-four-year-old railroad conductor's letter to Robert Ingersoll. The man's grandfather had been "a deacon in an Orthodox church" and an "out-and-out Puritan in his religious views," while his father, a minister, had progressed to Universalism. But even his father's liberal Christianity was too much for this skeptic, who confessed to Ingersoll his "strong dislike of so-called Bible religion," which he had never accepted because he believed that subjects like "God and immortality" and "life and death" were mysteries that no "man can solve." The journey from Protestant orthodoxy to agnosticism had been completed in three generations.[54]

Reform Jews faced a similar problem on their theological left flank. No sooner had Kaufmann Kohler, David Philipson, and other leaders of their generation secured the institutions of Reform Judaism than Felix Adler—the son of one of the nation's most prominent Reform rabbis and a man widely expected to become a leading voice for Judaism in his own right—proclaimed to a stunned community that "Judaism is dying." Adler rejected the Jewish conception of God and founded the Ethical Culture movement, which he allied with Higginson's Free Religious Association. Parallels between former Protestants and former Jews did not go unnoticed; observers highlighted a trajectory from evangelical Christianity to Channing's "spiritual liberalism" to the "ostentatiously undevout Ethical Culture."[55]

Against novel institutions such as the Free Religious Association and Ethical Culture, which offered systems of morals and ethics entirely detached from longstanding religious structures, the challenge faced by both Protestants and Jews became readily apparent. In thinly veiled critiques of systems like Ethical Culture, observers lamented that scripture was "losing power" in the face of competition from new "systems of individual ethics" and "theories of social progress." Critics charged that to the proponents of these new sets of belief "the motives and sanctions of religion" appeared to be "superfluous, or even obstructive."[56] The psychologist of religion and practicing Methodist George Coe observed that as a consequence of "the growth of ethical sentiment in conscious independence of official religion," never before had "the moral consciousness leaned upon religion as little as it does today."[57]

So aware were Protestants and Jews of their shared experience in this regard that one rabbi used the *Andover Review*, a Protestant theological journal, to decry the emerging acceptance of an "ethical sentimentalism, utterly removed from practical righteousness" that had been grounded in "belief in a Personal, Intelligent God."[58] Though some observers astutely noted important divergences in the Protestant and Jewish experiences with religious indifference—namely, that Protestants' problems stemmed from a growing unwillingness to accede to religious tenets, which was not a problem in Judaism given its lack of obligatory creeds—both traditions nevertheless shared the experience of people slipping away from religious communities and their long-standing teachings.

One additional development in America's religious culture provided a further impetus for Protestant affirmation of Judaism and Catholicism. Just as members of all three traditions grew accustomed to contending with competing belief systems that were even more theologically liberal, they increasingly faced strident opposition from more orthodox and conservative segments of their respective traditions. For the expanding wing of liberal Protestants, the specter of conservative opposition was never far away. The liberalizing project had begun in earnest during the 1870s and 1880s as more and more ministers and theologians accepted new scholarship on the origins and content of scripture and adopted new outlooks on the relationship between religion and science. Reaction from traditionalists was swift. In 1874, when the Chicago Presbyterian minister David Swing expressed the view that the historic creeds of Christianity were more human invention than divine inspiration, he was promptly charged with heresy. Although he was initially acquitted, the cloud of heresy continued to hang over Swing's head, and he eventually resigned from his pulpit and organized a congregation independent of the Presbyterian Church. The Swing trial captured national attention and left liberal Protestants embittered by the apparent intolerance within the denomination for modern religious thought.[59]

Heresy trials plagued America's Protestant denominations for several decades thereafter. In the early 1890s, Charles Augustus Briggs, another prominent liberal theologian who taught at the progressive Union Theological Seminary, was charged with heresy for, among other things, claiming that biblical texts were written by humans, and thus open to error in matters not essential to faith. After a prolonged process, the Presbyterian Church voted to suspend Briggs from the ministry, and his position at Union was saved only when the seminary's board of directors voted to cut formal ties to the denomination. For liberals, the lessons of heresy trials were clear: however much they might bask in their growing cultural authority and their increasing prominence as the public face of American Protestantism, within their own churches and communities they faced strong competition from conservatives who remained steadfast in their adherence to older theological ideas. And as much as liberals like Washington Gladden insisted that major religious questions "cannot be determined by a majority vote," that was precisely what many orthodox-minded Protestants sought to do.[60]

The gulf between liberal and conservative Protestants grew beyond a few heresy trials for prominent theologians. Optimistic, liberal voices had no sooner begun to secure the leadership of many major denominations than a distinct opposition developed. Theologians at places like Wheaton College in Illinois abandoned the progressive vision articulated by leading Protestant thinkers and instead fell in with the revivalist Dwight L. Moody. Moody, who cast his proclamations of biblical inerrancy and personal responsibility for salvation in the guise of a middle-class respectability lacking at early revivals, offered an interpretation of Christianity that stood in stark contrast to the message of progressive revelation and social emphasis of liberals. In the decades that followed, the revivalist tradition of Moody and his successor, the more flamboyant and less quick-witted Billy Sunday, coalesced with teachings of the growing Holiness movement. Holiness churches grew out of nineteenth-century Methodism and encouraged the quest for perfection through strict adherence to biblical teaching. Conservative Protestants were far from a monolithic force, but by the dawn of the twentieth century it was possible to see in the Holiness and revival traditions a coherent alternative to liberal Protestantism. This alternative received an intellectual foundation between 1910 and 1915, when twelve volumes of essays, entitled *The Fundamentals*, were published. These texts offered a coherent critique of the theological tenets affirmed by liberals, including their endorsement of biblical scholarship and their embrace of progressive revelation.[61]

In its growing division between traditional and progressive voices, American Catholicism was running on a parallel track to Protestantism. During the 1880s and 1890s, culturally accommodationist and theologically liberal leaders like James Gibbons, John Ireland, John Keane, and John Spalding gained prominence as the public faces of the Catholic Church in the United States, and the liberal-leaning *Catholic World* earned wide readership among Catholic and Protestant readers alike. Conservative church leaders grew restive. By the middle of the 1890s, the insistence of the Americanists that Catholicism could be easily reconciled with the cultural values of the contemporary United States drew loud critiques from Vatican officials and conservative American Catholics, notably the influential bishop of New York, Michael Corrigan. One element of American culture that particularly irked Catholic conservatives was the valorization of science and the view that contemporary scientific theories need not conflict with Christian teaching. "To some modern scholars religion and science are antagonistic; why should this be so?" asked Helen Sweeney, a Catholic writer who championed the liberal Catholic enterprise, especially the Catholic Summer School and the Catholic University of America.[62]

Not everyone agreed with Sweeney. The issue of liberal Catholicism came to a head in 1898 when Pope Leo XIII forced the American priest and scientist John Zahm to cease publication of his book *Evolution and Dogma*, in which he pugnaciously argued that Catholicism and organic evolution need not stand in opposition. The following year, the pontiff issued his declaration *Testem Benevolentiae*, which denounced a set of ideas that he labeled "Americanism." Though the letter mentioned no one by name, the ideas it condemned bore a striking—and not coincidental—similarity to those articulated by Gibbons, Ireland, Spalding, and others. The supposed Americanists backpedaled as swiftly as they could. Though their stature diminished in the worldwide Catholic Church (Ireland, for example, never attained his lifelong goal of becoming a cardinal), they remained popular in the United States, especially among Protestants like Lyman Abbott, who in 1911 declared Ireland, Spalding, and Keane "faithful and devoted servants" of both "the Roman Catholic Church" and "the American people."[63]

American Judaism likewise experienced the growth of a palpable division between those with a liberal religious outlook and those who held to more traditionalist views. After the seeming triumph of an acculturated Reform Judaism during the 1860s and 1870s, a backlash emerged, fostered by the arrival of more traditionalist European Jews like Alexander Kohut. Critics who charged that Reform rabbis like Kaufmann Kohler and David Philipson had sacrificed too much of traditional practice eventually established their own institutions, including the Jewish Theological Seminary in New York, and found a willing audience for their message in the many immigrants from eastern Europe who arrived at the close of the nineteenth century. The triumph of an unchallenged Reform tradition had once seemed inevitable; now it seemed a remote possibility.[64]

The conservative backlash pushed Americans from the liberal wings of all three traditions to identify more commonalities with one another than with traditionalists in their own belief systems. "The divisions of Christianity into Catholic and Protestant, of Protestants into orthodox and liberal, are paralleled in the divisions of Judaism," proclaimed the *Outlook*, noting that the Reform tradition represented the "Protestant element."[65] While many Jews would undoubtedly have preferred that their religion be defined on its own terms rather than in Christian categories, the fact that Protestants made such connections was nevertheless highly significant. It reflected the movement away from casting Judaism simply as a religious "other" and the growing embrace of views of common belief, practice, and experience. Similarly, liberal Protestants long observed a split in Catholicism between more progressive and traditional factions and had seen in men like Gibbons and Ireland "more hope for reform" than in many segments of Protestantism that seemed determined to cling to their "sectarian" convictions.[66]

In the early twentieth century, liberals came to perceive that the crucial division lay not between faith traditions but rather between liberals and conservatives within each. As David Philipson observed after the Fundamentalist-Modernist controversy in Protestantism reached its height in the 1920s, the issues under debate in Protestant circles "interest Jews no less than Christians." Both traditions were based on the Bible, and liberals in both faced divisive conflicts with conservatives about the inerrancy of the historical texts. Indeed, Philipson connected all of liberals' anxieties by linking the growing religious conservatism to the much-feared unbelief. "The intransigent attitude of the fundamentalists is driving thousands away from the churches," he declared, reconfiguring a longstanding argument among Reform Jews that clinging too firmly to tradition proved alienating. Just as the larger threat of skepticism and agnosticism had made the differences separating Protestants from Catholics and Jews appear less significant, so too did the specter of conservative elements in all three traditions make it seem to liberals that they had more in common.[67]

It was not the case, however, that religiously liberal Protestant, Jewish, and Catholic Americans came together only grudgingly as a result of dual fears of a secular culture and conservative forms of religious expression. The new relationship also reflected the view of many Protestants that Reform Jews and liberal Catholics were religiously kindred spirits, a view that resulted from new awareness of deeply held beliefs shared by members of all three traditions. This sense of commonality especially depended on Protestants' own shifting religious values. Just as Catholics and Jews had come to resemble American Protestants in their cultural practices, liberal Protestants modified their religious beliefs in a way that brought them closer to Judaism and Catholicism. Two elements of Protestant thought proved crucial in prompting this shift: first, the growing conviction that religion required concern for society as much as for the individual; second, and closely related, the view that a religious commitment was determined not by adherence to doctrines but by living an ethical life.

The downplaying of individualism that characterized late nineteenth-century American Protestantism marked a sharp departure from the tradition's longstanding values. A core tenet of the Reformation had been that the individual could gain access to religious truth by reading scripture without the mediating influence of the Catholic Church hierarchy. Protestants in the United States had ardently defended the principle of "private judgment" for centuries, and efforts to establish denominational hierarchies to provide even a modicum of oversight had met with considerable resistance. But as the nineteenth century progressed, private judgment was carried to such an extreme in the United States that committed Protestants began to wonder if individualism had gone too far. The major source of this anxiety was the rapid expansion of denominations; every year, it seemed, some minister claimed to have experienced some novel epiphany that led him to establish a new Protestant tradition that reflected what he perceived to be the height of religious truth. This phenomenon grew so widespread that by the middle of the nineteenth century there existed twice as many Protestant denominations in the United as there had been in 1800.[68]

Non-Protestant critics had long believed that the tendency toward multiplication represented a fatal flaw that would bring the anticipated downfall of Protestantism. Early in his career as a Catholic priest, John Ireland embraced the phrase "religious communism" as an apt descriptor of Protestants' tendency to splinter into anarchy and disorder, as nineteenth-century communists seemed wont to do. "A denial of authority is the very essence of the system," he declared. There was nothing that Protestants could do to correct the problem, Ireland noted, since private judgment represented the heart of Reformation ideology. Any effort "to impose a restraint upon license, to arrest the constant development of independent churches, of irresponsible ministries," would prove tantamount to "the effort to arrest with the hand the precipitous waters of the Niagara."[69] Other Catholic observers went even further. During the Civil War, some Catholics, including the widely regarded convert Orestes Brownson and Archbishop Martin Spalding (uncle of the Americanist John Lancaster Spalding), argued that the conflict itself resulted from Protestants' constant discord and disagreement. At its core, they charged, the war represented the inability of Protestants to reach consensus on what the Bible said about slavery. Unlike typical disagreements that only led to the splintering of denominations, however, this one led to the division of the entire nation.[70]

While Protestants never went so far as to blame their religious values for a war that left hundreds of thousands of Americans dead, they did slowly adopt the view that excessive individualism had wrought a deleterious effect. To be sure, many declarations along these lines were tentative and highly qualified. In an 1897 speech, Dartmouth College president William J. Tucker managed to affirm that "the church must make room for the largest and freest growth of the individual" while also insisting that the "individualism" that marked "the modern Church" was "not sufficient for present conditions or for those which are impending."[71] That Tucker tried to have it both ways is unsurprising. On the one hand, a key element of Protestants' response to skepticism—their endorsement of doubt and the accompanying insistence that churches needed to respect the beliefs and uncertainties of their members and not prescribe belief—required an even greater respect for individual judgment. On the other hand, constant splintering did not seem particularly beneficial to Christianity either.

It was the desire to split the difference on this point of tension that led Washington Gladden both to affirm the "old individualism" as a "necessary reaction against the hierarchical despotisms" that once characterized Christianity and at the same time to declare that "the force of this protest has gone quite far enough."[72] So, too, Newman Smyth mused that Protestantism had laid so much emphasis on "individual responsibility" and "personal salvation" that it had made "the kingdom of God identical with some sphere of life."[73] According to Smyth, many churchgoers had come to equate all religious truth with their personal beliefs. Another minister who worried that Protestantism did little to encourage concern for the larger social units of the family and the community put it even more bluntly. In many American churches, "nothing is heard or seen from one year's end to another's that is not an emphasis on the individual."[74]

Many liberal Protestants sought to expand their emphasis beyond the individual. Clergy, theologians, and laity increasingly proclaimed that a religious outlook centered primarily on the individual missed the point of Christianity. Because, in Washington Gladden's words, "it is in the use of his social relations that the spiritual activities of the man find exercise," it was incumbent on Protestants to turn their attention to society at large. "It is childish to suppose that we can shut ourselves within our conventicles and sing and pray and have a happy time all by ourselves, saving our own souls, and letting the great roaring world outside go on its way to destruction," he observed. Such an approach entirely "misses the true function of the church."[75] George Coe likewise insisted that "Jesus recognized no possible separation of the social from the religious impulse," and he proclaimed that the founder of Christianity had advanced the view of "a kingdom that comprehends in its scope all the so-called secular interests of life."[76] Countless others echoed this view. An Episcopal theologian announced that "the conditions under which men work and live between Sundays, are of direct concern to the Christian religion," while the editors of the *Andover Review* went even further in proclaiming that "the social hope of Chicago, New York, London, Berlin, and even Paris is in the intelligent service of the Church of Christ."[77]

These claims of Christianity's inherent social message signaled the inception of the Social Gospel, the movement that defined early twentieth-century Protestant thought. It stood on the foundation of the long-standing reform impulse in American Protestantism, which saw the uplift of the nation and its people as a fundamental component of the religious life. But the Social Gospel went further, offering a sophisticated theological argument that the salvation of the individual and society were intrinsically connected, and that personal redemption depended on a corresponding transformation of the broader world.[78]

A central metaphor in Protestants' Social Gospel rhetoric was the "Kingdom of God" or the "Kingdom of Heaven," an idea that had been refined by proponents of the New Theology, which gained popularity during the 1880s and 1890s as a Christian response to evolutionary theory and other scientific developments. These liberal theologians argued that God was immanent within the natural realm rather than distant from humans in a faraway heaven. Thus, God's kingdom could come to fruition on earth (it was precisely this conception of the immanent God that Leighton Parks had argued represented an evolved form of Hindu pantheism). In his 1883 book *The Freedom of Faith*, which offered the first systematic treatment of the New Theology, the Congregationalist Theodore Munger vehemently decried Christian doctrines that separated the divine force from the natural world it had created. "The New Theology does indeed regard with question the line drawn between the sacred and the secular,—a line not to be found in Jewish or Christian Scriptures, nor in man's nature," he wrote, adding that the existence of that false dichotomy "ignores the very process by which the kingdoms of this world are becoming the kingdom of God."[79] Munger's rhetorical linking of both Christian and Jewish scripture was crucial. It presaged the way in which language of God's kingdom underlay feelings of commonality among Protestant, Catholic, and Jewish Americans.

Over the next few decades, bringing the Kingdom of God on earth became the ideal for society toward which proponents of the Social Gospel worked. Though often frustratingly vague in their descriptions of this kingdom, liberal Protestants imagined the perfect world that would exist at the time of Christ's return as one in which all people would have equal access to economic opportunity and class tensions would cease to exist. Such ideas aligned perfectly with the seemingly bottomless well of optimism that characterized American life at the close of the nineteenth century. Many Protestants truly believed that the kingdom was within their power to grasp.

To be sure, the vision that Protestants articulated of the Kingdom of God was in distinctly Christian language. But the steps they proposed to bring it about proved broad enough to include Jews. More importantly, their commitment to a religious vision focused on social concerns rather than individual piety moved them much closer to their Catholic and Jewish neighbors in their understanding of critical aspects of religious belief.[80]

No Protestant thinker did more than the Baptist minister Walter Rauschenbusch to develop the view that the goal of Christianity was to inspire people to bring the Kingdom of God to earth. During the first two decades of the twentieth century (and before his untimely death during the global influenza epidemic of 1918), he popularized the Social Gospel by systematically articulating the ideals that first germinated during the 1880s and 1890s. Rauschenbusch, the son of an orthodox Protestant minister, rejected his father's traditional thought as he advanced in his own career as a clergyman. Rauschenbusch echoed the widely held view of his generation that Protestantism had somehow lost its way, and he insisted that "theology needs periodical rejuvenation." The remedy was not, as skeptics (like Robert Ingersoll) and spiritual eclectics (such as Felix Adler) suggested, the creation of new systems of ethics but rather the development of "a closer union of religion and ethics." For Rauschenbusch, the ideal religious life was not ascetic, individualistic, and "directed toward a future life" but was rather "social, political, solidaristic."[81] Ideal Christians were not meant to hide themselves away in order to secure their personal salvation; they instead needed to emphasize the ethical teachings of Jesus and work to bring the world into accord with his message.

The turn toward the social allowed Protestants to express new ideas and reshape their institutions in ways that afforded Catholics and Jews an opportunity to see commonality. In theological matters, an enormous gulf separated Protestantism and Catholicism, and little agreement existed on topics ranging from the appropriate structure of the church, to the function of clergy, to the nature of sacraments like baptism and communion—and whether or not other practices, such as confirmation and ordination, even constituted sacraments. When the emphasis remained on doctrine, commonality was difficult to find amid centuries of disagreement that tended to produce nothing but insult-laden rhetoric. The liberal Catholic Augustine Hewit, for example, insisted that Protestant ideas were nothing more than "parasites" and "heresies" responsible for "exaggerating, distorting, and altering the Christian doctrines."[82]

Yet Roman Catholicism had long boasted a rich tradition of social thought that gave priority to the social over the individual. John Ireland drew from this deep well of tradition when he called on his fellow priests to avoid "the tendency in the pulpit" to focus exclusively on "the individual soul," because each individual "is entangled in a hundred networks of most complex relations, the perils of which are its perils, the purification and elevation of which must ever be both the cause and effect of its personal sanctification." Protestants received concrete evidence of Rome's commitment to social action in 1891. The papal encyclical *Rerum Novarum*, issued by Leo XIII, articulated a comprehensive Catholic position on the rights of capital and labor in an attempt to ease one the most pressing social issues of the day.[83]

An emphasis on the betterment of society provided a vehicle by which Catholic and Protestant Americans could find a common cause. There was no reason, John Ireland declared, "why in efforts to do good to fellow-man the priest may not ally himself with others who are not of his spiritual flock."[84] So, too, Augustine Hewit affirmed that Americans who "take the side of Christianity," despite their "imperfect conceptions of its doctrines, un-Catholic prejudices, and their state of ecclesiastical separation"—in other words, Protestants—"may be regarded with us in one common and sacred cause," and Catholics should support all Americans who worked to "promote the welfare of the people" and to "remedy social miseries."[85]

But Catholics were not merely acknowledging a common desire to improve society; they increasingly credited Protestants with adopting a theology of social reform that mirrored Catholic teaching. When Washington Gladden offered his most sophisticated treatment of the Christian response to economic inequality and upheaval between workers and employers in his 1893 treatise *Tools and the Man*, the Catholic press noted the similarities between the positions advocated by the Congregationalist minister and those put forth by the pope in *Rerum Novarum*. "It is pleasant to note," one reviewer observed, "that the noble principles embodied in the encyclical of our great Sovereign Pontiff are finding adoption, acceptance, and imitation among the better class of thinkers."[86] Gladden himself likely chafed at the suggestion that ideas of social Christianity derived from a papal letter. Nevertheless, this endorsement of Gladden's sentiments stresses the extent to which an emphasis on social issues provided a basis of commonality between Protestants and Catholics.

The sea change in views of what constituted the heart of Christianity had even greater ramifications in the realm of Protestant-Jewish relations. For all of their theological quarrels, Catholics and Protestants shared the same religious faith and could agree on many of its essentials. The relationship between Christianity and Judaism was more complex. Because Christianity had emerged as an offshoot from Judaism, Christians often claimed that their tradition represented the evolution from a lesser form of belief and practice into a more advanced one.

Indeed, this line of argument was initially bolstered by liberal Protestants' newfound enthusiasm for the idea of progressive revelation as a rhetorical bulwark against skepticism and competing claims of other religious traditions. As long as Christians defined their belief system primarily in terms of doctrine, it was inevitable that they would clash with Jews in debates over which tradition proved superior. Even liberal Protestants like Washington Gladden and James Henry Snowden could fall into such a trap. In one sermon, Gladden accused "the Judaistic religion" of appealing to sense rather than intellect and of emphasizing "mere phraseology" rather than "the real meaning" of the biblical message, while Snowden more bluntly declared of Christianity: "We have all the light the Jews had and more."[87] Nor were Jews necessarily more sanguine in their views about

Christians. The equally progressive and inclusive Kaufmann Kohler pulled no punches in criticizing what he perceived as the erroneous innovations of Christians. He assailed their emphasis on creeds and dogma that bred an exclusivist spirit, which he deemed inferior to the Jewish message of "the Messianic promise of a common brotherhood."[88]

The Social Gospel and its accompanying ideas about the Kingdom of God shifted the emphasis of Protestantism away from the doctrinal and toward the ethical, thereby creating common ground for Protestants and Jews. Protestant liberals heralded Judaism's role in developing the conception of the Kingdom of God. This new idealization of Jews in turn led them to reformulate their understanding of the relationship between Jesus and the Jewish tradition to which he belonged.

In the new perspective of liberal Protestants, Jesus's understanding of the Kingdom of God did not differ in its fundamental nature from that of historic Judaism. The difference lay solely in whether it was the return of Jesus that would usher in the kingdom, or if its arrival would be marked by the coming of a different messiah. But Protestants were increasingly able to sidestep this thorny question. Social Gospel liberals held that Jesus actually taught that God's kingdom would develop not through "a revolution wrought by supernatural powers" but rather as a result of "human character rightly developed."[89] In other words, it would come when faith communities made proper ethics the central aspect of their message. The promotion of human development in the interest of cultivating this ideal society, noted one Protestant author, "is, or should be, the object of the Christian Church and the Christian minister."[90] This belief in gradual human striving toward the Kingdom of God, besides having the advantage of being entirely compatible with Progressive-era American cultural values, eliminated a major sticking point in Protestant-Jewish relations: the role of the Messiah in bringing the Kingdom of God. In so doing, it freed members of both traditions to affirm a common effort to improve the ethical values of society without engaging in disputes about the divinity of Jesus.

Jewish Americans recognized and enthusiastically embraced their Protestant neighbors' shift away from doctrine and believed this evolution signaled Christians' return to the ideals of the mother religion. The emphasis on the betterment of society rather than the securing of personal salvation was, according to David Philipson, "one of the main differences" that had separated the two traditions for nearly two millennia. Jews had championed the idea of "social salvation" throughout history. "If today the Christian churches have great programs of social justice and social welfare as indeed they have," Philipson declared, "they appear to be turning to the Jewish vision of life in this respect."[91] Protestants undoubtedly bristled at the suggestion that they were adopting a Jewish sensibility and certainly would have claimed that they had merely returned to the true message of Christianity. But the larger point is apparent: liberal Protestant and Reform Jews found themselves closer to one another in their understanding of the central purpose of religion than they were to the more conservative elements of their own traditions.

Leading Protestants became almost reflexive in their willingness to emphasize similarities rather than differences in their assessment of Judaism. "The unity of faith already exists," wrote the editors of *Outlook* in 1910, noting that "Jews and Christians" stood in accord "upon the most important . . . articles of faith." The essence of religion, the editors noted, was the belief "in one God, who is both the Creator and Ruler of the Universe"—a conviction not only shared by Jews, but also one that Judaism had first articulated, which therefore set it apart from many other religious traditions. "The belief in the unity of God, which the Jewish Church was the first to proclaim . . . has driven out, wherever it has gone, the old faith in multitudinous deities," they declared. References to "the Jewish Church," such as the one in this editorial, became common after the turn of the twentieth century and signaled the degree to which Protestants had come to view Judaism not as an unrecognizably different religion but rather as a variant of Americans' commonly held faith commitments. So, too, was there a common purpose uniting both religions. Not only did they emphasize "righteousness in life," but both were also in essence the same in that they constituted "an expression of the human soul seeking after God" as well as the "expression of our faith that God is seeking after us." Thus, there existed a common faith "in which all Christian believers and all Jewish believers unite."[92]

There was a final element that made new understandings of commonality possible. Not only were American Protestants moving closer to Jews and Catholics theologically with their emphasis on the social as the critical idea of religion, but they were also adopting non-Protestant ideals of worship practice. Protestant worship in the United States was as multifaceted as the denominational system that inspired it. But, with the notable exception of the Episcopal Church, which had always straddled the line between Protestantism and Catholicism, and certain segments of the growing Lutheran Church in the upper Midwest, worship practices were generally nonritualistic and centered on Bible reading and preaching. Indeed, many of the leading Protestants in nineteenth-century America had openly criticized ritualistic practices, suggesting, as Horace Bushnell did, that "reverential rounds and airs" and "priestly ceremonials" did nothing for the religious life except allow it to be "manipulated by our senses and sensuous tastes."[93] Anything that seemed formalized or ritualized—in other words, much of the religious experience of Roman Catholics and Jews—seemed to represent a baser form of religion than the intellectual faith of Protestantism.

As with other aspects of their religious thought, Protestant attitudes toward worship and liturgical practice grew more inclusive during the final decades of the nineteenth century. Lyman Abbott called on all Americans to study one another's religious practices. He noted that people might learn "the value of tradition from the Jew," a frank acknowledgment that progressive Protestantism had not always succeeded at preserving traditional practices.[94] The Congregationalist writer Mary Abigail Dodge acknowledged that people found a richer experience in "the solemn ceremonial of the Roman Catholic and the Episcopal churches."[95] So, too, James Henry Snowden told his Pennsylvania congregation to accept as useful and beautiful the "endless variety" of Christianity, noting that Presbyterians like him should not "look with suspicion on the Baptist or the Roman Catholic," who had equally valid forms of practice.[96]

In these same years, Protestant Americans became increasingly attuned to practices that they had previously eschewed for fear of seeming too "Catholic." Lyman Abbott pointed to liturgical practices other than preaching and noted that while Roman Catholics and Episcopalians (the Protestant denomination that most closely resembled Catholicism in practice) had "made relatively too much of the service and too little of the sermon," it was nevertheless true that "the Puritans and their descendants" were equally culpable for making "too much of the sermon and too little of the service." The result, he argued, was a seemingly narcissistic emphasis on preaching that denied the possibility of religious experience in other forms of practice. Abbott never suggested that formal liturgy should entirely supplant the nonliturgical, preaching-focused worship of most Protestant Americans. But he averred that because "certain spiritual practices" were "constantly repeated," there existed "a distinct advantage" in adopting, as Roman Catholics did, "a common phraseology for the expression of these common experiences." Abbott's *Outlook*, meanwhile, reported that some of those once-derided ceremonials, such as the recitation of the creed and Lord's Prayer, and the practice of undertaking a pilgrimage to the Holy Land, had found their way into Congregational churches. The practices so closely resembled those of Catholics that the editors joked that "the next thing will be submission to the Pope!"[97] For their part, Catholics noted the change. A priest in Boston observed the "constantly growing interest in the holy season of Lent" and the extent to which "non-catholic religious societies" had begun "following Catholic zeal in this direction."[98]

When one observer noted in the 1920s that "intelligent Protestants" had become "vitally affected by the beauty and dignity in the lives and practices of their Roman Catholic friends, and by the excellencies of contemporary Judaism," he touched on the reality that Protestants no longer believed they had a monopoly on religious practice. The affirmation of non-Protestant beliefs and practices had paved the way for a growing sense of commonality among all three traditions.[99]

There were, to be sure, crucial limits to Protestants' new affirmations of Judaism and Roman Catholicism. The expressions of commonality of this period were often limited to liberal religious leaders, and they were all too frequently offset by the still-pervasive anti-Semitism and anti-Catholicism. The widespread cultural idealization of a Judeo-Christian United States remained decades in the future.

Neither Protestants, Catholics, nor Jews in this period had become religious relativists, and all were convinced that their tradition was the most superior. Despite the increasing sense that Reform Judaism had much in common with liberal Protestantism, Kaufmann Kohler nevertheless averred that his tradition "set forth its doctrine of God's unity and of life's holiness in a far superior form than does Christianity."[100] For their part, Roman Catholics remained wedded to the view that their Church represented the true form of Christianity and that Protestantism was seriously error-laden. While a few particularly broad-minded Catholics might follow the lead of Thomas O'Gorman—"heaven forbid that I should say that grace is the monopoly of the Catholic Church," he declared—most were quite assured in their superiority.[101] This attitude manifested itself most clearly in the commitment that even the most liberal American Catholic leaders retained to the conversion of non-Catholics as their ultimate goal. Even John Ireland, the Catholic most beloved by Protestants and most seen as different in his beliefs and outlook, nevertheless declared that "the conversion of America" represented "a supreme duty" for Catholics "from which God will not hold them exempt."[102]

Liberal Protestants were perhaps the least inclined of all three groups to point out others' supposed errors (conservative Protestants remained quite eager to do so), but they too retained the conviction of their superiority. The aspects of Catholicism and Judaism that Protestants enthusiastically affirmed were the elements that seemed to suggest they were moving in the direction of Protestantism. While he conceded that some Protestant churches had adopted more ritualistic elements, Washington Gladden insisted that in reality "the ritualistic churches," including the Roman Catholic Church, were becoming more spiritual and ethical than before, thus following the model of American Protestant churches.[103]

Still, the different motives and interpretations that underlay this newfound commonality do not negate its significance. By the dawn of the twentieth century, liberal Protestants, Catholics, and Jews had built on a common cultural foundation and used shared anxieties about secularism and religious conservatism to reject notions of difference and instead affirm many common beliefs and practices. More significantly, this commonality did not remain limited to the intellectual realm. If members of all three traditions believed that the social represented the core of religion, it was only a matter of time before this shared outlook aligned with a broader cultural commitment to efficiency and inspired a range of interfaith efforts to advance progressive social reform.

4

DRAWING TOGETHER

The Cooperative Impulse in Liberal Religious Thought

At least once per year in the early part of the twentieth century, a group of Protestant leaders gathered in Maine for what to any onlooker would have seemed a highly curious undertaking. They consulted a large map of the state, moving town by town to evaluate the overall level of religious commitment and the amount of Protestant cooperation in each location. If a village had enjoyed rapid growth, these clergy and laymen (they were all men) devised a plan to allow one denomination and then another to establish churches in succession as the population could support them. Conversely, if a community had too many Protestant congregations, they set about trying to convince the churches of two or three denominations to combine their Sunday schools, share a common minister, or, in a few cases, unite into a new, single church.[1]

This might at first glance seem little more than another manifestation of Progressive-era America's obsession with efficiency. The United States of this period was, as the theologian Charles Briggs rightly noted, marked by "consolidation, centralization, and more efficient organization in business, in politics, and in education." In the same years that witnessed the mass consolidation of trusts like Quaker Oats, U.S. Steel, and Standard Oil, each with its emphasis on reducing needless waste in industry, this group in Maine sought to inspire a new wave of cooperation among religious groups in the state.[2] But in the final result, these Protestant leaders proved instrumental in doing more: they helped to foster a more inclusive, more cooperative religious culture throughout the nation. And what began primarily as an effort within Protestantism expanded to include Catholics and Jews as well.

The Maine Interdenominational Commission, as it was known, came into existence in 1892 when representatives of the state's five Protestant denominations—Congregationalists, Methodists, Disciples of Christ, as well as Baptists and their theologically liberal offshoot, the Free Baptists—joined together to combat the same decline of religious commitment that had worried Protestant leaders throughout the nation for the better part of two decades. Bowdoin College president William DeWitt Hyde served as the group's leader, while most of its tasks were handled by Alfred Williams Anthony, a seemingly indefatigable young Free Baptist minister who typified the theological liberalism of his generation. A native of Rhode Island, Anthony had attended Brown University and Cobb Divinity School (the precursor institution to Bates College). At the time of the Interdenominational Commission's founding he had just completed the well-worn trek to Germany for theological study at the University of Berlin.[3]

The commission's mission statement declared the group's intent "to promote co-operation in the organization of churches in Maine" and "to prevent waste of resources and effort in the small towns." Specifically, its members sought to encourage a sense among Protestants that they were not merely in the business of preserving their own denomination but rather were part of a larger whole. "No community, in which any denomination has any legitimate claim, should be entered by any other denomination," read the statement of principles, "without conference with the denomination . . . having said claims."[4] The commission looked askance at the frequency with which multiple denominations rushed to establish a presence in communities barely large enough for one church. When the various churches proved unsustainable, their congregants tried to poach one another's members, often, it seemed, leading residents to simply give up on religion in frustration. "It is not right," declared Anthony, "for us to have the church of Christ divided and distraught by cooperation and strife and struggle, if in any way, we can substitute the large-hearted spirit of Christian cooperation and friendly combination."[5]

The Interdenominational Commission offered a solution to the problem of religious competition, a phenomenon which inspired trepidation among American Protestants far beyond the small towns of the Pine Tree State. This divisiveness seemed especially short-sighted amid the intellectual and cultural threats that religion already faced from skepticism and the comparative study of other belief systems. One Presbyterian theologian likened Protestant churches to an "army among foes" in which "the contending factions" had become so wrapped up in their own disputes that they failed to note all sorts of challenges to Christianity, including "insurgent labor," "secularized charities," and "unchurched fraternities." Likewise, the nationally recognized psychologist of religion George Coe railed against the "denominational zeal" that produced a "vast amount of social machinery" that was nothing short of an "embarrassment."[6]

Almost immediately, the Maine Interdenominational Commission became the template for new efforts at "Christian cooperation and friendly combination." It was widely cited as the model for similar statewide and local federations of churches, which sought to replace the competition and disagreement that seemed inimical to religious faith with broad-minded cooperation and understanding. By 1910, Massachusetts, New York, Ohio, Rhode Island, and Wisconsin all boasted similar bodies built on the "need for increased efficiency among churches." These groups emphasized their common mission "to promote co-operation and comity and to prevent waste."[7]

Ultimately, the model of statewide cooperation paved the way for a national body founded on the same premise. William DeWitt Hyde and Alfred Williams Anthony were instrumental in developing the Federal Council of Churches, which was established in 1908 and counted over thirty Protestant denominations among its constituent bodies, including Baptists, Congregationalists, Disciples of Christ, Friends, Lutherans, Methodists, and Presbyterians (the Episcopal Church refrained from officially joining until 1940, though its representatives participated informally). The Federal Council's organizers acknowledged that local and state federations proved critical in reaching out to those Americans who seemed likely to fall away from the churches and from their faith. Indeed, the motivating principle behind the Maine Interdenominational Commission—that cooperation was essential for securing religious commitment—pervaded the organizing conferences that led to the creation of the Federal Council. "There must be somewhere and somehow found methods and ways of conversation, of common speech, of union not against one another, but against paganism and unbelief and unrighteousness," declared one participant at the meeting that laid the groundwork for the national body.[8]

The establishment of a national organization served in turn to advance further the development of additional state and local federations of churches. By 1913, ninety-six cities both big (New York, Cleveland) and small (Boise, Idaho, and Tiffin, Ohio) had their own ecumenical organizations.[9] Their prevalence prompted one observer to declare that "no community with two or more churches" could achieve "the largest results" without "some form of collective effort by which those elements of Christian work common to the whole community can be energetically prosecuted," while another noted that "it is no longer a question of whether or not the churches of a city will be federated—it is only a question of when."[10] Indeed, for a time, many observers believed that the executive secretary of interdenominational federations represented "a new Christian profession" that would become equal in stature with ministers as the public face of religion in the United States.[11]

Most significantly, these bodies did indeed seem to change how American Protestants viewed one another. The experience of cooperation rather than competition inspired new feelings of friendliness and commonality across denominational lines. James Henry Snowden observed that Washington, Pennsylvania, where he served as pastor, boasted a "Committee of One Hundred" who "carry on a cooperative Christian work in the town." Largely due to their efforts, "we have no fights or scandals, we live in peace and brotherly love, we work together and have a happy time all around."[12]

As time passed, these local and state federations grew increasingly inclusive in their membership. Although the vast majority of the formal institutions established in these years—including the Federal Council of Churches itself—did not include Catholics or Jews, some local organizations did. The Inter-Church Council of Ames, Iowa, noted that the town's Catholic church "cooperates in all social activities," while the New York Federation of Churches afforded full membership to Roman Catholics and associate memberships to the city's Jews (the result of a clause in the group's constitution that restricted full membership on a "Christian basis").[13] Moreover, Catholics and Jews frequently joined Protestants in cooperative enterprises even in locations where they did not seek formal membership in church federations.

Cooperation among Protestants, Catholics, and Jews represented the practical counterpart to the largely theoretical affirmation of Catholicism and Judaism that came to characterize American religious life at the end of the nineteenth century. The embrace of the two other major religious traditions in the United States had, like the acceptance of doubt and the employment of comparative religion, a clearly intellectual component. But Protestant Americans of the era were an active sort, busily developing reform organizations at home and missions abroad. It therefore followed that the embrace of pluralism would have a practical side as well.

These cooperative endeavors represent a crucial component of the process by which anxieties about religion's decline prompted liberal Protestants to embrace the diversity of faiths around them. These ecumenical projects emerged in response to the growing fear among Protestants that they themselves were partly to blame for diminished commitment because their quarrels and rivalries alienated potential churchgoers. Once Protestants started down the path of emphasizing cooperation, efficiency, and close ties among their own churches, it was a short step to bringing these views into alignment with the increasingly common affirmations of Judaism and Catholicism. Cooperative endeavors that included

WHY

AN INTER-CHURCH ORGANIZATION IN YOUR COMMUNITY?

THE CHURCHES OF YOUR TOWN

    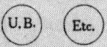

(Ad.) (Ba.) (Co.) (Di.) (Du.) (Ep.) (Ev.)
(Fr.) (Lu.) (Me.) (Prb.) (Re.) (U.B.) (Etc.)

MANY CHURCHES UNRELATED LEAVE EVIL FORCES UNDAUNTED

1. AMUSEMENTS
2. BROTHEL
3. GAMBLING
4. POVERTY
5. SALOON
6. DISEASE
7. DELINQUENCY
8. UNEVANGELIZED
9. UNECONOMIC CONDITIONS

THE MANY CHURCHES → CHRISTIAN FORCES UNITED IN SPIRIT AND ACTION → AS ONE FORCE

THIS RESULTANT OF GOOD FORCES CAN OVERPOWER THE VICIOUS INFLUENCES WHICH NOW COUNTERACT THE GOOD INFLUENCES OF HOME AND CHURCH.

THERE ARE OTHER REASONS.

THE COOPERATION OF CHURCHES WINS THE SUPPORT OF MEN ALIENATED OR UNTOUCHED BY RIVAL CHURCHES.

JESUS PRAYED—"That They May All Be One Even As We Are One."

Write for the reports of successful efforts in Christian Cooperation to

REV. ROY B. GUILD, *Exec. Sec.*
105 East Twenty-Second Street
New York City

FRED B. SMITH, *Chairman*
JAMES A. WHITMORE, *Field Sec.*

WHY

THE COMMISSION ON FEDERATED MOVEMENTS

OF THE

FEDERAL COUNCIL OF THE CHURCHES OF CHRIST IN AMERICA?

BECAUSE

OF

THE DISINTEGRATION OF CHRISTIAN FORCE.

"DIVIDE AND DEFEAT."

THE PROCESS OF DIVISION.

ROMAN CATHOLIC CHUCRH

PROTESTANT CHURCH | ROMAN CHURCH
(Evangelical)

1. ADVENTISTS (6 Bodies).
2. BAPTISTS (15 Bodies).
3. CONGREGATIONAL.
4. DISCIPLES OF CHRIST (2 Bodies).
5. DUNKARDS (6 Bodies).
6. PROTESTANT EPISCOPAL (2 Bodies).
7. EVANGELICAL (2 Bodies).
8. FRIENDS (4 Bodies).
9. LUTHERAN (20 Bodies).
10. METHODIST (16 Bodies).
11. PRESBYTERIAN (12 Bodies).
12. REFORMED (4 Bodies).
13. UNITED BRETHREN (2 Bodies).
14. TOO MANY OTHERS TO NAME.

CHRISTIAN COOPERATION HAS BEEN DEVELOPED BY MEMBERS OF THESE DENOMINATIONS SUPPORTING NATIONAL AND LOCAL INTER-CHURCH ORGANIZATIONS SUCH AS Y. M. AND Y. W. C. A., INTERNATIONAL S. S. ASSOCIATION, LAYMEN'S MOVEMENTS.

THE GREATEST PROBLEM OF CHRISTIANS IS TO UNIFY AND DIRECT THE ABOVE FORCES IN CORRECTING UNCHRISTIAN CONDITIONS IN OUR COMMUNITIES.

An informational pamphlet produced by the Federal of Council of Churches in the early twentieth century encourages the formation of interdenominational organizations in communities to challenge "evil forces." Brochures such as this one encouraged the development of local federations throughout the United States. Presbyterian Historical Society, Presbyterian Church (U.S.A.), Philadelphia.

Catholics and Jews emerged during the late nineteenth century. Like interdenominational efforts among Protestants, these too drew energy from pervasive emphasis on mutual work during World War I.

The turn toward cooperation with one another, let alone with Catholics and Jews, marked a sharp departure from the long-standing modus operandi of American Protestantism. Before the end of the nineteenth century, Protestant leaders, churches, and denominations in the United States had far more experience with discord and division than they did with cooperation and mutual effort. This was perhaps a natural consequence given the very nature of Protestantism. Its rejection of hierarchical authority and its emphasis on the right of believers to interpret scripture for themselves did not exactly encourage uniformity of thought. From the earliest days of the Reformation, Protestant churches faced the problem of splintering. No sooner would a set of doctrinal beliefs and liturgical practices take hold than some new reformer would come along and offer a new system as the *true* form of Christianity.[14] In Europe and colonial America, this tendency was largely held in check by the presence of established churches. When one denomination held the favor of a monarch or a colonial legislature and thereby received government support, powerful incentives existed—in the form of both direct coercion and the power of popular opinion—to belong to the established church.

American independence changed matters considerably. The federal constitution prohibited the establishment of a national church, and established state churches did not outlive the early republic. The emergence of the Baptist and Methodist denominations in the early part of the nineteenth century undercut the authority of the more entrenched denominations, including the Congregational churches of New England and the Episcopal Church in the South. Within a few decades of independence, even the last holdout states of the Northeast had completed the process of disestablishment, inaugurating what scholars have called the "free market religious economy." And once the process of splintering started, it was nearly impossible to stop.[15]

Each new denomination offered its own exclusivist claim that it and only it possessed the highest form of Christian truth, and the religious landscape in the United States was soon marked by sharp divisions among Protestants. For much of the nineteenth century, most Protestant churchgoers identified themselves not as part of a larger Protestantism but as a member of their specific denomination, and denominations bitterly competed with one another for members.[16]

To be sure, even amid this fierce rivalry instances of ecumenical cooperation did occur. As early as the mid-eighteenth century, Protestant leaders in the

American colonies had expressed frustration about the widespread discord among churches of various denominations. Many clergy sought to emphasize the areas in which they agreed rather than their points of disagreement. Likewise, against the backdrop of the denominational fracturing of the antebellum religious free market, Protestants from different traditions banded together to fight social ills such as prostitution and intemperance. Perhaps the most noteworthy ecumenical organization to emerge in these years was the Young Men's Christian Association. The YMCA movement began in England in the 1840s and reached the United States less than a decade later. By the outbreak of the Civil War, two hundred YMCAs existed throughout the nation, providing physical activity in a Christian setting that was intentionally nondenominational.[17]

Ecumenical cooperation peaked during the Civil War, as Protestant denominations of both the Union and the Confederacy set aside their differences in support of their respective causes. In the North, the prominent clergyman Henry Ward Beecher cheered signs that denominations had begun to move away from discord. This constituted an enormous departure, he noted, as "until recently the wall between the denominations was a wall so solid, that all the artillery of love could not batter it down." Yet even the war did not entirely end denominational squabbling. In an 1864 collection of sermons, the liberal Protestant theologian Horace Bushnell lamented the "scandal" of "discordant opinions and strifes of doctrine endlessly propagated."[18] Though some interdenominational cooperation certainly continued after the war—the YMCA continued to grow; the Evangelical Alliance, with its emphasis on cooperation in the mission fields, took root in the United States under the leadership of Josiah Strong; and the American Missionary Association coordinated efforts of several denominations to evangelize former slaves—Protestant quarrels largely resumed following the Confederate surrender.[19]

Within two decades, though, the liberal Protestant leaders who were already on edge from the challenges of skepticism and eclecticism began to suspect that their denominational division might be an additional source of their trouble. Their basic premise was that the competing claims of various Protestant denominations pushed Americans away from churches. Within this broad argument, however, there were two variants: one focused on the state of religion in burgeoning urban areas; the other centered on religious life in rural communities.

In the urban sphere, Protestants grew anxious about the rapidly growing number of immigrants who seemed to have come entirely untethered from any religious community. Whereas previous generations had worried that new arrivals would bring an increase in the prevalence of Catholicism and Judaism, liberal Protestant leaders had by the late nineteenth century come to accept if not fully embrace the continued presence of Jews and Catholics in the United States. As millions of immigrants poured into the nation in each of the decades between 1880 and 1910, the new concern was the large percentage that seemed to lack any religious affiliation.[20]

The fears of the largely Protestant middle-class establishment were exacerbated by the perceived connection between the new arrivals and the wave of labor upheaval that struck the nation in these same years. From 1870 to the century's end, the United States underwent massive industrialization, which saw the rise of mechanization, a diminished role for skilled workers, and a growing reliance on unskilled labor. This upheaval in the American workforce coincided with the broader trauma of the prolonged economic downturn of the period between 1873 and 1897. As workers grew anxious about their prospects, they increasingly joined labor unions. Unions, in turn, grew ever more militant.[21]

As conflicts developed between capital and labor, Protestant churches faced intense pressure to side with the business owners, who often provided the financial backbone of churches. But more and more religious leaders proved reluctant to do so. They believed that socialist labor leaders had already begun to instill a culture of irreligion among workers. Abandoning workers would inevitably mean abandoning cities and industrial centers to the forces opposed to religion. In 1886, a year that saw fourteen hundred strikes involving fifty thousand workers throughout the United States, the minister Newman Smyth denounced socialism with its "creed of present life for all" as a political and economic manifestation of the increasingly popular materialism that left no room for religious belief. Moreover, he assailed socialism's "more pronounced representatives" whom he found to be "outspoken in their enmity against all religion."[22] Soon after Smyth's declaration, a protest in Chicago's Haymarket Square turned violent when a bomb exploded, killing seven or eight police officers and injuring dozens of bystanders. Protestants took the Haymarket riot as an ill omen of what would befall the nation if they lost control of the working class to irreligious socialists.[23]

With the benefit of historical perspective, it is clear that socialism would not have succeeded in winning the allegiance of large numbers of the immigrant working class, nor was it truly the case that religious faith was in such grave danger. As a few perceptive ministers at the time acknowledged, many immigrants who did not affiliate with an American church still sought "to maintain a degree of religious life" that reflected familiar beliefs and practices.[24] Moreover, despite the tendency of the middle class to envision the new migrants as a single amalgam, ethnic and cultural divisions persisted among these communities well into the twentieth century. Ethnic identity impeded the emergence of a class consciousness. Finally, anxious Protestants overestimated the effectiveness of the socialists' rhetoric. Most socialist leaders proved to be more concerned with ideals, such as workers' ownership of factories, than they were with practical matters. Laborers swiftly lost interest in a movement that seemed unwilling to advocate for shorter workdays and improved conditions.[25]

Fears about the declining cultural authority of their churches and institutions won the day, however, and Protestants fell over themselves trying to reach the urban working class. As they fretted about the "estrangement to the methods of religious and ethical influence" that pervaded poor city neighborhoods, Protestants began to believe in the existence of "an almost organized resistance to moralizing influences."[26] They responded to this imagined conspiracy by undertaking a massive effort to shape community life in urban America. In what became known as the "working church" movement, they added gymnasiums, kitchens, and libraries to their buildings to bring wholesome activities to cities. They also established chapels and mission churches in the heart of immigrant neighborhoods, which had their own ministers, and offered kindergartens, clubs for children, and activities and classes for adults.[27]

Indeed, so many churches rushed to establish a presence in urban neighborhoods that it created an overabundance of religious institutions. This, in turn, provided Protestants with a ready-made excuse when their outreach efforts failed. Whenever a church of one denomination "plants a chapel in some promising field," Washington Gladden observed in his massive 1898 study of the working church movement, "it may confidently expect that before the paint is dry" another denomination would construct its own building and "divide . . . a constituency which is not large enough to support one enterprise."[28] Other Protestants agreed, noting that the "friction and waste" of denominational competition represented "one of the chief reasons why churches decay and die in the poorer sections of the cities."[29]

If Protestants had engaged in greater self-reflection, they might have discovered that the true cause of workers' alienation was the fact that the pillars of their congregations were the very business owners who so unfairly treated their employees. Occasionally a Protestant critic did perceive that the result of unfair or paternalistic treatment from "professedly Christian men" was "intense aversion to Christianity."[30] But overall, even the most theologically liberal of Protestants chose not to grapple with their relationship to social elites or their condescension toward immigrants. Instead, they emphasized the problem of denominational rivalry. Specifically, Protestant observers complained that each church insisted on having its own Sunday school associated with its mission chapel, all of which were held at difference times of day because the organizing churches thought of nothing besides their own convenience. Children would bounce from one to another, often securing financial assistance from many at once, but never appearing to be "in any way under effective and continual church training."[31] Nor, critics charged, was the behavior toward children lost on the adults that the churches wished to reach. Washington Gladden decried the "pushing rivalry" and the "egoism" of competition among Protestant churches, which, instead of winning people to Christianity, repelled them with its uncharitable character.[32]

While urban ministers formulated their critique of the deleterious effect of denominational competition on their efforts to reach immigrant city dwellers, clergy and religious leaders concerned with the country offered a parallel argument. Observers detected the same drift away from religion that seemed prevalent in cities and larger towns. "It needs hardly be said that the religious life in the church is not what it should be," lamented one minister in Maine. He pointed to both a decline in new members and a spirit of apathy among existing congregants as indicative of a lack of "vitality in the spiritual work of the church."[33] In part, such sentiments reflected a broader malaise that had set in over many rural sections of the United States as residents abandoned country towns for bustling metropolises. One New England minister noted that "the loom has left home for the distant manufacturing town" and with it had gone "the shoemaker, tailor, and blacksmith."[34] Even for those who did remain, the role of the church diminished. The growing distribution of newspapers to rural areas, for example, rendered "the old mingling of the people in church and at the lecture less necessary."[35] Religious organizations that had once served as the nexus of community life and provided a hub for gossip became outmoded.

Protestant leaders anxious about denominational competition complained that there had been no reduction in the number of churches to match the diminishing rural population. They expressed concern about the viability of such institutions. In an effort to discover why so many churches seemed to be struggling, George Coe attempted to calculate the precise number of clergy and churches in the United States. The Methodist psychologist determined that in 1890 there existed 154 Protestant churches for every 100 Protestant ministers, which meant that nationwide a whopping 49,000 churches lacked a minister. Coe deduced that the majority of these churches were in rural areas with populations that were either small to begin with or were in decline.[36]

Not all of Coe's contemporaries accepted the validity of his calculations, but his claims supported widely cited anecdotal evidence of towns with "twice as many churches as the population requires or can support." His argument also seemed to be borne out in the experience of individual churches.[37] The lay leaders of the First Congregational Church of Waucoma, Iowa, which boasted only one hundred names on its membership roll, told their minister (on Christmas Eve, no less) that they could afford to pay him no more than two-thirds of his salary. Not surprisingly, the minister left soon after. Over the next several decades, the church went through a series of ministers, and it remained mired in financial distress (at times the church met its financial obligations only because of loans and gifts offered by the women's guild; despite their absence from the ranks of church leaders and their overall silence in discussions about pluralism, women clearly played a pivotal role in American Protestantism in this period).[38]

The story of Waucoma's Congregationalists played out in small churches throughout the nation, much to the chagrin of Protestant leaders who unfavorably contrasted the actions of churches with those of other institutions. "When business doesn't pay, business men combine, and limit production to a paying basis," lamented William DeWitt Hyde of the Maine Interdenominational Commission. "But when churches are too numerous to pay expenses, benevolent Christians make up the deficit, and prolong indefinitely the agony of cut-throat competition."[39]

Critics pointed to denominational rivalry as the reason that so many financially unsustainable churches continued to exist in rural areas. They offered numerous reasons why such rivalries contributed to the decline of religion. First, many Protestants argued that because churches failed to pay their ministers a livable wage, short pastoral tenures like those in Waucoma became the norm. But when ministers came and went with frequency, they were not able to forge the meaningful relationships needed to secure the commitment of existing members, let alone win new people to the church. Washington Gladden, who early in his career served churches in several New England towns, noted that "only a minister who lives among them, and visits them often," could inspire those who were apathetic or uncertain about Christianity to affiliate with a religious community.[40] Another minister echoed this view, noting that "half-paid pastors" lacked the time to look beyond "their own people" to "the lost sheep on the mountains."[41] So, too, rural churches remained in such dire straits financially that they focused all of their attention on raising funds, thereby precluding the possibility of community outreach.

The most damning critique of denominational rivalry, though, applied equally well to urban and rural communities. Critics echoed Gladden's critique that needless competition had served to "paralyze the Christian church in this land." The constant bickering among churches simply proved off-putting and encouraged people to abandon religion entirely.[42] The Presbyterian James Henry Snowden effectively summarized the problem. The project of trying to interpret scripture had "given rise to a great number of doctrines and creeds," which had "divided the Christian church into many branches and sects." Snowden observed that when a "thoughtful man" took note of "how the church is all divided and torn," he might well begin to wonder "whether there is any certain truth in religion and may excuse himself from believing anything."[43] The Episcopalian bishop Charles Anderson lamented that when people "find it difficult to make a choice, they cut the Gordian knot by choosing none," and he insisted that "our many church labels are proving to be libels against Christianity."⁴⁴ Another Presbyterian, Henry Van Dyke, encapsulated the critique of many American Protestants. "The Kingdom of Christ is not helped, but hindered, by a multitude of hair-splitting creeds, exclusive claims and ecclesiastical rivalries," he declared. Van Dyke, who was also a professor of English at Princeton University, blasted those "Christians who hope to meet in heaven" but "shut each other out from their communions and pulpits on earth," and chided Protestants for the excessive number of churches that they had allowed to develop in the United States. "The resources of Christianity are wasted, its modes of efficiency are hampered, its clarity and simplicity obscured," he observed. His final point represented the strongest indictment of denominational division: that it jumbled what should have been a straightforward, appealing message and instead sent people away in frustration.⁴⁵

The ubiquity of these critiques of Protestants' internal division reveals that no solution immediately solved the perceived problem. Yet efforts to combat denominational competition, or "sectarianism," as it was known, occupied the attention of Protestant liberals for decades. They discussed, debated, and attempted to enact a range of models that would replace rivalry with cooperation.

The first popular articulation of a solution for this problem came in a series of short stories, "The Christian League Club of Connecticut," that Washington Gladden published in the *Century* magazine in 1882. Set in the fictional community of New Albion, Connecticut, the story focused on the growing concern about the town's "churchless classes" and the pervasive sense, in the words of one character, that "something must be done or we shall lapse into heathenism." The problem's solution came through a new organization, called the Christian League Club, which included ministers and lay leaders from all of the town's Protestant churches, ranging from the Seventh-day Adventists on one end of the theological spectrum to the Unitarians on the other and all denominations in between. In Gladden's story, the group assumed responsibility for devising a plan by which churches would canvass neighborhoods and reach out to nonchurchgoers without competing with one another.⁴⁶

Gladden's "Christian League Club" struck a chord with readers, not just at the time he published it, but also for decades to come. In 1907—a full quarter-century after the initial publication—the muckraking journalist Ray Stannard Baker noted that he still recalled the series and observed that "the discussion which it awakened in our family circle stirred me in a way that I have never forgotten."⁴⁷ Gladden received letters of praise for "The Christian League Club" as late as 1910. In a 1916 article in the *American Journal of Theology,* Alfred Williams Anthony credited the series with awakening the spirit of cooperation and Gladden with many of the ideas that underlay the Maine Interdenominational Commission, the Federal Council of Churches, and countless other organizations large and small that sought to make the ideals of the stories a reality.[48]

There was a complicating factor, however, which made real-life cooperation more difficult than that imagined in New Albion. However much liberal Protestants like Gladden wanted their denominational rivalries to be insignificant, real divisions defined by actual theological issues did exist. It was fine to insist, as Gladden's fictional characters did, that "doctrinal or theological discussions of any kind" would never be allowed to disrupt ecumenical endeavors.[49] But making such a policy work in practice proved a formidable task. The Maine Interdenominational Commission, which had only a small number of constituent churches encompassing a narrow field of Protestant theology, nevertheless endured constant challenges when it sought to bring together churches from denominations with different ideas of authority. Its Baptist, Congregationalist, and Free Baptist members emphasized the autonomy of the local church and had weak denominational institutions. Methodists, by contrast, possessed a more developed hierarchy, which included bishops who oversaw local ministers.

Differences of hierarchy presented a particular problem in the matter of clergy assignment. Methodist bishops typically appointed ministers to churches, whereas Congregationalist and Baptist churches selected their own clergy. When the commission sought to combine a Methodist congregation and a church from a denomination with a less-developed hierarchy, its members had to navigate difficult terrain.[50] Ecumenical organizations with greater diversity of Protestant denominations, such as those that tried to balance the flexibility of Unitarianism with the liturgical rigidity of the Episcopal Church, had an even more complicated project.

Protestant leaders determined to stop denominational rivalry identified two possible solutions to the problem of disagreement in matters of doctrine and institutional polity. The first option was to find some theological common ground, often described as the "essentials" of Christianity, on which to meet. Such efforts rarely met with success, in part because Christian churches all diverged greatly in matters related to doctrine (was communion—the Lord's Supper—merely commemorative or was Jesus spiritually present in the elements?), denominational structure (should it have a hierarchy of ministers, local associations, and bishops?), and practice (should the sermon or the Lord's Supper be the focal point of the worship service?). The editors of the *Outlook* emphasized the scope of this problem. They noted that while the "High Church Presbyterian puts the Presbyterian Creed and Assembly above the Bible, and the High Church Anglican the Prayer-Book and the rubrics above the Bible, and the Roman Church the authority of the Pope above the Bible, and so long as other Christians insist upon the right of private judgment in the interpretation of the Bible," overcoming division would prove difficult.[51]

A still larger impediment was the general unwillingness of most American Protestants to codify their beliefs, essential or otherwise, into new statements of faith. This problem had particular force because the Protestants most supportive of ecumenical efforts were the very liberals who were least tolerant of rigid codes of doctrine. Many, like Lyman Abbott, found creeds to be impediments to religious life because they prevented Christians from considering fundamental questions of religion for themselves. "The creed stops thinking," he bluntly declared.[52] As James Henry Snowden observed, Protestant churches of this era had recently begun to pay "less attention to theological speculation and controversy and more to practical doctrines and work."[53] Beyond presenting an impediment to this practical work, creeds also undermined one of the favored tenets of liberal theology: progressive revelation. Creedal statements choked progress by committing churchgoers to doctrines that were centuries out of date. Hence, American Protestants advocated setting aside the "antiquated and metaphysical statements of faith" and not replacing them with new ones, however broad or inclusive they might be.[54]

Since codifying an essential Christianity proved impossible, most Protestants favored a second solution to the problem of denominational rivalry: ignoring divisive questions of doctrine and polity in the hopes that they would go away. The Maine Interdenominational Commission was adamant in its desire to avoid wading into theological controversy. The charter of the Federal Council of Churches included the proviso that the body had "no authority to draw up a common creed or form of government or of worship, or in any way to limit the full autonomy of the Christian bodies adhering to it."[55]

While few Protestants desired any effort to create uniformity of belief and practice, they were enthusiastic about cooperation, which explains why the early twentieth-century ecumenical movement had a decidedly practical nature rather than a theological one. When churches combined, the decision to do so was typically cast in the language of efficiency rather than in theological terms. In North Dakota, for example, the Congregational and Methodist churches devised a list of struggling churches that each received money from the domestic mission funds of the denomination. When they found twelve towns in which both denominations had a presence, each decided to close six churches. The Federal Council of Churches proclaimed the success, noting that in the twelve communities, "the one new church generally had more members than the other two old ones, and the church was more respected."[56] Building on the strong social impulse that guided liberal Protestant theology in these years, interdenominational bodies also emphasized that they were more successful than individual churches in combatting social ills. One Federal Council report noted that "in such cities as Cleveland, Indianapolis, St. Louis, Louisville, and Pittsburgh, the hand to hand grapple of the church with the vice problem has produced wonderful results," and that ecumenical organizations had addressed other issues, including juvenile delinquency, the intemperate consumption of alcohol, and the need for better charity work.[57]

To be sure, America's Protestant churches had spent the better part of a century cooperating on social issues, ever since the birth of the first wave of reform organizations from the Second Great Awakening, which also focused on encouraging temperance and curtailing vice. The difference between those groups and the ones that exploded in number in the early twentieth century related to their underlying goals. In the case of most nineteenth-century organizations, social reform represented the fundamental impetus of the work. The desire to effect change overcame intense sectarian rivalry, which led to ecumenical cooperation.

Cause and effect were reversed in the countless state and local federations established during the early twentieth century. Here, reform was perceived as a vehicle for the larger goal of diminishing religious division. In optimal circumstances, social causes provided a means, not an end. Cooperation paved the way for the acknowledgment of a common Christianity across denominational lines, as the Federal Council observed in a report that beneath all practical efforts "is the desire to perform community tasks in the spirit and power of Christian fellowship."[58] The Presbyterian minister Henry Van Dyke explained how the two went together: a "closer fellowship, a freer and fuller cooperation in work and worship," would serve as the first step toward "a removal of the dividing walls" and "a coming-together" of U.S. churches.[59]

To the extent that it is ever possible to identify clearly defined generational shifts in history, World War I provided one such moment within American Protestantism. To be sure, there was some continuity of leadership, as people who had attained prominence—including Alfred Williams Anthony, Francis McConnell, and George Coe—remained active for years or decades after the war. Nevertheless, many of the figures who guided the nation's Protestant churches through the turmoil of the late nineteenth century either died (Gladden, Rauschenbusch) during the war years or retired from public life (Abbott). The man who two decades earlier had arguably stood among the foremost theological thinkers in the nation had become "dear old Dr. Newman Smyth," the elder statesman of theology who turned up at meetings run by much younger men.[60] This rising generation of religious leaders had not lived through the height of the Victorian crisis of faith and had not experienced firsthand the threat to religious belief when the threats of agnosticism, comparative religion, and a secular culture were most potent.

Yet the entry of the United States into World War I did not alleviate Protestants' anxieties about losing their cultural authority. Their fears that religion might cease to be central in the nation's life did not diminish but rather came to be spurred by different sources. A lack of religious commitment among the nation's troops became the new cause of concern during the war. Protestants' anxieties that the absence of religious influence would lead to immoral behavior by soldiers supplanted earlier worries about the morality of urban and rural Americans who were alienated by the bickering of churches. Some observers noted that in military training camps "so large a percentage are not members of our churches"; in fact, "the large proportion of the young men were not even attendants of the church at home."[61]

During World War I, the growing peril of communism—especially in the aftermath of the Bolshevik Revolution and amid ongoing labor upheaval—became a source of anxiety. Communism combined two long-standing fears of American religious leaders: labor upheaval that threatened to undermine the social order and materialistic philosophies that offered intellectual alternatives to Christian belief. In the face of tumult at home and revolution and war abroad, liberal Protestants did not abandon the cooperative enterprise. Rather, they redoubled their efforts to meet the new challenges, albeit with more confidence than they had exhibited in the late nineteenth century.

From the war's outset, Protestant leaders strove to set denominational differences aside. In July 1917, members of the Federal Council issued calls for a new organization that would "coordinate and federate all the activities of the Protestant denominations in relation to the War."[62] The immediate context was different, but the model of cooperation bore a striking resemblance to the same ideals put forward to respond to poverty and vice in the nation's cities. Two months later, the Federal Council established the General War-Time Commission of the Churches, which in its mission of seeking "to avoid all waste and friction and to promote efficiency" drew on the same language that had guided the interdenominational movement for decades.[63]

The General War-Time Commission remained active throughout the conflict, holding regular meetings to encourage cooperation among its constituent Protestant churches. Once again, mutual effort seemed critical to Protestants' claims for cultural authority, because it appeared that the only options available to them were working together or not working at all. Religious leaders grew anxious as "those who are close to the army and navy" issued warnings about "provincial denominationalism." Federal Council leaders noted that military officials had grown annoyed as "so many different churches and organizations" sought to present "their own peculiar tenets and methods." These military brass had begun to question the wisdom of allowing ministers into the army camps. Given their own anxieties about soldiers' lack of connection to religious institutions, such an outcome was tantamount to disaster. "Unless we work as a unit there is danger of our losing the opportunity for good in and about the great camps of the country," warned a pamphlet produced by the Federal Council.[64] This was little more than a variant of the same argument that liberal Protestants had made in other contexts for decades: denominational rivalry and competition were highly alienating, and ultimately undermined the ability of the nation's churches to advance the moral and religious good.

Cooperation became the hallmark of religious life in the nation's war camps. At the national level, denominations joined together to raise funds to construct camp facilities. At Ohio's Camp Sherman, Baptists, Congregationalists, Lutherans, Methodists, and Presbyterians expressed willingness to pool resources to build a "community village," which included a shared place of worship.[65] Before the development of the formal organization of the army and navy chaplaincy corps in the late spring of 1918, churches in the vicinity of military camps generally took responsibility for overseeing the religious needs of trainees. The Federal Council offered clear guidelines calling for "larger denominations" to serve as "hosts of the workers of the smaller denominations" and for "the closest cooperation between the churches." The organization left no question of its motives, calling for "weekly meetings . . . for conference and prayer," which, its members believed, "will not only insure cooperation but . . . will obviate the appearance of sectarianism."[66] Robert E. Speer, the head of the General War-Time Commission, remarked that the cooperation among Protestant churches represented an important aspect of religious culture in the United States. He lauded his fellow Protestants for curtailing any "sectarian spirit" and for not allowing each denomination to pursue "its own glory and ends instead of the glory and ends of the whole."[67]

The idea that each Protestant denomination represented one element of a larger whole was enormously significant. In part, it reflected the broader wartime spirit of national unity and cultural assimilation. Theodore Roosevelt, a close friend to many liberal Protestant leaders, repeatedly denounced the hyphenated Americans whose desire to maintain some loyalty to their country of origin was "incompatible with patriotism" and incompatible with "Americanism."[68] But such language was also the product of two decades of interdenominational cooperation that had led liberal Protestants to examine the very nature of denominationalism. Despite claims that, in the words of Alfred Williams Anthony, the goal was not "the disregard of denominational standards and denominational organizations" the existence of such cooperation forced a reconsideration of the meaning of denominational separation.[69]

Indeed, few Protestant leaders considered the nature of denominational identity as extensively as Anthony did. Much of his concern centered on the question of whether an individual Protestant of one denomination could be expected to attend a church of another. This question had considerable relevance in light of the Maine Interdenominational Commission's efforts to consolidate and combine churches. Anthony concluded that it caused "no injustice" for someone to worship or join "a denomination which would not be his primary preference."[70] It was less important "that one particular type of church should be created or preserved" than that "the Master be honored and served."[71] Statements like these helped to demolish the exclusivism that had defined Protestant denominations for much of the nineteenth century. Anthony reinforced the emerging consensus that differences that separated Protestant churches dwarfed their common mission and purpose.

Despite their protests that the existence of individual denominations was not up for discussion in ecumenical efforts, liberal Protestant clergy and laity nevertheless continually evaluated and ultimately redefined their understanding of division. They increasingly articulated the view that each Protestant tradition possessed a partial amount of religious truth. Only when denominations were considered together did the larger whole appear. In this spirit, Anthony called on his fellow Protestants to reject "the conviction that our denomination is the sole repository of truth" in favor of a spirit of "fellowship and cooperation" for a greater purpose.[72]

Such views became nearly ubiquitous in the liberal circles of major Protestant denominations. "The doctrines of different churches are not so many conflicting absolute truths," as they had been considered in previous generations, noted Francis McConnell. Rather, the Methodist bishop continued, they constituted "different paths of approach to truth."[73] Lyman Abbott concurred that "no denomination possesses the truth," but that each one held "a fragment of truth," and it was up to various churches to undertake the project of "piecing these fragments together."[74] Abbott even proved willing to concede the impermanence of his own denominational tradition. "When Congregationalism has done its work, fulfilled its mission, contributed its share, it may march off the stage and give place to other polities."[75]

An inherent contradiction existed in the two conclusions about denominationalism expounded by Protestant ecumenists like Abbott, McConnell, and Anthony. If each tradition contained some unique element of a larger truth, the differences among them were not insignificant—as rhetoric often claimed them to be—for without the existence of each denomination, might not some aspect of truth be lost? Advocates of ecumenism finessed this contradiction by once again resorting to the same strategy that justified their acceptance of doubt: they invoked the person of Jesus. One Congregationalist minister who was active in the Federal Council believed that because of varying human "temperaments" it was impossible "that a number of men may study the word of God to find one polity for all." In other words, human nature would invariably lead people of different backgrounds, educations, and worldviews to draw different conclusions from scripture about the proper organization of a church and the correct practices for worship. The seeds of future relativism had begun to seep in.

For the moment, though, liberal Protestants believed that as long as people kept "looking toward the Lord Jesus Christ" such differences need not matter.[76] Denominational difference simply became a matter of personal taste. While "a good man" might "have been nourished on doctrine which is distasteful to the rest of us," people had "no right to object overmuch to his spiritual food," declared Francis McConnell.[77] At Boston's Old South Church, George Gordon told his congregation that denominations represented "natural expressions of the admirable variety of the human spirit" that proved beneficial, offering "themselves to original and divine Christianity as modes of bringing the power of that Christianity to bear upon the people."[78]

This evolving view on Protestant denominationalism was not simply the case of a few clergymen and theologians whistling in the wind. Rather, as had happened with new understandings of doubt, it had a profound effect on the nature of church membership and affiliation in the United States. As liberal ministers and lay leaders ceased to believe that their particular denomination held a monopoly on correct religious belief, the bar for church membership was lowered. Movement among denominations—at least among liberal churches in the major denominations—became far easier. By the dawn of the twentieth century, transferring membership from a church of one Protestant denomination to that of another was no longer cast in terms of seeking greater religious truth. Rather, it was seen as part of the quest for greater personal satisfaction in one's religious experience.

Perhaps this result was to be expected given the broader culture in which liberal Protestants operated and which they frequently embraced. The same years that saw the development of the ecumenical movement also witnessed the emergence of a new culture of consumerism in the United States, which emphasized personal choice and buying to satisfy personal desires. So, too, it became acceptable to shop among Congregational, Methodist, and Baptist churches. Religion, declared George Gordon, "would be much more effective if every Christian were to recognize his obligation and became a member of that particular church which most strongly appeals to him and through which he can best express his personal faith and conviction." Gordon believed that Boston's Old South Church, which he served as pastor for much of his career, benefited enormously from its members who "came to us from other religious communities," noting that "they have brought with them inexpressible additions to our power, our richness of life, our friendship, our fellowship and happiness."[79]

The growing acceptance of membership in more than one denomination also reflected these evolving views. In the *Outlook*'s advice column, one reader offered the scenario of a young man who had been raised in a Congregational church, but as an adult had moved to a city where he preferred to attend an Episcopal church. The reader asked the editors if this meant that the man would need to abandon the Congregationalism of his upbringing if he wished to become a member of his new Episcopal church. "Why could he not keep his old relation with the Congregational church in his old home (for there are many things in that church that he still loves, as he is broad enough to see the good in both), and be confirmed in the Episcopal Church, that he may have more entire sympathy with those among whom he now prefers to worship the same God?" read the letter. Lyman Abbott, Hamilton Mabie, and the *Outlook*'s other editors saw no problem with the young man keeping one foot in each church, and they did not expect other ministers would disagree. "In such a case we think it probable that . . . he would encounter no objection; at least we earnestly hope there would be none."[80]

Nor were things different for clergy, who increasingly moved from one denomination to another as their careers progressed without viewing such changes as the result of a profound shift in their religious views. The records of a local association of Congregational churches near Boston show that a number of ministers moved with relative ease between that denomination and Presbyterian, Methodist, and Episcopal churches.[81] Here, too, the *Outlook*'s advice column proved instructive, suggesting that since the purpose of denominations was to "best promote Christian interests," there existed no reason why ministers should be "restricted to a single means." Thus, ministers did not undercut denominations by affiliating with more than one church at a time. "A man may belong to several scientific bodies, and with equal reason to several religious bodies. The reason is the same in matters of science and religion: the bodies he belongs to are not competitive."[82]

It was during World War I, though, that such attitudes were put into practice in the largest and most systematic way. Religion was an integral element of how Americans understood the conflict. President Woodrow Wilson's foreign policy was largely shaped by his Presbyterian faith and commitment to the expansionist ideal of foreign missions. Moreover, popular rhetoric cast the war as a conflict between a sacred, god-fearing United States and a materialistic, godless Germany. American soldiers imbued their daily experiences in the war zone with religious significance and devoted considerable attention to reflecting on spiritual matters.[83]

At the forefront of Protestant leaders' concerns was the preservation of religious faith and morality among American soldiers. In many respects, this anxiety represented a variant on the long-standing concern about declining religious authority. But in the context of wartime France, these long-standing fears had practical consequences. Religious faith seemed to be the only thing standing between American troops and the prostitution and other vices that pervaded the war zone. Protestant leaders lamented the "moral and religious problem on the other side of the sea" and insisted that they would play an active role in ensuring that American soldiers did not succumb to immoral temptations as French soldiers had.[84]

The desire to preserve soldiers' religious commitments coalesced with the new spirit of interdenominational cooperation in the method devised to help American soldiers abroad to affiliate with a church at home. This was a relatively simple process when there was a chaplain or minister from a soldier's own denomination readily available. But the logistics of a war zone rendered such a scenario impossible. It was therefore important, War-Time Commission leaders believed, that "an ordained minister of any evangelical denomination" be able "to act for other communions than his own" in accepting a soldier's confession of faith and sending word back to the home church. Thus, all chaplains were advised to "receive any man's confession of faith, baptize him if he has not already been baptized, administer the Lord's Supper," and then send all the information to the man's home church, which was instructed to respond "in the same fashion" as if the soldier "had appeared at the church to make his confession in person."[85] To be sure, the exigencies of wartime and the urgency of solidifying the faith statements of soldiers might have encouraged a greater flexibility of rules than Protestants would ordinarily have accepted. But the perceived interchangeable nature of clergy of different denominations and the ease with which it was assumed they could act on behalf of a church of another Protestant tradition signaled that a profound shift had already occurred.

It was certainly true, as James Snowden observed, that cooperative efforts ensured that "the old sectarian strife" had been "killed off" and made it "no longer respectable or decent for Presbyterians and Methodists and Baptists and Episcopalians to oppose and abuse each other."[86] Ultimately, though, these efforts transcended Protestantism. Even before World War I, the newfound focus on combined action among religious groups expanded to include the Catholics and Jews with whom liberal Protestants increasingly proclaimed their religious commonality. To be sure, the major institutional manifestations of cooperation—including the Federal Council of Churches—remained limited to Protestant

STATEMENT OF THE CHAPLAIN

OR OTHER MINISTER RECEIVING THE CONFESSION OF FAITH

I Certify that ....
has personally made to me his confession of faith in Christ, has expressed his desire to become a member of the Church, and has answered the questions in the foregoing manner.

I have..baptized him.
(If baptism by immersion, so state. If already baptized, so state.)

....

I have..administered to him the Lord's Supper.

(Signed) ....
(If not a chaplain give other official title)

Field address ....

The parents (or next of kin) of the applicant are

....

Address ....

....

The official form provided by the General War-Time Commission of the Churches to chaplains. The form emphasized simplicity to ensure that any chaplain of any denomination could arrange for a confession of faith to be sent to a soldier's home church. Presbyterian Historical Society, Presbyterian Church (U.S.A.), Philadelphia.

denominations. But actual cooperative projects frequently included Jewish and Catholic Americans as well, a natural consequence of the turn to the social in Protestant thought. Because affirmations of Judaism and Catholicism were predicated on a shared view among all three traditions that religion's primary focus should rest on society, it followed that Protestants, Catholics, and Jews would find common purpose in the cause of social reform. And so they did. The organizers of the Parliament of Religions in 1893 noted that their work had been made far easier by the fact that it had become "no uncommon thing" for "Catholic and Protestant, Christian and Jew, orthodox and non-orthodox, to confer and even work together along lines of moral reform."[87]

In practice, given that Catholics far outnumbered Jews in the United States, instances of combined Catholic and Protestant action proved more numerous than those of Protestants and Jews or of those that included members of all three traditions. One of the first issues that brought Catholics and Protestants together, just as the earliest stirrings of Protestant interdenominational discussion were occurring, was divorce policy. During the 1860s and 1870s, a number of states had relaxed their laws, thereby making it easier to dissolve a marriage. As early as 1879, a coalition of Protestant and Catholic reform groups united to amend Connecticut's state laws to make the process of attaining a divorce more onerous. These efforts helped inspire the formation of the National Divorce Reform League, a coordinating body for antidivorce efforts, which boasted that its effort transcended denominational difference and that "its membership includes representatives of all leading bodies, (including Catholic)."[88]

Another favorite cause for collaborative action was temperance reform. While Catholics and Jews typically opposed outright prohibition, a cause often advanced by hostile nativists, there was a sizable population of both who joined with Protestants seeking to curtail alcohol consumption. In 1884, the Citizens' Reform Association of Buffalo, New York, which included Protestant, Catholic, and Jewish clergy among its members, filled the city's largest venue to capacity when it invited John Ireland to speak on behalf of temperance legislation. The Minnesota bishop's speech was filled with vivid language casting "the liquor traffic" as "demoniac" and blaming it for "virtue destroyed, souls damned, earth cursed and eternity turned into darkness and despair."[89] At the conclusion of Ireland's fiery address, James O. Putnam, the founder of the University at Buffalo, who decades earlier had been a leader of the virulently anti-Catholic Know-Nothing Party, affirmed this newfound commitment to ecumenical cooperation on social issues. "If our dogmas are as many as the waves," Putnam declared, "our citizen feeling and purpose on this transcendent question, is one as the sea."[90]

Over the next few decades, Ireland and others associated with the Catholic Total Abstinence League frequently took part in Protestant events and campaigns

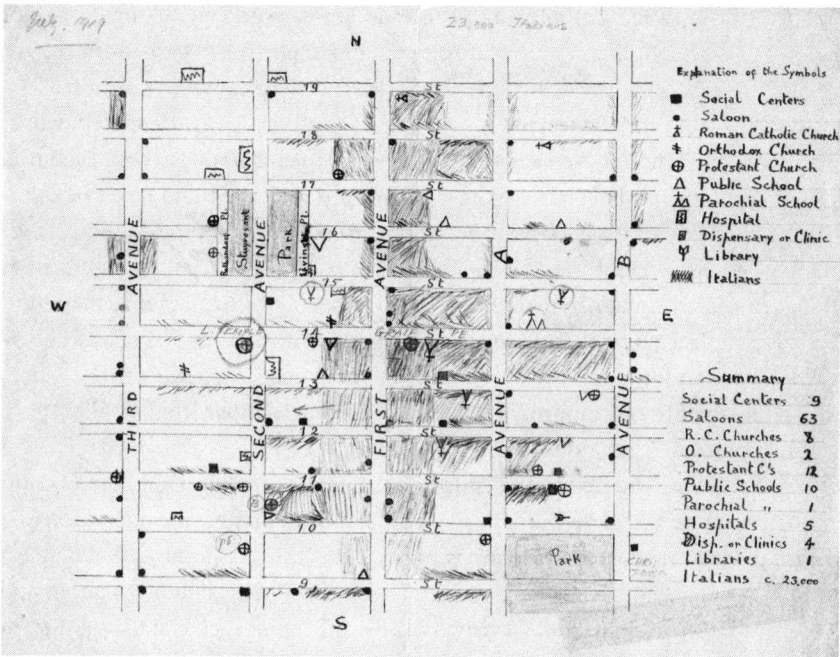

A 1917 map of the neighborhood around New York's Labor Temple indicates a spirit of interdenominational cooperation and the anxieties that inspired this new approach. Protestant, Catholic, and Orthodox churches are noted—yet their numbers are far outweighed by the number of saloons in the neighborhood. Presbyterian Historical Society, Presbyterian Church (U.S.A.), Philadelphia.

to combat the intemperate consumption of liquor.[91] Noted temperance advocate Frances Willard cheered the involvement of members of both traditions in the efforts of her Woman's Christian Temperance Union, offering examples of instances in which Catholic priests supported her campaign and "Catholic and Protestant women made common cause."[92] Many Americans credited such ecumenical efforts with achieving results when previous campaigns had failed. Roy B. Guild, the Federal Council of Churches' field secretary for federation work, reported that in Duluth, Minnesota, "the Catholic churches, the federation of churches and the most prominent labor leader united to banish the saloons after all other attempts had failed."[93]

Guild's mention of a leader in the labor movement spoke to the area of greatest cooperation among Protestants, Catholics, and Jews in response to concern about declining religious authority in American life. The rampant labor upheaval continued largely unabated after Haymarket, culminating in the Pullman Strike of 1894, and leaders from all three traditions remained worried. Here, too, cooperation between Catholics and Protestants was especially strong, and once again John Ireland played a pivotal role. Ireland and other liberals from the so-called Americanist wing of the Catholic Church adopted the same position about labor organizing and strikes that most Protestant progressives articulated: workers should be allowed to unionize and go on strike if absolutely necessary, but in general walking off the job was to be avoided, and violence could never be tolerated. Theodore Roosevelt lauded Ireland's efforts: "He can speak about labor matters, about socialism, and all, in a way that no other man can, because there is not an honest workingman in the country who does not recognize him as a friend." For his part, Ireland frequently encouraged mutual effort in all sorts of areas. "The fields of action for common well-doing are numerous," Ireland wrote, "where all members of the community may unite in action without [the] smallest peril to one's particular religious faith."[94]

Liberal Protestants and Catholics even succeeded in finding a measure of common ground on what had perhaps proved the most divisive issue of religion and policy during the nineteenth century: public education. Protestants had long insisted that the religious instruction in the nation's schools be nonsectarian and cover teachings on which all Christians agreed. Despite such claims, significant anti-Catholic biases existed. Lessons frequently valorized historic Protestant figures while casting Roman Catholicism in a negative light, and the Protestant King James translation of the Bible was almost exclusively used when scripture was read in the classroom. The refusal of Protestant teachers and administrators to respond to Catholics' misgivings about such one-sidedness prompted the establishment of a system of parochial schools.[95]

Yet many of the more acculturated liberal Catholics sought to prove their allegiance to American society by supporting public education. John Ireland, for example, enthusiastically endorsed a plan, devised in Poughkeepsie, New York, and implemented elsewhere, by which a municipality funded two Catholic schools with Catholic teachers, on the condition that no religious instruction took place during normal school hours. Parents received assurance that their children would not be subjected to the prejudices of Protestant instructors. For their part, Catholic leaders like Ireland could have the best of both worlds. This model provided the benefits of parochial schools for Catholic students, but allowed Catholics to demonstrate their commitment to American public education. Protestants in Poughkeepsie likewise supported this approach to public education.[96] Innovative endeavors appealed to Protestants like George Coe, who bemoaned the "secularization of education" that had occurred as social scientists eliminated prayers and scripture readings from schools. He believed that religious instruction would return only when Catholics and Protestants joined together to stress the need for an emphasis on faith in schools and ceased arguing about points of difference.[97]

At times, cooperation served not a specific social cause but the larger social concern that Americans had grown unconnected from religious institutions. Building on its record in other ecumenical activities, Buffalo's Charity Organization Society followed a model advocated by other interdenominational groups. The group divided the city block by block for a religious canvass, and various churches were assigned a specific block. Each took responsibility for learning the affiliation of all residents, and, if they did not attend church, for putting them in touch with one of their choice. Washington Gladden applauded the willingness of Catholics to take part in this project. "The animosities of Protestant and Catholic will be hard to overcome; but this alone would be a great and beautiful achievement," he wrote. "If, by a plan like this, in which surely no theological questions are raised, these two great divisions of Christians could be brought together in friendly labor for the poor, the gain to the kingdom of God would be of unspeakable value."[98] A similar ecumenical effort to encourage people to attend church occurred in Toledo, Ohio, where the Roman Catholic bishop and the secretary of the federation of Protestant churches took out a full-page advertisement in the local newspaper "urging people to attend Sunday services."[99]

Perhaps the most ambitious institutional manifestation of this spirit occurred in New York City. At the urging of Charles Stelzle, the Presbyterian Church allocated funds to establish a new church in Manhattan's Union Square. According to Stelzle's plans, this would be a "distinctly Christian" body, but would adopt a different approach. "The workingman who has been alienated from the Church cannot be attracted by an insistence upon more of the same thing that alienated him," Stelzle wrote, noting the large Jewish population in the neighborhood and the general sense that Christians were hostile to Jews.[100]

Stelzle's church became known as the Labor Temple, and as it grew during the 1910s its leaders moved away from the expectation that everyone associated with it would ultimately be won over to Protestant Christianity. It drew the support of leading liberal Protestants, among them William Adams Brown, and under the leadership of Jonathan C. Day it came to include members of the neighborhood who retained their commitment to Catholicism or Judaism. The purpose of the Labor Temple, as it came to be understood, was to continue the project of combatting irreligious sentiments among poor Americans by providing "the essential message of religion to industrial workers" who might otherwise "come under the influence of Marxist and other radical currents of thought." The best way to conduct this work was to form a committee of "clergy and lay members of all denominations and both Gentile and Jewish members." At least in this one instance, the cooperative impulse provided the foundation for a novel religious institution.[101]

Just as World War I inspired combined effort of Protestants, the conflict also provided a major impetus for cooperation among Protestants, Catholics, and

Jews. On the domestic front, mutual efforts centered on the "war production communities" that sprung up to meet the industrial needs of the nation at war. These included Gary, Indiana; Hamilton, Ohio; and Erie, Pennsylvania, as well as shipbuilding sites on the East Coast and logging camps in the Northwest. The rapid development of these communities with essential industries stoked old fears about the spread of irreligion among laborers with socialist leanings, especially in lumber camps where, according to a report submitted to a Federal Council committee, "the loggers are almost solidly radical and overwhelmingly I.W.W. in convictions."[102] This invocation of the Industrial Workers of the World signaled deep anxieties and once again highlighted the view that cooperation seemed the only antidote to religious institutions losing sway over workers. But now the solution reflected common practice. The first step was to create some sense of Protestant unity, either through an existing federation of churches or by forming a "wartime committee consisting of the pastor and one layman of each church." The Federal Council encouraged such groups to "invite the cooperation of Catholic and Hebrew." Combined groups of Catholics, Protestants, and Jews also organized canvasses of workers to determine religious needs in the community.[103]

The Federal Council sought to conduct detailed surveys of life in war production communities, and they shared the fruits of their research with Catholic and Jewish organizations. In places that were built from the ground up for the sole purpose of war production, the War Department ordered Protestants not to start constructing churches of every denomination. In a development that foreshadowed the emergence of the ideal of the United States as a Judeo-Christian nation after World War II, the federal government stipulated that "there should be only one Protestant, one Catholic and one Hebrew church" in each location. The Protestant church was charged with "representing American Protestantism" in its entirety.[104] Denominational affiliations were noted on the membership rolls of the one Protestant church, but leaders accepted as entirely reasonable the request of the federal government that one church, along with a Catholic parish and a Jewish synagogue, would sufficiently secure the religious needs of these wartime communities.

Other elements of the nation's wartime experience likewise reflected this commitment to cooperation. The General War-Time Commission included "all Protestant, Catholic and Hebrew churches" in its 1917 campaign for the Red Cross.[105] As part of this campaign, a rally was organized in Arlington, Massachusetts, that included "every clergyman in Town" and an assembly "of Catholics and Protestants."[106] Members of all three traditions likewise combined for worship services during the duration of the war, such as a Thanksgiving service in Rochester, New York, in 1917 that included forty-three hundred people from eighty-six churches, both Catholic and Protestant, and two Jewish synagogues.[107] At Long Island's Camp Upton, the primary site where American soldiers were housed and trained before departing for Europe, five Protestant denominations contributed to the construction of a chapel that was ultimately used "by the Catholics for their confession and the Jews for their Friday evening service."[108] The service of dedication for the chapel reflected its interfaith mission. It opened with an invocation from a Catholic priest, included prayers led by Episcopalian and Presbyterian ministers, and concluded with a benediction offered by a rabbi.[109] The spirit of combined effort for the religious good of the nation that had begun with mutual efforts among relatively similar Protestant denominations had blossomed into a phenomenon that encompassed Catholic and Jewish Americans as well.

Enormous cooperation existed among Protestants, Catholics, and Jews in the realm of military policy. An informal group, known as the Committee of Six, which included a priest, a rabbi, and four Protestant ministers, met monthly throughout the war at the urging of Secretary of War Newton D. Baker.[110] Its members advocated for the expansion of the military chaplaincy, for the suppression of immoral activities in the war zone, and for the extension of draft exemptions to all theological students. In their activities, Committee of Six members—the prominent liberal William Adams Brown among them—frequently noted that in their cooperative work they were speaking for "all the Protestant, Catholic, and Jewish churches."[111]

The spirit of interfaith cooperation also found its way to Europe. The chief of the chaplaincy corps, the Episcopalian Charles H. Brent, emphasized his desire "to promote . . . a spirit of brotherhood among the Chaplains." He made it his policy that each one would "minister to the needs" of soldiers "irrespective of their religious affiliation" and "look upon the conviction of his brother with the same respect as his own."[112] Under Brent's leadership, images such as "the Jew carrying the crucifix to a dying Catholic" helped to define the nature of religion during the war.[113]

These efforts at combination were not unhindered by obstacles. The majority of these projects involved only Protestants, and even in these limited efforts longstanding theological and denominational barriers could not always be transcended. This became especially true as lines between religious liberals and conservatives hardened. One point of contention was whether or not to include Unitarians, the most liberal of America's Christian churches, in city federations. In some cities, such as Cleveland and Indianapolis, they were included, but in Detroit they were prevented from joining. In Boston, matters proved more complicated, because Unitarians refused "to give generously" because of the dominance of more conservative evangelical churches. But the evangelicals likewise did not contribute to the effort, for fear that "the Unitarians will modify the program of

Evangelism." In Providence, the debate over the inclusion of Unitarians and Universalists grew so contentious that the cooperative organization collapsed. Such instances forced Roy Guild of the Federal Council to conclude that "the only way to form the federation is to follow the natural lines of cleaving," or, at least, "the existing lines."[114] The result was that someone was always left out of cooperative efforts. If theological liberals ran the combined organization, they might include Unitarians, Universalists, and even Catholics and Jews at the expense of more theologically conservative Protestants. When more traditional evangelicals took charge, nonevangelicals and their liberal allies found themselves left out.

Nevertheless, three decades of closer cooperation had altered America's religious landscape, and the highly visible combination of effort during World War I served only to confirm the significance of the shift. Even before the war's conclusion, the Federal Council of Churches—never missing, it seemed, the opportunity to form yet another committee—established the Committee on the War and the Religious Outlook, which sought to chart a course for American Christianity in the aftermath of the conflict. Its members believed that cooperation would flourish into something greater. "One of the most hopeful effects of the war," declared Robert Speer, the commission's chair, was "the new spirit of cooperation among the churches, and their desire for still greater unity in the approaching days." Noting that they were "drawn together more closely than ever in prayer and activity," Speer lauded that "in the work of the churches during the war there was a degree of cooperation hitherto unknown."[115] Speer and many others anticipated that the new sense of common purpose would only grow after the war.

Ultimately, this project of forging closer religious ties would expand to include Jews as well, but in the immediate aftermath of World War I, the focus remained within Christianity. For some liberal Protestants, cooperation no longer sufficed. William Adams Brown, a theologian at New York's Union Seminary, the secretary of the General War-Time Commission and its liaison to the Catholic War Council, declared that "the impulse to Christian union is more deep-seated and fundamental" than an emphasis on practical work. Jesus, Brown declared, had proclaimed "a single spiritual union" among all his followers, and "to those who hold such a conception of Christianity, a divided Christendom is a contradiction of terms." Brown was not alone in thinking such thoughts. In fact, for several decades a number of religious intellectuals had devoted considerable attention to the question of Christian unity. But in the aftermath of the war, as Americans increasingly sought to give "outward expression" to such feelings, it ignited yet another discussion about religious difference—specifically, could Protestantism and Catholicism be reunited?[116]

5

A LARGER VISION
The Quest for Christian Unity

Few American Protestants changed their views about the nature of religious difference over the course of their lifetime as much as Newman Smyth did. In his early years, Smyth showed few signs of being the theological liberal he would become. He received his training for ministry at Andover Seminary during its final days as a bastion of Protestant orthodoxy and during the late 1860s continued his studies at the University of Berlin, anticipating the path that George Coe and Alfred Williams Anthony would follow two decades later. Upon returning to the United States, Smyth began his pastorate at the First Presbyterian Church of Peoria, Illinois, where, in 1876, he unequivocally proclaimed that Catholicism was "alien to our traditions and hostile to the Christian State." He laced the sermon containing this pronouncement with familiar anti-Catholic tropes, including labeling the recent pronouncement of papal infallibility "a declaration of hostility against the authority of the modern nation."[1]

A decade letter, Smyth had traded his Illinois Presbyterians for New Haven's prestigious Congregationalist Center Church ("I care very little for the harness in which I work so long as it does not rub in the breeching" was his explanation for switching denominations, a statement indicative of his views on the differences within Protestantism). He remained in its pulpit until his retirement, shaping the religious ideas of countless Yale University students. He also emerged as one of the foremost leaders of the New Theology movement, which offered an alternative to traditional orthodoxy and provided the intellectual basis for liberal Protestantism.[2]

Perhaps most notably, Smyth also exchanged his hostility to Catholicism for the view that the continued vitality of religion in the United States required the abandonment of hostilities among Christian traditions. "We must Christianize the American union . . . by the sacrifice of whatever is useless, uneconomical, finical or notional, in our inherited customs, methods, and ecclesiasticisms," he declared.[3] By the end of his career, Smyth would prove quite willing to abandon as useless many elements that had previously been central to Protestant Christianity. Indeed, he and others became convinced that the future of Christianity required moving beyond the division of Protestants and Catholics and bringing them together into a single, united Christian church. The very title of one of his later works, *Passing Protestantism and Coming Catholicism*, suggested his vision. Protestants needed to accept their responsibility for maintaining the detrimental schisms within Christianity, and then they needed to dedicate their full effort to inspiring unity in "a Christianity divided in its own house against itself."[4]

During the first quarter of the twentieth century, a small cohort of Protestant clergy and theologians followed Smyth and championed a reunion of Christianity into a single church. This was not merely the combination and cooperation favored by the Federal Council of Churches and similar organizations. Indeed, Smyth assailed those Protestants who advocated "resting in still sectarian or merely denominational federations, loosely connected while admitting only as some distant idealism the real unity of the whole Church."[5] The quest for "organic unity," as this ideal became known, never gained popularity beyond a small circle that consisted primarily of educated, theologically liberal Congregationalists, Episcopalians, and members of the Disciples of Christ.

Despite the small number of supporters for Christian unity, their efforts provide crucial insight into liberal Protestants' engagement with the religious diversity within Christianity. The campaign for unity simultaneously marked both the culmination and the ultimate limit of Protestants' reimagining of religious difference. In their effort to end centuries of division between Protestantism and Catholicism, these theologians embodied the belief that the difference between the two Christian traditions was far less significant than historically thought. By imagining a universal church, advocates of unity suggested that there were no points of disagreement within Christianity that could not be overcome.

These efforts at Christian union drew strength from the broader political culture of the early twentieth century. Just as advocates of religious cooperation and combination drew parallels to the emphasis on consolidation in American business, Smyth and other advocates of unity attempted to use the spirit of national solidarity during World War I to foster support for their cause. In the immediate aftermath of the conflict, they cast their argument in terms of internationalism and global peace. Ultimately, the campaign for unity achieved little, yet even in its failure it reflected American Protestants' enormous shift in their views about religious diversity. The very desire of Protestants to unite with Catholics marked a significant departure from the staunchly anti-Catholic attitudes that were commonplace a few decades earlier. Meanwhile, many liberal Protestants who rejected the calls for unity did so because they saw nothing wrong with different forms of belief and practice within a divided Christianity—including the beliefs and practices of Roman Catholics—which itself was evidence for greater enthusiasm for pluralism.

The movement for Christian unity represented the culmination of two other phenomena that characterized America's religious culture in the late nineteenth and early twentieth centuries: the affirmation of Roman Catholicism and the growing commitment to combined action and effort. The foundation of the project rested on Protestants' more inclusive views about one another and about their Catholic neighbors. The essayist Mary Abigail Dodge typified evolving views when she expressed opinions that would have been unheard of from a New England Congregationalist decades earlier. "Christ established no church," she declared, "neither Catholic nor Congregational, nor any church between the two." Beyond difference of personal preference, all forms of Christianity stood on equal ground.[6]

When Dodge was writing at the end of the nineteenth century, "unity" and "union" had already come to pervade Protestant rhetoric, yet they remained ambiguous terms. Depending on the context and the person employing them, they connoted everything from the closeness of spirit that Protestants and Catholics increasingly felt toward one another, to simple cooperation in reform efforts, to combined worship services. In 1889, when a group of clergy and theologians set out to examine the question of "church unity," its members simply reflected many of the same concerns that inspired the establishment of the Federal Council of Churches and dozens of similar state and local bodies. One of the participants observed presciently that "the organization of the Christian denominations against menacing social evils" would soon "become a social as well as an ecclesiastical opinion," and the emphasis would need to rest on practical concerns.[7]

Some members of this group, which included such luminaries as Washington Gladden, the Episcopal bishop of New York, Henry Potter, and Columbia University president Seth Low, seemed content to keep "unity" in the realm of practical cooperation. Others, most notably the Presbyterian theologian Charles Augustus Briggs, aimed for something larger and more ambitious in its scope. This latter group embraced the term "organic unity" to encapsulate their dream of a return to a single Christian church unburdened by denominational cleavages. Briggs employed the language of nearly all of his liberal contemporaries who saw closer ties and better organization as tools to secure the religious commitment of Americans. An efficient, united church would prove better suited to combatting "irreligion and infidelity in Christian lands," he noted. In its current form, he argued, "the church of Jesus Christ lags behind, too conservative in its methods to be efficient."[8] But Briggs imagined something vastly greater than the interdenominational cooperation advocated by Protestants like Alfred Williams Anthony. In part, this reflected his weak personal commitment to any one denomination; Briggs had been largely alienated from the Presbyterianism of his early years since his heresy trial, and in his later years he flirted with Roman Catholicism before ultimately joining the Anglican Church.[9]

Briggs longed for the consolidation of all of Christianity and remained optimistic that such a feat was achievable. He highlighted the many points of commonality that existed between Catholics and Protestants, noting that the "common faith" of both was summarized in the Apostles' Creed of the early church, the worship of both emphasized the teachings of the Lord's Prayer, and the "morals" of both drew from the Ten Commandments and the Sermon on the Mount. "Who will venture to say," Briggs asked in a spirit that reflected the broader attitude of affirmation that marked Protestant thought, "that the Roman Catholic Church is not as faithful to these foundations of our common religion as Protestants?"[10]

While Briggs hinted at a union of Protestantism and Catholicism, his longtime friend Newman Smyth—the two had studied together in Berlin—produced the most exhaustive treatment of the subject. In 1908, while many of his fellow Protestants were busily institutionalizing the ideal of interdenominational cooperation in the Federal Council of Churches, Smyth published *Passing Protestantism and Coming Catholicism*, which argued that neither branch of Christianity could survive in its present form. Smyth reiterated the well-worn critique that the division of Protestants into denominations served only to diminish the cultural authority of their institutions. "Protestant churches," he observed, "are not maintaining their influence over considerable areas of thought. It is not simply that worldliness and unbelief are coming in; but much religion is withdrawing from the churches."[11] Smyth departed from most of his contemporaries, though, in his lack of confidence that cooperation of the sort put into practice by the Federal Council would do much to solve the problem of Christian division. He sought a deeper, more meaningful unity. The inclusion of Roman Catholics was essential, and Smyth had little patience for organizations made up solely of Protestants for mutual work on social issues. He considered the Federal Council to be at best a distraction and at worst an impediment to the progress of unity.

The real impediment to the goal of people like Smyth and Briggs, however, was that their views of the Catholic Church did not reflect reality. Like many liberal

Protestants, both men welcomed the presence of theologically progressive, acculturated Catholic leaders like John Ireland and John Lancaster Spalding, and they rejoiced at the willingness of Catholics to engage in common political and social projects. But Smyth and Briggs erred in assuming that such interactions signaled a newfound willingness to respect the theological claims of Protestantism. For all his boasting of close relationships with Protestants and his efforts to foster combined action on issues such as temperance, Ireland also maintained his conviction that the nation's "hope is in the Catholic Church," and he insisted that "the conversion of America" was a "supreme duty" for all members of the Church.[12]

Another prominent Catholic, Connecticut Supreme Court judge William C. Robinson, exemplified the way in which these two views could exist side by side. Robinson participated in an event hosted by a Congregational Church seeking to improve understanding between Catholics and Protestants, and he wrote in an article in the widely read *Catholic World* that "the day is passed when attacks on so-called 'Protestant errors' can serve any useful purpose." But these sentiments did not reflect any live-and-let-live attitude. Rather, Robinson believed that honey would win more converts than vinegar. The best way to "gather in this wonderful and precious harvest of loyal loving souls" that the United States offered Rome was through a cordial process of defining "the truth" that Protestants "already possess" and then supplanting their erroneous beliefs with the tenets of Catholicism.[13] Among liberal Protestants, goodwill and cooperation reflected a new commitment to affirming the inherent value of Catholic belief and practice (though in their more honest moments a good number of those Protestants would not have turned down conversions of Catholics); for liberal Catholics, they represented a tool to the desired end of converting the United States to Roman Catholicism.

An even greater problem stemmed from the transience of liberal Catholicism. During the 1890 and early 1900s, Briggs, Smyth, and even other Protestants who were less invested in a reunion of Christianity convinced themselves that the Catholic Church was running on a parallel track to Protestantism. Specifically, they believed that liberalism was ascendant and that within a short time Catholics would toss aside old religious ideas that no longer had relevance. Washington Gladden praised the Catholic Church for what he perceived as a turn away from pointless "liturgical tendencies" toward "purely spiritual and ethical elements," which would result in "improved morality" as well as a "vital piety."[14] Protestants, it seemed, imagined Roman Catholicism remaking itself in their own image. For a brief time during the 1890s, as liberals like Ireland and Spalding stood at the forefront of the American Catholic Church, this position was perhaps tenable.[15]

But Protestants retained this vision for far longer than they should have. Briggs and Smyth both shared the view that the papacy represented the primary obstacle to Christian unity, noting that the existence of a hierarchical institution with absolute authority in spiritual matters represented "the point where reconciliation seems most impossible."[16] As long as Catholics adhered to a doctrine of papal infallibility and granted broad powers to the pontiff, prospects seemed bleak. Unfortunately for liberal Protestants, a series of events revealed that Ireland, Spalding, and their ilk did not represent the future of the Catholic Church and that the pope was determined to use his power to clamp down on stirrings of liberalism.

The trouble for liberal Catholics began in 1893 with their participation in the Parliament of Religions. Ireland, along with other prominent liberals, including Baltimore's Cardinal James Gibbons and Catholic University of America president John J. Keane, not only attended the event but also gave speeches at it, participated in its worship services, and enthusiastically championed its goals. Pope Leo XIII objected to Catholic leaders appearing in a setting that seemed to suggest that there might be sources of religious truth outside Catholicism. The attacks on liberals continued unabated for the next fifteen years. In 1898, the pontiff ordered the American scientist John Zahm to cease publication of his *Evolution and Dogma*, which suggested to the liberal Protestants who accepted evolution that the Vatican had greater interest in preserving doctrine than in reconciling Christianity with modern science. In 1899, Leo issued the pastoral letter *Testem Benevolentiae*, which denounced a set of ideas that he labeled "Americanism." The letter condemned the idea that Catholic teaching should be brought into line with American ideas of government and society, especially the separation of church and state. Liberal Catholics quickly backpedaled and denied that they had ever advocated such ideas. But the message was clear: the Vatican looked with disapproval on any effort to make Catholicism more palatable to Protestant Americans.[17]

Even more problematic for proponents of Protestant-Catholic unity was the fact that, by the standards of late nineteenth-century Protestant thought, many of these liberal Catholics were not all that theologically liberal. A large gulf separated the religious views of Spalding and Ireland from those of Smyth, Briggs, and other liberal Protestants. The latter held fast to a progressive worldview, not only in their politics, but in religion as well. They believed in the infinite capacity of humans to transform society for the better. More importantly, through their affirmation of progressive revelation, they expressed the expectation that religious knowledge would develop over time. Liberal Catholics talked about progress a great deal (John Ireland blustered about the wonders of America's upward trajectory with great frequency), but, in reality, they did not share the expectation of continued upward development. "As it would be absurd to imagine that a human being, in this present existence at least, might continue to grow forever, it would not be less extravagant to believe that a people or the race might continue indefinitely to make progress," wrote Spalding. What went up, he declared, must come down. Therefore "mankind, to whatever heights they may rise, must rise but to fall."[18] This was hardly the heady optimism that liberal Protestants extolled. This darker, more cynical view of human potential also left liberal Catholics more committed to institutional authority. If social progress could not be counted on to be beneficial, traditional religious bodies like the Catholic Church served as an important counterbalance.

By the dawn of the twentieth century, it was becoming increasingly clear that Ireland and Spalding's cohort of acculturated Catholics would not unite with Protestants for anything beyond cooperation on social and political issues where agreement already existed. For a short time, another option presented itself in the so-called Catholic modernists, a transatlantic network of scholars who explored in a more sophisticated manner the Americanists' idea that Catholicism could be reconciled with modern thought. In the United States, modernism took root at St. Joseph's Seminary in New York and in the pages of the *New York Review*. These intellectuals embraced new biblical scholarship—something that earlier liberals like Ireland and Spalding had rejected—as well as modern scientific theories and, most importantly, closer ecumenical ties within Christianity. Most strikingly, the modernists held a genuinely progressive view of religion. Roderick MacEachen, a professor at the Catholic University of America and a frequent correspondent with George Coe, exemplified the critique of Catholicism. MacEachen retained his commitments to modernism throughout his career. "There is no leeway for new spiritual experience—for new knowledge concerning God," he wrote of Catholic teaching. In the view of the Vatican, "revelation" was considered "a closed book."[19] For a brief moment in the early twentieth century, modernists believed they could change the Church's opinion.

Charles Briggs and Newman Smyth were ecstatic at these developments in Catholicism. Smyth hailed the modernists' effort as "a renovating movement" that, according to some, was "destined to be the greatest religious movement since the Reformation."[20] Briggs went further. In a 1909 volume that examined the question of "the reunion of Protestantism with Rome" with the hope of creating "nothing less than the unity of entire Christendom," he suggested that the emergence of modernism created the sought-for opportunity for unity. The aging theologian described the Catholic Church as divided between the modernists and "medievalists," a bifurcation that he observed "is precisely the same conflict that has been in progress all over the Protestant world." Unity would thus emerge because "the old lines" between Catholics and Protestants had "become indistinct," replaced by the division in each tradition between traditionalists and modernists.[21]

Unfortunately for Briggs and Smyth, the modernist moment in Catholicism had passed even before their manuscripts on unity reached their publishers. In

1907, Pope Pius X, who had succeeded Leo in 1903, condemned the modernist movement, thereby effectively ending its influence on the Catholic Church. Modernists like Roderick MacEachen who chose to remain within the fold of Catholicism found themselves silenced or relegated to a career of publishing anonymously and looking over their shoulders.[22] While the movement crumbled rapidly, Protestant advocates of unity failed to perceive just how much had been lost. Writing two years after the pope's denunciation of modernism, Briggs acknowledged that difficulties remained, but he believed that as Protestants' "denominational lines become thinner and the sectarian fences become lower," they would become more open to the project of reuniting the whole church.[23]

Briggs especially failed to grasp how little support he had within either Protestantism or Catholicism for his project. After 1900, the theologian's views on the papacy shifted dramatically, and not in a direction likely to win the approval of even those liberal Protestants who looked on Catholicism with a generally favorable disposition. He declared that "the Papacy has a much firmer basis in a number of texts of the New Testament and in Christian history than most Protestants have been willing to recognise," and in so doing undercut the long-standing Protestant claim that the office of the pope represented a perversion of scripture.[24] He did not stop there. Briggs criticized historical Protestantism and insisted that any movement toward unity necessitated Protestant acknowledgment of the "revolutionary and illegal character" of the Reformation.[25]

Even the most liberal Protestants undoubtedly bristled at Briggs's assertion that they occupied "a false position which must ultimately abandoned" in their opposition to the papacy. But his proposals for unity proved no more satisfying to Roman Catholics. The theologian's call for the abandonment of the doctrine of papal infallibility and the creation of a "constitutionalized Papacy," in which the pope would accept the checks and balances of an independently elected Council of Bishops, drew the scornful reproach of John Ireland. In a highly public exchange in the pages of the *North American Review*, Ireland asserted that the papacy could not "change the vital principles of its being," which meant that the pontiff would neither "reduce himself to be merely the Executive head" nor allow "that a Constitution be framed defining and limiting" its authority. As a proposal for unity, Briggs's platform failed to please Catholics and Protestants alike. It revealed the enormous theological and institutional gulfs that separated even the theologically liberal members of both traditions.[26]

Charles Briggs died in 1913 and was spared having to witness the extent to which the prospects of a liberal movement in Catholicism diminished in the aftermath of the condemnation of modernism. For his part, Newman Smyth remained cautiously optimistic that those who hoped to overhaul the Catholic Church would somehow prevail, noting the "internal reformation already working beneath the surface in the Roman Church." But he also acknowledged that the culmination of such a project remained a "distant achievement."[27]

As prospects diminished for a direct reunion of Protestantism and Catholicism, the American proponents of Christian unity considered a new approach: using the Episcopal Church as a mediator to broker a union between the two strands of Christianity. During the 1910s, Smyth enthusiastically adopted this approach. He was encouraged in this endeavor by Disciples of Christ minister Peter Ainslie, a theological liberal and peace activist who served as pastor of the Christian Temple in Baltimore. Smyth's new ally likewise had a long history of participating in efforts to reconsider religious difference, including his service as a member of the advisory council for the Parliament of Religions in 1893. In 1910, Ainslie and Smyth joined Episcopalians and other representatives of the Congregational Church and the Disciples of Christ to form a Joint Commission on Unity, which sought to organize a worldwide conference to advance a reunion of Christianity.[28]

For Episcopalians like Chicago bishop Charles Anderson who were committed to unity, necessity dictated looking toward other Protestants. Episcopalians had long sought closer ties with Catholicism and felt that under Pope Leo XIII the possibility existed that "a bridge might be built over the chasm that separates the Roman Catholic Church from the rest of Christendom." Following Leo's death, they too perceived the emergence of "a reactionary policy" which rendered it "impossible for the non-Roman world to pursue the subject except on a basis of intellectual suicide."[29]

Meanwhile, to Protestants like Smyth and Ainslie, there was considerable logic in the idea that the Episcopal Church could serve as an effective mediating body between Roman Catholicism and Reformed Protestant churches such as Presbyterians, Congregationalists, and Baptists. Episcopalians, and the worldwide Anglican Church to which they belonged, represented a microcosm of Christianity with their High Church and Low Church factions. High Church Anglicans viewed themselves as one small step removed from Roman Catholicism, and they embraced much of the highly ritualized worship and hierarchical governance of Rome. Low Church Anglicans more closely resembled Protestants in their less formal liturgy and relative indifference toward hierarchy. American Episcopalians suggested that their tradition's ability to keep these two groups at peace within one denomination provided evidence that they held the key to reconciling all of Christianity. The bishop of Connecticut, for example, observed that these "two contending tendencies" held "the possibility of a wider and a larger sympathy" among Christian churches. "Is there not demonstration of the possibility of

Christian unity on a larger scale in the fact that, already, within one Christian body are these wide divergencies?" he asked.[30] If the Episcopal Church could hold together such dissimilar conceptions of belief and practice, perhaps a united Christianity could do so as well.

The problem, however, was that this method of fostering unity was a highly academic enterprise that consisted primarily as a debate about theological minutiae that never explored the practical side of religion that mattered so much to Americans of the early twentieth century. The starting point for discussions of unity was an 1886 document prepared by the Episcopal Church, known as the Lambeth Quadrilateral, which sought to reduce Christianity to four essential principles: the Bible as the "revealed word of God"; the creedal statements of the early church as the sources of the fundamental truths of faith; Baptism and the Lord's Supper as the two sacraments; and the Historic Episcopate, that is, the belief that a line of continuity existed from Jesus through the Apostles to all bishops throughout history.[31]

As an effort to bridge the barriers within Christianity, the Lambeth Quadrilateral was a nonstarter. Other Protestants saw the proposal as, in the words of one, "hardly more than a gracious way of inviting them all to become Episcopalians."[32] The document served only to highlight the many points on which Episcopalians differed from other Protestant denominations. All Protestants agreed that scripture was the word of God and accepted the two sacraments (for their part, Catholics believed there were seven sacraments). But most Protestants, who had already negotiated closer ties with one another, had already determined that they had little interest in using systematic articulations of belief as the basis for unity. One of the guiding principles of the Federal Council of Churches was that it would not seek unity through any "creedal statement."[33] Even the Presbyterian theologian James Henry Snowden, who was more open than many of his contemporaries to the continued use of creeds, saw these expressions of faith from the early church as the first in a series of "mile-stones of theological progress." Subsequent documents had "brought out some Scripture doctrine more clearly" or "freed it from some error."[34]

The Historic Episcopate proved an even more futile basis for unity. Episcopalians, Roman Catholics, and Eastern Orthodox churches (a major force globally but not in the United States) held fast to its importance and believed that the legitimacy of ordination required that it be officiated by a bishop who could trace his lineage back through to the early church. Most Protestants not only rejected the importance of such a historical institution, but assailed the very notion that a separate class of clergy existed above the minister. The belief that the Historic Episcopate constituted an essential principle of Christianity flew in the face of hundreds of years of Protestant teaching.[35]

The question of legitimacy of ordination had practical consequences for relationships between Episcopalians and other Protestant denominations. Conflicts arose that served only to highlight the degree to which efforts for a theologically negotiated Christian unity were at odds with practical cooperation. In 1914, the Congregational and Episcopal churches of Lenox, Massachusetts, proposed a number of practical points of union between their congregations: combining the men's groups from both churches, merging the two Sunday schools, holding a combined service every Sunday evening, and uniting for the Sunday morning service when attendance declined in the winter months. Leaders in both denominations heralded the Lenox proposals as indicative of just the kind of unity to which they aspired. Yet denominational leaders believed that cooperation in Lenox would succeed only if it rested on a theological foundation, which proved to be highly elusive. Consequently, the Episcopal Church refused to sanction any closer ties in Lenox.[36]

Moreover, the very element of the Episcopal Church that made it the model for church unity—that is, its blend of Roman Catholic and Protestant elements—increasingly seemed to be just as much of an impediment. The Joint Commission on Unity witnessed a growing divide among its Episcopalian members. Its Low Church segment argued that the path to unity would come through the Episcopal Church joining with other Protestant traditions, and then approaching Rome as a united Protestant church. By contrast, the High Church members bristled at the involvement of representatives of the Congregational Church and the Disciples of Christ and suggested that Episcopalians negotiate with Rome directly. The priest William T. Manning, whose Trinity Church in New York had long been a hub of High Church Anglicanism in the United States, ignited the controversy when he refused to allow the Episcopal Church's Board of Missions to meet with representatives of corresponding bodies from other Protestant churches. Manning claimed that such an act would jeopardize the relationship between the Anglican Communion and Rome. Similarly, when the bishop of Connecticut allowed clergy in his diocese to invite Congregationalist ministers to preach in their churches, Manning vehemently objected. Speaking for Congregationalists, Newman Smyth objected to Manning's success at "converting what was intended as a gracious act into a cause of irritation" that had sown doubts among Congregationalists about the seriousness with which the Episcopal Church approached the subject of Christian unity.[37] Doubts swirled around the entire project until an event occurred that seemed to offer more hope for unity than anything before it: the United States entered World War I.

World War I inspired feelings of mutuality and common purpose throughout the United States. Robert E. Speer, the head of Protestants' General War-Time

Commission, heralded "the harmony of relationship which has prevailed between the Protestant and the Roman Catholic Churches."[38] Advocates of Christian unity could not help but hope that they could parlay such sentiments into support for their cause. Moreover, the bloodshed in Europe provided a potent rhetorical tool. Peter Ainslie saw the division of Christianity as a source of world conflict and warned that unless steps were taken to alleviate it, "God pity us and save us from a world catastrophe, to which the present war shall be but a nursery game."[39]

Amid the cooperation among Catholics and Protestants that characterized the nation's wartime experience, Newman Smyth and Peter Ainslie saw an opportunity to overcome one of the long-standing impediments to closer ties. Specifically, they hoped that the feelings of common purpose and moments of shared ministry by army and navy chaplains would inspire Protestant leaders to recognize ordination in one denomination as sufficient grounds to conduct the rites and rituals of any other. In December 1917, the two took a first step with their "Appeal to All Our Fellow-Believers in All the Churches," which called for all Christian churches to ordain all the military chaplains, so that they would be perceived as representing "the whole Church of God" and not just one denomination.[40] In part, this effort to ensure that chaplains had full ministerial standing in the Episcopal and Congregational churches reflected a commitment to providing the best available pastoral care to the American armed forces. But it also represented an effort to use circumstances to provide a practical impetus to the flagging campaign for unity. "I have come to the clear conviction," Smyth confessed in a letter soliciting support from Washington Gladden, "that something now . . . should be done to bring this work from the air to some definite point of possible action."[41]

It quickly became apparent that the longed-for goal of Christian unity would remain elusive. Though a number of prominent Americans did sign on to the appeal for joint ordination, many of those solicited by Smyth and Ainslie declined to give their support. For some, the lack of Episcopalian action on the Lenox proposals and similar efforts suggested that the denomination was not serious about unity. The Congregationalist George Gordon of Boston's Old South Church was among those who were highly skeptical. Despite his staunch theological liberalism and his many close friendships with Episcopalians, including one with the *Outlook* editor Hamilton Mabie that went back decades, Gordon remained unconvinced that the leaders of that church were seriously committed to unity. "I have no confidence whatever in the generosity or sincerity of purpose entertained by the Episcopal leaders," he wrote.[42] Another prominent Congregationalist theologian who was active in the movement for church unity likewise declared Smyth and Ainslie's proposal a nonstarter. "I have no notion that the Episcopalians will look with any favor upon any plan of joint ordination at the present time," he wrote.[43] Such assessments proved prescient, as no prominent Episcopal Church leader signed the proposal. Even Chicago bishop Charles Anderson, who advocated unity as "the will of Christ" and "a fundamental dogma of the Christian religion," refused, noting that the joint statement "would raise fundamental questions of doctrine and order and canon law" and would also "create confusion and fail so utterly at what we both have at heart."[44]

An even greater obstacle to unity rested in the very success of the high level of religious cooperation that had developed among American churches. Many Protestants were so pleased with the progress they had made through cooperative efforts that they saw little need for the more radical step of church unity. Alfred Williams Anthony, one of the founders of the Maine Interdenominational Commission and a leader of the Federal Council of Churches' campaign for church federation, admitted his "general sympathy with the general purposes" of the call for joint ordination, but objected to its coming in wartime with the "characteristics of an alarmist's cry." Anthony astutely observed that while American clergy and churchgoers generally supported cooperative endeavors, most did not share the vision of unity. "I am quite sure that in these sections where parts of the great church have not caught the larger and better vision," he wrote, "an appeal of mere words would irritate rather than alleviate the difficulty."[45]

Indeed, some of the most vehement objections to the appeal for joint ordination came from the Federal Council of Churches. Its leaders accused Smyth of willfully ignoring all that had been done to forge closer relationships among Protestant churches in order to advance his own agenda. Smyth and others who sought greater unity during wartime held that view because of a "lack of knowledge" about how much cooperation was already taking place, observed one Federal Council official.[46] Even Smyth's fellow Congregationalists scorned his efforts as distractions. "It is true that the Church is divided from the point of view of organic church unity. But it is also true that the Church was never so united in the prosecution of distinct and moral spiritual ends," one theologian declared. This critic added that ordinary Congregationalists had begun "to feel impatient with what they call our 'flirtations' with the Episcopalians, and our neglect of the Federal Council and what it is doing to bring about unity of action upon the part of all evangelical Christians."[47] The campaign for unity seemed little more than a quixotic effort to develop a romance between a small cohort of denominational leaders whose views on the nature of religious affiliation seemed increasingly distant from those of the vast majority of Protestant Americans. The plea for joint ordination in wartime went nowhere.

The advocates of organic unity remained undeterred, and they found a new ally in Charles Henry Brent, an Episcopal bishop who served as chief of chaplains of the American Expeditionary Force in Europe during World War I. A Canadian by birth, Brent had moved to the United States and quickly established himself in circles of religious and political prominence. In 1901, he received an appointment as the missionary bishop to the Philippine Islands, recently acquired by the United States. There he made the acquaintance of General John Pershing, and the two remained friendly thereafter. Brent reluctantly agreed to return to the United States to become bishop of western New York just as the nation entered World War I, and what began as a brief tour in France with the Red Cross turned into an appointment—at Pershing's request—to lead the newly established chaplaincy corps.

By the time Brent arrived in Europe, he had developed a long-standing commitment to breaking down barriers among Protestant churches. The bishop reported that he made it a habit in the Philippines of offering communion to "any communicants of other Christian churches who might be present."[48] Such a view was likely to provoke controversy in the Episcopal Church of the early twentieth century, especially among the High Church element, for whom Brent already lacked sympathy for their tendency to "cripple themselves by reading out of their fellowship those who do not agree with them or in carping criticism of others."[49]

Charles Brent's commitment to unity grew stronger as he witnessed the strong feelings of camaraderie between Protestant soldiers and Catholic chaplains, and vice versa. From his own experience leading a chaplaincy corps of "priests and ministers of all faiths," he "found no considerateness, no brotherly love more marked than that exhibited by large numbers of the splendid men contributed . . . by the Roman Catholic Church."[50] He observed that ordinary soldiers expressed similar sentiments. In one instance, Brent was puzzled to find a machine gun battalion in which every single member claimed to be a Roman Catholic. Finding such a situation enormously unlikely given the religious diversity of the American army, he investigated. "The boys said," he recounted after the war, "'we had a good chaplain and we were afraid you would take him away from us. He is a Roman Catholic and so we said we were Roman Catholics, and for the duration of the war we are Roman Catholics.'"[51]

Episodes like this convinced Brent of the inherent unity within Christianity. While he admitted that he did not support the particular details of the proposal for ordination of chaplains put forth by Newman Smyth, he nonetheless chided his fellow Episcopalians for their "cold and uninspiring and negative reaction to the proposal."[52] He returned to his diocese of western New York determined to advance the cause of church unity.

Indeed, the movement for unity drew on a range of anxieties and hopes circulating in the days during and after World War I. The war breathed new life into old fears about the deleterious effect of emotional trauma on religious commitment.

Charles H. Brent (center), Herbert Hoover (far right), and General John J. Pershing (far left) all received honorary degrees from Columbia University in 1920. The three men worked together closely during World War I, and all were committed to the interfaith efforts that resulted from the war. Columbia University Archives, New York.

Amid "the hardest facts of life—the awful reality of evil, the tragedy of suffering, the uncertainty of the future, the mystery of death," observers noted, "the conventional formulae and traditional faiths of some have been shattered."[53] Peter Ainslie, the Disciples of Christ minister and champion of unity, lamented that "the condition of the Church today is not a subject over which one may become enthusiastic" and predicted the prospect of "the loss of many" from America's religious communities.[54]

Meanwhile, as some Protestants worried about the return of a Robert Ingersoll–style skepticism, others saw the Bolshevik takeover of Russia and the growing visibility of communism in the United States highlighted by the Red Scare of 1919 as indicative of a resurgent threat of irreligious worldviews. Charles Brent noted that communism was "the grossest materialism" but possessed "all the passion of religious devotion." Only "new unity among the churches of Christ" would stop the "hideous waves of terror" that would otherwise "roll over the people of the next generation."[55]

Still other Protestants grew apprehensive that the wartime's "expression of benevolence in physical care and welfare beyond anything ever witnessed in history" would show that charitable efforts could be detached from religious institutions. Such secularized benevolence, observers noted, "creates a possibility of eventual peril not only to all Christian Churches, but to all people everywhere, if it is permitted to become a substitute for strong progressive, evangelical, evangelistic Christianity."[56] Old fears that a divided Christianity would prove inadequate to meet the competition of non-Christian institutions, thereby causing a further weakening of Protestants' influence on society, rushed to the surface.

On the other hand, the sense of optimism and possibility that characterized the postwar world pleased the champions of unity. "In these days when all things are possible," declared Charles Brent, "I can conceive of a measure of unity being much nearer to us than most men think."[57] Although the Federal Council of Churches had cast a wary eye on Smyth's ordination scheme during the war, its Committee on the War and the Religious Outlook emphasized the desire for closer ties among various denominations. In his final report, the committee's chairman, William Adams Brown, observed a more ardent yearning to unite for things other than "practical work." The Presbyterian minister and Union Theological Seminary professor noted that the desire for union was "found in the very nature of the Christian religion itself."[58] The experiences of cooperation during the conflict had given new enthusiasm for unity.

Indeed, the postwar emphasis on unity drew on a longer rhetoric that linked religious unity with international cooperation. A quarter-century earlier, the organizers of the Parliament of Religions had situated their work of religious comparison in a broader internationalist spirit. Because the "tendencies of modern civilization were toward unity," they wrote, it made sense that religious understanding should be fostered "to bring men together in a wider brotherhood" beyond that fostered by diplomacy or commerce.[59] A few years before the outbreak of World War I, the Protestant minister Henry Van Dyke declared "world-peace" and "church-union" to be "fruits of the same tree."[60] Following the armistice, many of the same Protestants supported the League of Nations, and they believed that the international body that served as the cornerstone of the Versailles Treaty signaled a new era of political unity in the world. Charles Brent encapsulated the shift in view with his declaration that henceforth people would see "the national on the background of" not merely the "international" but rather all of "mankind."[61] Brent and others believed that its ideals would carry over to the religious world. "The churches must come together. If the nations can do so, the churches can," Brent declared.[62]

The new international focus also alerted Americans to efforts elsewhere in the world to foster Christian unity, including, it seemed, among Roman Catholics. Observers believed the time had come to "wake up the United States" to the project, in the hope of advancing the cause worldwide.[63] If the nation was to take its place as a world leader, its churches needed at least to match the efforts of those in other countries to foster greater union within Christianity.

For some observers, religious unity was not simply a possible result of internationalism but rather a necessary condition for the success of the political transformation of the world. Peter Ainslie pointed to the hugely unsuccessful effort of Pope Benedict XV to broker peace during the war and attributed its failure to "the weakness of the Church" that resulted from its disunion, lamenting that the pontiff's plan earned "little more than a polite bow, really creating no more interest than if it had come from the Sultan as the spokesman of the Mohammedan religion."[64] Likewise, the Federal Council of Churches issued a statement declaring its understanding of "the value of 'Leagues of Nations,' 'Treaties' and 'Parliamentary agreements,'" but cautioning that "they will all fail" unless "they be leavened with the truth of Christ," a task that "cannot be done worthily by unrelated churches and organizations."[65] Charles Brent, who had seen firsthand the consequences of international hostilities, concurred. "I myself am of the conviction that if we succeed in reaching a unified world through Internationalism and fail to realize a unified church, the future will be pretty hopeless," he declared.[66]

In 1919, advocates of Christian unity initiated efforts to jump-start the project of organic unity. A committee that included three Episcopal Church bishops and the moderator of the National Congregational Council—acting by their own admittance "without any official sanction and purely on our private initiative"—drafted a series of "Proposals for an Approach toward Unity."[67] Central to this was what became known as the Concordat, which established a simple mechanism that would allow Congregationalist ministers to receive ordination in the Episcopal Church by appealing to the bishop of the diocese in which they lived. The committee hoped this would push the denominations over the hurdle of differences in understanding of ministry, thereby creating a model for wider Christian unity, and they met with success as the Congregational Church quickly endorsed the Concordat.[68]

The advocates of Christian unity soon discovered what Woodrow Wilson and countless other hopeful Americans had already realized. The optimistic rhetoric of the period after World War I inspired no more change in the religious realm than in the political sphere. Just as the U.S. Senate defeated hopes for greater political unity among nations with its rejection of the Versailles Treaty and the League of Nations in 1919, the House of Deputies of the Episcopal Church sounded the death knell for the immediate hope of Christian unity when it killed the Concordat in the autumn of 1923. Newman Smyth, who had spent the better part of two decades advocating unity and was nearing the end of his life, lamented "the advanced position which was thus gained and lost," and observed that the failure of the Concordat served only to reinforce "the feeling generally prevailing" among

Congregationalists "that the Episcopalians mean nothing by all their talk and prayers for unity but the absorption of our churches in theirs, making us all Episcopalians."[69] A campaign designed to bring Christians closer together had served only to raise their suspicions and distrust of each other.

At various points during the 1920s, it appeared that progress might be made in the international realm, as negotiations continued between Rome and the Church of England.[70] Brent and others pushed on with plans for the World Conference on Faith and Order, which took place in Lausanne, Switzerland, in 1927. In some respects, this conference represented an enormous triumph for liberal Protestants from the United States who championed the cause of Christian unity. American religious leaders undertook more than their share of the work of planning and organizing the conference. Yet the interpretation given the conference by its very participants suggested a significant step back from the optimism about unity expressed during the 1910s. One of the Congregationalist representatives to Lausanne conceded that the event was "idealistic." It was worth doing "not because of immediate gains," which seemed unlikely, but rather to present an outward sign of the "impelling faith in the inevitableness of the coming Kingdom."[71] A conference that was imagined as a concrete step toward a united Christianity instead came to be understood as expressing a symbolic desire to advance the much-desired Kingdom of God.

Yet even with its more limited scope and amorphous goals, the Lausanne Conference accomplished little. Roman Catholicism—one-half of the equation of a reunited Christianity—was not even represented after the Vatican chose not to send official delegates. Soon after the conference concluded, the pope denounced it and other similar gatherings for fostering a relativistic view that denied the superiority of Roman Catholicism.[72]

It is difficult to look on the quest for Christian unity as much more than a prolonged flight of fancy. While it consumed the attention of a small cohort of clergy and theologians, the movement never won widespread enthusiasm among either ordinary ministers or churchgoers in the United States. This largely resulted from the fact that the liberal Protestants who advocated unity failed to grasp that, unlike with the issues of doubt, comparative religion, and combined practical efforts with Catholics and Jews, the outright unity of Christian churches was of little practical interest to the majority of religious Americans. In the 1890s, James Snowden proclaimed that Christians did not desire "an outward unity of form in which all the Christians in the country or world are to be consolidated into one huge organization" because "it would be unwieldy and unworkable and would tend to stifle liberty and growth."[73] Other Protestants went even further. A federation of churches in central Pennsylvania, which boasted a successful record of cooperation to advance specific practical goals, explicitly dismissed "organic unity" as a "chimerical idea" in its statement of purpose.[74]

In reality, advocates of Christian unity would likely have agreed with Snowden and would have claimed that they did not seek to create a monolithic institution. But what precisely they did seek was difficult if not impossible for most Protestants to imagine. In making their case, the advocates of unity often drew on sophisticated knowledge of the intricacies of scripture and church history that most clergy—let alone laity—lacked. The early champion of unity Charles Briggs conceded that commitment to the cause was guided by unique elements of his life and training. His vast knowledge of "the doctrine, polity and worship of the Presbyterian and Reformed Churches" allowed him to imagine avenues for making unity possible, his time living in England made it possible "to overcome early prejudices against liturgy and ceremony," and his "several residences in Rome" provided his chance "to enter into sympathy with Roman Catholic doctrine and worship." Briggs conceded that no one could "understand and state with accuracy the theology of any other religious body" without having "lived with them, and thought with them, and worshipped with them in sympathetic union."[75] Briggs apparently did not think through the full import of his words. By his own admission, the prospects for meaningful understanding, let alone unity, remained bleak unless ordinary Protestants could have access to the same diversity of religious experiences that he had enjoyed as a leading theologian.

Despite years of negotiation and argument (and apparently a large amount of prayer), proponents of unity never overcame the most basic impediments to their effort. They never solved the problem of divergent understandings of the nature of ordained ministry and the essential elements of Christianity. Nor could they articulate what Christian unity would look like in practice. Proponents dismissed the possibility of universally held belief or practice—"there is no hope whatever of uniformity of worship," Briggs declared—and affirmed that there need not exist a forced unity that destroyed the "manifold and rich fruits of the life of the Church."[76] But simply repeating the phrase "unity in variety" accomplished little. The Federal Council of Churches advocated "organic unity" as a project by which churches would "act as one organization in all matters, whether many or few, which are designated for union effort."[77] It was clear that Briggs, Smyth, Brent, and others imagined vastly more significant changes, but they never explained how those changes would work in practice. Would a single Christian denomination exist, in which individual churches could choose their preferred style of worship? Or would local churches of various denominations be combined into a single institution that would hold multiple services in different styles? Questions like these went unanswered year after year, perpetually deferred by advocates of unity.

But without clarity, ordinary Protestants had little understanding of how a united Christianity would function in practice.

Yet even in its failure, the campaign for unity illustrates just how far Protestants' attitudes about religious diversity had shifted during the late nineteenth and early twentieth centuries. Convoluted as their work became, champions of unity sought first and foremost to bring Protestants and Catholics together in a single Christian church. That any prominent clergy or laity would even contemplate such an enterprise marked a significant departure from earlier attitudes. It demonstrated that the two branches of Christianity seemed far less different than they had a half-century earlier.

Even more indicative of shifting attitudes on pluralism are the reasons why so few Protestants supported the cause of organic unity. Simply put, they saw little reason for it. "Christians are many in creeds and churches," declared James Henry Snowden in a sermon he repeated during the 1890s and 1900s. "They have never been of one mind in doctrine or of one form in worship."[78] Supporters of unity faced the irony that their cause was hindered by the fact that Protestants had already become much closer and had ceased worrying about differences and divergences within Christianity. Indeed, those differences were seen as beneficial.

The lesson most Protestants had learned over the previous decades was that religious pluralism was something to be celebrated, not eliminated. "We would all be glad to make Christians of one mind by making others like ourselves," Snowden observed. Because "the truth is vast, too many-sided, too far-reaching and mysterious," the Presbyterian theologian believed that "each one sees a different side or fragment of the truth" and thus "we cannot be one, but must be many."[79] For his part, Lyman Abbott employed nearly the same language as Smyth to argue that Christ had not intended for denominational distinctions to divide his followers. But while Abbott shared the same starting principle as advocates for unity, he drew a vastly different conclusion from it. "Religion is not a great furnace that melts all men into molten metal and then pours them into one mold," he wrote in 1889, as the movement toward unity began to grow in earnest, and his views changed little through his remaining career. The existence of "distinctive denominational peculiarities," Abbott wrote in 1917, simply meant that such peculiarities did not constitute "essential elements of Christianity."[80] In 1920, as negotiations over the Concordat reached their height, George Gordon likewise affirmed that fundamental unity was possible even amid denominational division. "All the forms of the Christian church have room to work in this land," he told his Boston church, noting that "the Greek Orthodox," "Roman Catholic," and "all varieties of Protestantism" were "all regiments in the institutional army of the Lord Jesus Christ." There was thus no need for the "annihilation of these denominations."[81]

Central to this critique was a long-standing feeling that it "would tend to stifle liberty" were "all the churches in the country or world to be consolidated into one huge organization."[82] William Adams Brown of Union Theological Seminary noted the particular irony of the effort to promote unity. Not only did Christians "differ in their views of what Christ has brought to the world and what He requires of His church" and interpret the different denominations as attempts at "a complete and adequate expression" of Christian teaching. They also disagreed about the very nature of unity, so the project of fostering it inevitably also bred division. "The very intensity of this motive to Christian union creates an obstacle in the way of its own fulfillment," Brown declared.[83] Fortunately, Protestants had taken to heart a half-century of reflection about religious difference, and the inability to overcome difference mattered little.

Not all advocates of organic unity shared the single-minded focus of Newman Smyth. Charles Brent and Peter Ainslie saw other means for overcoming difference. Both men applauded the work of the Federal Council of Churches, which Ainslie praised for fostering unity "on the practical basis of working together in a common service for the good of the whole Church and the community."[84] In the decade after World War I, Ainslie, Brent, and many others would join in organizations that sought to bring Protestants, Catholics, and Jews together to foster interfaith understanding and strengthen the place of religion in American life. The campaign for Christian unity failed, but many of its champions found a new cause in the idealization of a truly pluralistic society.

6

PROCLAIMING COMMON GROUND

The Goodwill Movement and the Shaping
of a Jewish-Christian America

On the evening of February 23, 1926, six hundred "Jews and Christians in about equal numbers" gathered at the tony Hotel Astor in New York for the first ever "goodwill dinner." The meal was kosher, and contemporary accounts of the event stressed that it marked "the first time in the history of the Christian Church that such consideration has been given" by Christians "to the convictions of Orthodox Jews." The evening's festivities were organized by a special committee, consisting of representatives of the Protestant Federal Council of Churches and the governing bodies of Orthodox, Conservative, and Reform Judaism. Presiding over the dinner was Charles Evan Hughes, the former Supreme Court justice and secretary of state. "Ours is a nation which was founded in neither race nor creed, but rather in the adherence to principles of liberty and brotherhood," Hughes told the audience, calling on Americans to "dedicate ourselves anew" to showing "mutual understanding, friendly accord, and earnest cooperation for the common good." Speakers for the evening included a number of noted civic and religious leaders, which helps to explain why the event "attracted wide attention throughout the country." Among those who spoke were New York mayor James J. Walker, Federal Council of Churches president S. Parkes Cadman, and Cyrus Adler, who served as president of the Jewish Theological Seminary. Cadman, who had served as an army chaplain during World War I, lamented the tendency of people "to emphasize our difference and minimize our agreements," and he called on all Americans to reverse that tendency and to "labor for the development of a common mind."[1]

Many of the gathered guests had long supported efforts that cultivated a public rhetoric of enthusiasm for America's religious pluralism. One of the event's Protestant organizers was Alfred Williams Anthony, who had been instrumental in launching the Maine Interdenominational Commission and had actively participated in the Federal Council of Churches since its founding. In the early 1920s, Anthony turned his attention to Christian-Jewish relations. The Baptist clergyman expressed his desire to use "the double foundation of a better understanding and closer conformity" in order to "cultivate kindliness and goodwill and substitute confidence and cooperation for suspicion and hate."[2]

The Goodwill Dinner built on a series of efforts at the local level to move beyond the now decades-old cooperation on social issues into the realm of deeper interfaith respect. In 1907, an informal group of Christians and Jews gathered in Cincinnati to evaluate songs and readings that were performed in public schools in order to "come to a better understanding" and ensure that there was no "stirring up of needless religious and race feeling" with the use of material that Jewish families might find offensive.[3] Similarly, when Russell Stafford succeeded George Gordon as pastor of Boston's Old South Church, he received a welcome from a city club that included Christian and Jewish members. "It is my hope that I shall not be thought of simply as a Congregationalist; nor, if I may say so without being misunderstood, simply as a Christian," Stafford declared. "It is with the thought of all we have in common with our Hebrew friends, that I venture this protest against an exclusively Christian emphasis."[4] Such interaction found its way into pulpits, as Jewish and Christian clergy preached in one another's churches and synagogues with growing frequency. "So spiritually uplifting is this service that, if it represents the best of your religious teachings," the rabbi Abram Simon told worshippers at a Congregational church with an invocation of scripture, "'thou almost persuadedest me to be a Christian.' Were you to attend my services, I am inclined to believe that in the openness of your noble hearts you may be tempted to say, 'I believe I am a Jew.'"[5]

Likewise, New York City's Labor Temple—the ecumenical institution established under the auspices of the national Presbyterian Church—invited ministers and rabbis to participate in its lecture series and to address audiences consisting of both Christians and Jews. Jonathan C. Day, the minister who served as the organization's superintendent, believed the appeal of these speeches to mixed audiences lay in the "large common interest" that bound the two traditions together. "Neither the rabbi nor the Christian minister can speak of a thing bearing upon the religion of either that is not common to both," Day wrote. He interpreted this shared spirit as evidence of a sea change in cultural values. "The bitter hatred of past conflicts is being relegated to the junk heap. There is a spirit of fraternity and fellowship abroad in the world," the clergyman added.[6]

The Goodwill Dinner thus embodied this larger spirit of interfaith comity while also reflecting a new development of the 1920s, namely, the desire among liberal Protestants to establish national organizations with Catholics and Jews to promote appreciation of the religious diversity in the United States. These efforts marked the culmination of Protestants' affirmation of Catholicism and Judaism and built on the various instances of cooperation and combined effort that emerged in the early twentieth century. They also marked the beginning of the widely documented project of the 1930s and 1940s to combat hostility and prejudice, especially against Jews. These efforts in turn produced the cultural consensus of the 1950s that the United States was a "Protestant-Catholic-Jew" nation.[7]

Yet as much as these goodwill organizations of the 1920s were a prologue to what would come later, they also reflected the success of nearly fifty years of effort by leading liberal Protestants to articulate a favorable message about the country's religious diversity. Many of the founders of this interfaith movement were the clergy and laity who had shaped liberal Protestant values for decades, and they forged fruitful partnerships with Jewish and—to a lesser extent—Catholic leaders who shared their outlook.

The nascent interfaith movement is best considered through the lens of three groups that encompassed its breadth of ambitions and organizational models: the Federal Council's Committee on Goodwill between Jews and Christians, the American Association on Religion in Colleges and Universities, and the Amos Society. Taken together, all three groups demonstrate how decades of Protestant affirmation of Jews and Catholics paved the way for members of the three traditions to enshrine those values in permanent institutions. These new organizations provided the bridge connecting the evolving attitudes about pluralism among liberal Protestants of the late nineteenth and early twentieth centuries with the values of a Judeo-Christian America that would emerge in the years after World War II. They thus reflected older ideas and values as well as new ones. The groups rested on the now-familiar rhetoric of anxiety about the declining place of religion in the nation's life and collapsing levels of faith commitment. They also reflected a continued sense of religious superiority among liberal Protestants that would not dissipate fully until the latter half of the twentieth century.

But these goodwill groups forged new ground by depicting the religious culture of the United States as one shaped equally by Protestants, Catholics, Jews. They also cautiously expanded their embrace of diversity beyond the realm of the religious into areas of race and ethnicity, categories that had been held as distinct from religion at events like the World's Parliament of Religions. Both of these developments presaged the view of pluralism that would take root more widely in Protestant thought—and in American society at large—following World War II.

In many respects, the events of the decade after World War I belied the embrace of religious diversity that had become widespread among the liberal elite of the nation's mainline Protestant denominations. After 1918, the nation experienced a sharp upsurge of anti-Semitism, which grew stronger in the 1920s and continued unabated until the nation's eventual reckoning with its attitudes toward Jews in the aftermath of World War II and the Holocaust. While less pronounced, anti-Catholicism also returned with considerable force.

The early 1920s witnessed Henry Ford's publication of a series of editorials based on the wildly anti-Semitic forgery *The Protocols of the Elders of Zion*. In these articles, which appeared in his nationally read *Dearborn Independent*, Ford blamed Jews for nearly every ill of modern society and accused them of scheming to take over the world. During the same years, many colleges and universities, most notably Harvard and Princeton, initiated strict quota systems that dramatically curtailed the number of Jewish students admitted. In the halls of government, rhetoric surrounding the passage of the 1924 immigration restrictions made clear that many political leaders wanted the entry of Jewish and Catholic migrants into the country sharply curtailed. A resurgent Ku Klux Klan expanded beyond its earlier preoccupation with terrorizing African Americans and began to target Jews as well as Catholics. As the American Protective Association had done three decades earlier, the Klan draped its nativism in the cloak of Protestant Christianity. "A wave of Protestant, Anglo-Saxon Americanism is beginning now to gather force," announced one Klan pamphlet, which proclaimed that soon "a torrential flood" would "sweep every disloyal papist and Christ-hating Jew from the face of our beloved land."[8]

Jewish Americans particularly perceived the increasingly vitriolic hostility directed toward them. Abram Simon, the rabbi of a prominent Reform synagogue in Washington, D.C., who served as president of the Central Conference of American Rabbis during the 1920s and who on several occasions offered the prayer of invocation for sessions of the U.S. House of Representatives, called attention to the "flood of venom and misunderstanding" that had "been released since the war." In a radio address that attracted the attention of New York senator Royal S. Copeland, Simon decried the "malignant hatred bequeathed us by the world tragedy" and expressed particular regret that "the brunt of this resurgent ill will has had to be borne by the people of Israel."[9]

Much of the anti-Semitism of the post–World War I years stemmed from the commonly held view that advocates of communism were Jewish. In the aftermath

Abram Simon (far left) was enormously influential in building support for interfaith efforts among Jews and in fostering a religiously inclusive culture in the nation's capital. Here he is pictured at a meeting with Herbert Hoover at the White House. The Jacob Rader Marcus Center of the American Jewish Archives, Cincinnati, americanjewisharchives.org.

of World War I, Americans remained anxious about the threat of communist ideas, and some Protestants had come to believe that communism represented the most potent manifestation of the secular threat to religious belief. Because some of the leaders of the Bolshevik Revolution in Russia were Jewish, many Americans leaped to the conclusion that Jewish radicals had concocted a similar plan to overthrow the U.S. government. This view underlay the Red Scare of 1919 and 1920, in which Attorney General A. Mitchell Palmer oversaw waves of arrests and deportations of suspected radicals. Anti-Semitism tinged the expressions of even some Protestants who had previously offered enthusiastic endorsements of religious diversity. The Episcopal priest Leighton Parks, who had been instrumental decades earlier in shaping favorable views on Hinduism and Buddhism, explained his support for the Russian Orthodox Church by noting that it represented "the only organization which the Jewish leaders of the Soviet government have been unable to destroy."[10] Princeton University professor and Presbyterian minister Henry Van Dyke drew a distinction between the "true Jew" and "the renegade, godless Jew," who was "the most dangerous man in the world." He denounced the "infidel and false Jew" for attacking Christianity in Russia, and he warned that "there are perhaps thousands of half-baked communists in America who half-heartedly sympathize" with what had been done in Russia.[11]

Meanwhile, the anti-Catholicism that had percolated throughout the decade boiled over in 1928 when the Democratic Party nominated Al Smith for president. The first Roman Catholic nominee for America's highest office drew widespread scorn, including from some prominent religious leaders. Disciples of Christ minister Charles Clayton Morrison, who edited the widely read *Christian Century* magazine, denounced Smith as unfit to be president because Catholicism represented "a culture sharply alien" to American values.[12]

As had been the case during the previous wave of American nativism in the 1880s and 1890s, prominent liberal Protestants were not the champions of such attitudes but rather some of their most vocal opponents. At the outset of this latest upsurge of intolerance, Jonathan Day of New York's Labor Temple offered an almost elegiac reflection in a Jewish periodical. "As a Christian minister I want to express my gratitude to the Hebrews who have lived through nineteen centuries of misunderstanding, misinterpretations, and relentless persecution," he wrote. Day inverted the common anti-Semitic trope that the Jews killed Christ by instead suggesting that Jesus's sympathy would be with modern-day Jews because he empathized with their suffering. Moreover, they had demonstrated a willingness to forgive their persecutors. It was Jews, and not Christians, Day wrote, who "have taught me the meaning of the prayer of my Master on the cross when He prayed, 'Forgive them, for they know not what they do.'"[13]

During the 1920s, as it became clear that the postwar anti-Semitism and anti-Catholicism continued to blight society, more and more liberals echoed Day's words and denounced the intolerant spirit. Charles Brent, the Episcopal Church's bishop of western New York who had served as the chief of chaplains of the American Expeditionary Forces during World War I, declared that he had "not a grain of confidence" in Attorney General Palmer, who had denied "common, decent justice" to suspects in the Red Scare.[14] Brent and others assailed not only Palmer's methods but also the broader spirit of intolerance that undergirded his actions. Alfred Williams Anthony likewise declared, "Americans are not ruled by old world prejudices, musty and foul," and thus did not believe the claims of *The Protocols of the Elders of Zion*. "Henry Ford has been crying in a wilderness and his voice has returned unto him void," Anthony observed.[15] Meanwhile, many Protestants swiftly denounced the anti-Catholic invective directed toward Al Smith. The aging Henry Van Dyke, by this point a self-described "unimportant old Presbyterian minister," lambasted "the loud vociferation of the Howling bigot," as well as the "gentle murmurs of mild Congregational ministers who merely suggest that it is not improper to let your ecclesiastical prejudice control your vote," and especially—a clear reference to Morrison's *Christian Century*—the pronouncements of "a religious newspaper of liberal reputation." In a pamphlet published by the Democratic National Committee, he announced his intent to "always resist" attempts "to arouse and array religious prejudice and hostility."[16]

The Federal Council of Churches emerged as a leading voice against the Ku Klux Klan. In 1922, the ecumenical organization's administrative committee issued a statement denouncing the secret society, and they forcefully disavowed the Klan's claims to represent Protestant Christianity. Noting that its activities posed "grave consequences to the Church and to society at large," Federal Council leaders insisted that the goals of the Klan were "consistent neither with the ideals of the churches nor with true patriotism."[17] When one rabbi objected to the limied scope of the Protestant organization's statement and insisted on "action not words" in responding to individual Protestants who supported the Klan (a near impossibility given the Federal Council's lack of authority over its constituent denominations), he nevertheless received a sympathetic hearing from the general secretary. "I quite agree with you in feeling," replied Samuel McCrea Cavert, "that the authoritative bodies of all Protestant churches ought to deal with this matter in a vigorous way."[18] To some extent, Cavert got his wish. Several major denominations issued statements or resolutions condemning the Klan.[19]

While the Federal Council was unable to exert direct control over denominations, its leaders became proactive in another way. Reflecting the commitment to large-scale institution building that had pervaded society at large, liberal Protestants committed to fostering a favorable view of pluralism aspired to create major institutions that would seek to improve mainstream attitudes toward religious minorities such as Jews and Catholics. These groups would have responsibility for, in the parlance of the day, creating religious goodwill.[20]

While the desire to combat anti-Semitism and anti-Catholicism represented a critical impetus in the formation of theses institutions, it was not the only impulse that prompted their creation. They were manifestations of what by the 1920s was a long-standing commitment among liberal Protestants and their Catholic and Jewish allies to the notion that interfaith interaction represented a critical tool in the effort to secure the vitality of religious faith in the United States. "The need now is to co-operate in concrete deeds to combat the influences of materialism, lawlessness and irreligion," which, according to Alfred Williams Anthony, seemed as though they might "engulf Jews and Christians alike." Emphasizing a mutual foe but also a shared identity, the Baptist minister observed that Christian and Jewish Americans had "common perils to avoid and a common country and humanity to serve."[21] So, too, the rabbi Abram Simon invoked the familiar anxiety of declining religious commitment. "There are thousands of men and women, Christians and Jews," he declared, "who have knowingly or unknowingly slipped from the tether of church or synagogue; they have no home!" He believed that organizations of Christians and Jews could solve the problem by providing a place "where Jews and Christians can not only think together, can not only speak together, can not only dwell together, but also work and worship together in peace and unity."[22]

Simon's invocation of "peace and unity" also signaled the extent to which interfaith institutions were further buoyed by the same internationalism that had encouraged Brent and other Protestants to advocate for Christian union. A few years before his indictment of the "bad Jews" of Bolshevism, the Presbyterian Henry Van Dyke told an assembly of Jews that it was a shared "doctrine of Judaism and Christianity" that inspired the victors of World War I to develop "a league of international power."[23] Abram Simon called for a "League of Religions" that would meet alongside the League of Nations.[24] His fellow rabbi David Philipson, who had actively participated in interfaith efforts since the 1890s, cheered the emergence of the "international mind" during the 1920s and suggested that an "inter-religious mind" be encouraged alongside it. "We shall think in terms, not only of our special ism or doxy," Philipson declared, "but shall accustom ourselves and those who come into the sphere of our influence to think of men and women of all other religions as children of the One Father." The rabbi encouraged religious Americans to study one another's traditions, focusing particularly on "the splendid achievements which men of other creeds have done."[25]

Champions of such sentiments also drew inspiration from the widespread reports of interfaith cooperation on the front during World War I, which often contained language of "brotherhood." During the war, reports appeared in the U.S. press extolling the "wonderful and hitherto unprecedented way in which the common universal elements of Judaism and the various forms of Christianity are emphasized as never before."[26] Amid the carnage of the conflict, it became "almost matters of everyday" experience that chaplains would provide care for soldiers regardless of religious affiliation. "I, for one, have read psalms at the bedside of dying Protestant soldiers. I have held the cross before a dying Catholic. I have recited the traditional confession with the dying Jew," recalled a Jewish chaplain. He added that the experience had confirmed in him the feeling that "we are all one in a very real sense."[27]

While participants in the goodwill movement often cast their inclusive statements in extremely broad language, in practice they restricted their focus to Protestants, Catholics, and Jews, who accounted for the overwhelming majority of religious adherents in the United States. Moreover, for theological reasons, membership in these organizations consisted primarily of liberal Protestants and

Reform Jews. The 1920s saw the emergence of a resurgent conservatism in Protestant thought, and liberals (who nevertheless remained the public face of Protestantism for respectable middle-class Americans) endured growing criticism as the fundamentalist movement became increasingly organized. Newly empowered conservatives lambasted the liberals who dominated the Federal Council of Churches for issuing "more favorable" statements "about Jews than about orthodox Christians."[28] Orthodox Jews, who were typically more recent immigrants, had less interest in interfaith efforts, as did members of the nascent conservative movement. Catholics, still reeling from the papal condemnations of Americanism and modernism, took part in some activities of the goodwill movement, but their roles were typically smaller than those of Protestants and Jews.

Despite their shared goals, the goodwill organizations of the 1920s differed significantly from one another. Three of the most prominent groups—the Committee on Goodwill between Jews and Christians of the Federal Council of Churches, the American Association on Religion in Colleges and Universities, and the Amos Society—diverged in the nature of their membership and in the ambitiousness of their scope. Yet considered together, all three organizations illustrate the commitment of liberal Protestants in the 1920s to building institutions that enshrined their embrace of religious pluralism in American life.

Of these various interfaith organizations, the Federal Council's Committee on Goodwill between Jews and Christians was the most active. The committee was the brainchild of Alfred Williams Anthony, who in 1921 assembled an informal network of individuals to respond to the virulent wave of anti-Semitism plaguing the nation. In 1923, the Commission on International Justice and Goodwill, a major committee within the Federal Council, authorized the incorporation of the group into an official subcommittee.[29] "Perhaps no page of history," mused the author of an early document of the Committee on Goodwill, "bears more blots and stains upon it than that which records the relations of Christians and Jews during almost two thousand years."[30] Anthony quickly sought to make reality reflect the group's rhetoric and invited representatives of the Central Conference of American Rabbis, including David Philipson, to participate. As an indicator of the gulf that still separated the two traditions, Jewish representatives elected not to join the Federal Council's committee but instead to meet with its members on a regular basis.

Anthony's goals for the committee fit within the model favored by the Federal Council of Churches: placing emphasis on areas of practical cooperation in order to avoid controversial disagreements of belief and practice. In addition to the desire "to combat anti-Semitism" (and, according to Protestants, "anti-

Christianism" among Jews), the Committee on Goodwill sought to identify "the things that we can do together, the possibilities of service for the common good."[31] Anthony made clear that the group would not "enter into doctrinal controversy" and would not "presume to speak for any group in the Christian Churches, either about Christology, or any other doctrinal or organizational matters."[32] Early on, the group also sought to allay the fear among Jews that the Federal Council intended the committee to serve as a tool for conversion. "Because of our mutual respect for the integrity of each other's religion and our desire that each faith shall enjoy the fullest opportunity for its development and enrichment," the members declared, "we have no proselytizing purpose."[33] For their part, Jewish leaders cheered the decision to organize the committee's work "along practical lines." This course of action seemed to offer "a very definite program for the removal of grounds of mistrust between the Jews and non-Jews."[34]

Within six months of its inception, the Committee on Goodwill boasted a significant workload of practical activities. Its members addressed students at major Protestant theological seminaries, and in ten cities its representatives helped to establish "forum councils" that brought Christians and Jews together for informal discussion. In so doing, Anthony and other committee members discovered the existence of "similar movements in different cities in different parts of the country," which they "brought into alliance" with their own efforts. The vitality of such local organizations suggested a broader interest in the ideal of religious comity among Jews and Christians. This message seemed especially popular in the Midwest, where local efforts developed in Cleveland, Des Moines, Indianapolis, and Iowa City, a reflection of the general openness to interfaith conversation that had existed in the rapidly growing interior states which lacked the entrenched religious interests of the East Coast.[35] Another midwestern city, Detroit, provided a fruitful location for another of the group's goals: pulpit exchanges between ministers and rabbis. A stone's throw from Henry Ford's anti-Semitic *Dearborn Independent*, over forty such exchanges occurred each year in the mid-1920s.[36]

The committee also devoted attention to areas outside of major cities, which reflected the reality that the goodwill movement was not merely the product of a few northeastern cities. It arranged a series of events "in rural churches," where representatives of Judaism explained their beliefs in the hopes of allowing "Christians to cultivate a more appreciative understanding" of Judaism.[37] Though most of its efforts remained limited to Protestants and Jews, the committee occasionally won the support of Catholics, especially in securing "pronouncements and publications in papers, religious and secular," for events such as "thanksgiving observances," which appeared "over the signatures of an outstanding Jewish Rabbi, Roman Catholic priest, and Protestant clergyman."[38] One of the first effects of the committee noted by Jewish Americans was "a growing sense of shame on the part of high-minded Christians at the stupidity and vulgar display of bigotry and unfriendliness."[39] The goodwill movement did not succeed in ridding American society of anti-Semitism, but it made it far less respectable.

The Committee on Goodwill took particular pride in a program of "student group conferences conducted by young people," which offered the hope that religious diversity had already become a core value of the next generation of American leaders. By the late 1920s, Cornell, Yale, Smith, Columbia, and the University of Chicago stood among the schools where studies of Jewish-Christian relations were planned. The committee hoped that initial discussions would "develop larger enterprises on each campus, and in each college town."[40] So, too, its members encouraged closer ties among future members of the clergy by endorsing programs like one in Chicago that brought together students of four Protestants seminaries and a Jewish theological school. In a series of lectures, the students examined "those principles which are held in common without going into theological controversies" in order to "lay a foundation for understanding and respect in our future religious leadership."[41]

This emphasis on shaping the views of the next generation of Americans through efforts on college campuses provided the guiding impulse for another major interfaith endeavor, the American Association on Religion in Colleges and Universities. Like the Federal Council's Committee on Goodwill, the American Association emphasized concrete, practical goals, and it drew its inspiration from long-standing anxieties about the decline of religious influence in the United States. Nowhere was this phenomenon more apparent, its organizers believed, than in the nation's academic institutions. Because religion held "primary importance in all character building programs," its declining influence in the academy did not bode well for the spiritual or moral vitality of the country.[42]

Drawing on the same argument that had been previously employed by Protestant advocates of both church federations and Christian unity, the American Association insisted that overemphasis on differences of belief and practice had proved deleterious to religion itself. But they expanded this familiar argument to include not just differences within Protestantism, but also differences among Protestants, Catholics, and Jews. "Students and faculty unfortunately frequently see divisions and competitors, if not indeed strife, between the rich variety of denominations and faiths, rather than the undergirding unity of all these differences," noted its organizers.[43] They argued that the constant emphasis on division and disagreement served only to alienate Americans from religious communities.

The model for the American Association on Religion derived from the Council of Church Boards of Education, which Protestants had developed as clearinghouse of information on the best approaches for religious education. Ora Delmer Foster, a Congregationalist minister, took this idea and expanded it. Steeping his rhetoric in the parlance of efficiency and professionalism that characterized many ecumenical institutions, Foster proposed a "central agency" of Protestants, Catholics, and Jews in which "all elements could meet, formulate policies, and execute programs." Specifically, he envisioned an organization that could "determine how far common interests existed" among the three traditions and examine the degree to which those interests "could be promoted cooperatively" in the nation's academic institutions.[44]

The American Association on Religion differed from other interfaith groups in its frank acknowledgment of the changed religious landscape of the United States. According to its proposals, "all great American University communities are composed of three natural religious groupings of agencies responsible for the moral and religious culture of the University family; Catholics, Jews, and Protestants."[45] Even in an era of vastly improved interreligious relationships, this statement marked a rare acknowledgment that Protestants no longer held sway over the nation's religious culture. This outlook manifested itself in the governance of the organization. The association's board included four Protestants (including Charles Brent), four Jews (including Abram Simon, David Philipson, and Cyrus Adler), and four Catholics. Catholic involvement was precarious, a reflection of the anxiety within the Church about any interfaith activities. One representative temporarily left the group when his superiors claimed that its work undercut Catholic educational institutions.[46] The organization further showed its inclusiveness by appointing four additional representatives of university administrations, in part to provide a voice for "minority groups not specifically included in the three great religious groupings" of Protestantism, Catholicism, and Judaism.[47]

The major success of the American Association on Religion came at the University of Iowa, where the group proved instrumental in establishing a school of religion in 1926. Because the goals for the school included offering classes that presented "a wholesome view of religion" and encouraged "an expectancy for men and women to choose religious callings as a vocation," university officials concluded that funding it with public money constituted a violation of the separation of church and state.[48] Ora Delmer Foster convinced the Rockefeller family to finance the school, and he brought together Protestant, Jewish, and Catholic leaders in Des Moines to elect a board of trustees for the new institution.[49] A rabbi involved in the selection process noted that "not a discordant note of any kind marred the deliberation" of the various religious leaders and lauded the "fine, broad spirit of cooperation" that marked the election of the trustees.[50] Even a few years earlier, such an institution would have been unimaginable. It had now not only come to fruition, but it had done so with almost entirely no rancor.

The School of Religion at the University of Iowa marked the greatest achievement of the American Association on Religion, but the group did provide guidance to numerous other academic institutions, including Stanford University, the University of Oregon, UCLA, and Indiana University. After a 1927 visit to Indiana, a representative of the association reported that five Protestant denominations had joined with Catholic and Jewish groups on campus. In so doing, they "brought a new spirit into the religious work of the university."[51] Though the scope of its focus remained narrow, the American Association on Religion succeeded in presenting interfaith activity as a project that included Protestants, Catholics, and Jews equally.

Of the various goodwill organizations, the Amos Society proved to be the most ambitious in its efforts not only to foster practical cooperation but also to articulate a common theological platform for Christians and Jews. It also had the distinction of being one of the few interfaith organizations of the 1920s initiated by a Jew rather than by Christians. Founded in 1923 by Isidore Singer, a Moravian-born Jewish intellectual who had risen to fame with the *Jewish Encyclopedia* he had published two decades earlier, the Amos Society existed largely on paper. But the lack of an institutional apparatus did not prevent Singer—who despite his self-relegation to the position of "literary editor" was in fact the principal spokesman for the organization—from setting out lofty ambitions. He sought "to induce Church and Synagogue to initiate spiritual unification, first of the American people and, in the course of time, of all mankind."[52]

As with his Protestant counterparts, Singer's desire for "spiritual unification" arose from anxieties about agnosticism and atheism.[53] Invoking the scriptural account of the ancient Israelites fighting the Canaanites, he declared that "the Canaanites whom the Church and Synagogue of to-day have to contend with, are religious indifference and crass materialism."[54] Amid such a threat, neither Christians nor Jews had the luxury of keeping to themselves. "The Church is in the same boat with the Synagogue," Singer declared, noting "a spiritual disintegration of ecclesiastical Christianity analogous to that eating at the vitals of rabbinical Judaism." In their current form, entirely independent of one another, neither tradition would survive the assault of irreligious forces.[55] But while the boat might have been taking on water, it was not necessarily doomed to sink. The solution would come through greater cooperation between Christians and Jews (which in practice meant Protestants and Jews, since Singer had little patience for Roman Catholics, blaming them for centuries of violence and accusing them of ignoring Jewish pleas for closer cooperation).[56]

Specifically, Singer sought for members of both traditions to embrace the spirit of the prophetic texts of the Hebrew Bible, which he thought would provide a stronger theological foundation for his enterprise than other interfaith groups.

These books—which included Isaiah, Ezekiel, Jonah, and, most importantly for Singer's purposes, Amos—offered a religious message far less centered on ritual and more concerned with ethical living. In a nod to Christians, Singer situated Jesus as the last in the line of the ancient Jewish prophets. Rather than engaging in centuries-old debates about whether or not Jesus was the Messiah, Singer instead focused on the ethical content of Jesus's teachings. He believed this message diverged little from the core tenets of Judaism and belonged in the synagogue just as much as in the church.

In earlier generations, such declarations would likely have fallen upon deaf Christian ears. But by the 1920s, most liberal Protestants, although far from willing to deny or ignore the divine nature of Jesus, nevertheless proved quite ready to emphasize his ethical teachings over his role as Messiah. For decades, theologians like Newman Smyth had insisted that Christ's teachings were primarily "ethical and religious" rather than "metaphysical and theological."[57] Although Christians retained the view that Jesus was distinct from earlier prophets, this emphasis on ethics nevertheless laid the foundation for a shift in the tenor of Protestant-Jewish dialogue. Such conversations ceased to focus on quarrels about the nature of Jesus and instead affirmed shared interpretations of his ethical message.

In the early twentieth century, liberal Protestant thinkers made the biblical prophetic texts central to their understanding of ethics. Walter Rauschenbusch, who popularized the concept of the Social Gospel, described "the thought of the prophets" as "the spiritual food that [Jesus] assimilated in his own process of growth."[58] The Methodist bishop Francis McConnell, who during the 1920s served as president of the Federal Council of Churches, likewise endorsed a simplification of Christian theology, and he called on Protestants to spend more time studying the books of the Old Testament.[59]

Isidore Singer sought to capitalize on this shift in Protestant thought in his effort to advance the cause of greater comity between Christians and Jews. Under the banner of the Amos Society, he issued a series of Christmas and Easter messages to American Christians, in which he reaffirmed his conviction that Judaism and Christianity were, at the core of their teaching, identical religions. "Whenever I read the Gospels in their Hebrew re-translation . . . I am unable to suppress the feeling that the whole disastrous break between Church and Synagogue, between 'Jew' and 'Christian,'" Singer wrote, "was a useless waste of energy." The division resulted from "an appalling misunderstanding," by Jews and Christians alike, of "the true religious philosophy of the Hebrew Prophets and the Psalms, whose popularization Jesus considered as his life's mission."[60] In reality, Jesus "was fed exclusively upon the spiritual sap of the Old Testament," particularly "the Prophets who were his inseparable companions and admirers." Even beneath their "folkloristic embellishments," the Gospel narratives of Jesus's life contained "the faithful echoes of the flaming exhortations and messages of our, of your, Amos and Hosea; of our, of your, Isaiah and Jeremiah."[61]

Given both the clear theological tenor of the Amos Society's messages, which stood in stark contrast to the practical focus of other interfaith organizations, and the extent to which he downplayed the uniqueness of Jesus, one might expect that Singer was largely preaching to himself. Yet his message won considerable support from Protestants and Jews alike, which reflected the increasingly widespread acceptance of the values he articulated. Alfred Williams Anthony viewed Singer's organization as a helpful ally of his own Committee on Goodwill. Anthony applauded Singer because he "treats Jesus and his teaching reverently and sympathetically," and affirmed that "agreement in history and ethics is a good basis for the beginning of friendship."[62] Peter Ainslie, the Disciples of Christ minister who was a major supporter of the campaign for Christian unity, wrote approvingly of Singer's endeavor. So, too, did the Congregationalist minister and Federal Council of Churches president S. Parkes Cadman. Cadman declared his "belief that the Jewish Ecclesia and the Christian Ecclesia and their ministries are more closely related than is commonly supposed." The president of Chicago's McCormick Theological Seminary, one of the theological schools that participated in the Federal Council's goodwill program, went further. He proclaimed his conviction that "were Jesus here to-day . . . he would announce some common ground that would unite unselfish, truth-seeking Jews and unselfish, truth seeking-Christians in a movement for correcting social wrongs and for the bringing in of an era of social righteousness." Prominent laity, including the presidents emeriti of Stanford and Brown universities and the sitting presidents of the University of Wisconsin, the College of the City of New York, and the Carnegie Institute, also endorsed Singer's program.[63]

Jewish leaders proved no less exuberant in their assessment of the Amos Society. Central Conference of American Rabbis president Abram Simon cited the willingness of Protestant and Jewish leaders to support Singer as evidence for the viability of his message. "I am very impressed with the possibility of multiplying small Amos groups in every large city as radiating centers of practical, scholarly and fraternal work," Simon declared.[64]

Despite their successes and the widespread support they enjoyed, these three organizations—and the larger cause they represented—faced enormous headwinds as the 1920s progressed. These impediments suggested the limits of Americans' new outlook on religious pluralism. For its part, the Federal Council's Committee on Goodwill faced increasing opposition from more conservative denominations in the larger ecumenical body. In 1929, the General Assembly of the United Presbyterian Church reduced its annual appropriation to the Federal Council as an act of protest against its "liberal" programs, which included interfaith efforts. When the committee planned a series of books and pamphlets on Christian-Jewish relations, its leaders decided that the books needed to be written by Christian authors. "What Christians say is more important to the conservative Christians than what Jews say," they conceded.[65]

Ultimately, the Committee on Goodwill achieved its greatest success by inspiring the formation of the National Conference of Jews and Christians (later the National Conference of Christians and Jews) in 1928. The new group counted among its members many of the liberal Protestants who had not only fostered closer ties with Jews but who had contributed more broadly to the embrace of pluralism in its various forms. Alfred Williams Anthony, Francis McConnell, and Charles Brent all served on either the executive board or the advisory committee of the new organization.[66] In its stated purpose, the National Conference of Jews and Christians closely matched that of the Federal Council's Committee on Goodwill, but it drew language from the Amos Society in declaring its mission to forge interfaith cooperation "based on those ideals of justice, fellowship and peace which are common to the prophetic traditions of Jew and Christians alike."[67] The National Conference enjoyed greater flexibility since it was unhindered by conservative Protestants. It also proved more inclusive with the addition of Roman Catholics. Among its Catholic participants was the priest John A. Ryan, who had been ordained by John Ireland and would rise to fame during the 1930s for his support of Franklin Roosevelt's economic policies.

Meanwhile, the group that had been most inclusive of Catholics from the beginning, the American Association on Religion in Colleges and Universities, likewise faced significant obstacles. Its broad constituency of Jews and Christians discouraged significant investment of time and resources from any one group. When Ora Delmer Foster sought additional funding from the Rockefeller family, he was turned down because the group lacked widespread support. A representative of the family cheered the interfaith ideals of the group as "a wonderful idea," but noted that the organization "consists of only the idea and the Trustees."[68] The constituency for an interfaith campaign in colleges and universities remained quite narrow.

Nor did the Amos Society fare much better. In part, this resulted from the fact that many of Singer's Protestant and Jewish supporters did not grasp the full import of his message. Observers lauded his "effort to create a deeper mutual understanding between Jew and Christian" and his work "to promote Justice, Peace and Fraternity by means of impartial and scholarly presentations of the Jewish and Christian contributions to civilization."[69] But they were treating his message as though it was simply an attempt to advance practical cooperation. Singer's more ambitious attempt to define a common theological ground for Jews and Christians went largely unnoticed.

Beyond the specific impediments faced by each interfaith organization, the larger movement suffered from lingering exclusivism on the part of its Protestant members. Despite their increasing enthusiasm for religious pluralism, most liberal Protestants nevertheless retained a commitment to the superiority of their beliefs. Alfred Williams Anthony discovered the tensions that could result from these somewhat incongruous perspectives. Although he clearly supported improved ties between Jews and Christians and saw the inherent value of Jewish tradition, Anthony routinely put his foot in his mouth by making statements that conveyed an underlying discomfort with Jews.

In 1922, Anthony expressed his desire "to help Jews find their Messiah." After considerable criticism, he expressed contrition for his statement, which he acknowledged was not in the spirit of interfaith understanding.[70] The following year, however, the Baptist minister submitted an editorial to the widely read *Jewish Tribune* in which he once again illustrated the prejudices that threatened to obstruct future progress. While he averred that "to a certain point the religion of Jews and Christians is common and the philosophy underlying the religion of both is nearly the same," he nevertheless insisted that certain "complaints concerning Jews" were legitimate. Among the problems he identified were ill manners, dishonest business practices, and a refusal to adopt American customs, among which he included the Sunday Sabbath. This was particularly problematic, as it highlighted the extent to which Anthony expected not merely acculturation but the acceptance of Protestant religious practices.[71] Anthony's article drew a gracious but forceful rebuke from a Reform rabbi, and the Committee on Goodwill declared the exchange a contribution to a growing "literature of understanding."[72]

Anthony's attitude toward conversion inspired a heated exchange in the summer of 1929 between the Baptist minister and Louis Marshall, a highly regarded New York lawyer who served as president of the city's largest Reform synagogue. Marshall publicly attacked the Federal Council's Committee on Goodwill, claiming that its true purpose was the conversion of Jews. He told Anthony that while he found goodwill "desirable," he feared that young men and women "are likely to be swayed by the conversionist efforts of men who are regarded as in every way honorable and conscientious."[73] In other words, Marshall believed the interfaith movement of the 1920s had accomplished little more than making it easier for Christians to convert Jews, because they had replaced Jews' fear and suspicion of Christians with undeserved trust.

In his reply, Anthony appeared to confirm Marshall's worst fears. He noted that most Christians believed it their duty to preach the Gospel to anyone who would hear it, though he did not admit to holding such a view himself. Anthony further exacerbated tensions by noting that some Protestants still sought to convert one another and thus could reasonably be expected to try the same with Jews. "Do the Jews wish to have Christians discriminate against them and say, 'We have no interest in Jews'? To many Christians such an attitude would mean abandoning Jews to what they would call a 'lost' condition," he declared.[74]

Anthony's view reflected the values of liberal Protestantism. While he considered his religious beliefs to be superior, Anthony held that it should be up to every American to choose his or her own religious affiliation. While a sharing of beliefs might lead some Jews to convert to Christianity, it was equally possible that some Christians might choose to embrace Judaism. But what Anthony likely intended as a declaration that Protestants made little distinction between their fellow Christians and Jews was read differently by Marshall, who labeled Anthony "delightfully frank and naïve." "I feared, but now I know, that so far as the Churches are concerned they are principally interested in good-will as a mechanism for the attainment of their conversionist ends," Marshall wrote.[75] The creation of institutions to advance enthusiasm for religious pluralism had failed to eliminate entirely feelings of separation between American Protestants and Jews, as one official of the Federal Council noted when he reviewed the correspondence between Anthony and Marshall. Lauding "the attempt of two sincere and brotherly men" to work through their disagreement, he nevertheless conceded that their "points of view" might "not be reconcilable."[76]

Despite the mixed record of success of the goodwill organizations founded during the 1920s, they nevertheless proved highly influential in shaping Americans' attitudes to pluralism. The heated exchange between Alfred Williams Anthony and Louis Marshall ultimately confirmed the liberals' growing conception of the religious culture of the United States as defined in equal measure by the nation's Catholic, Protestant, and Jewish citizens. Moreover, in their attention to religious diversity, the goodwill organizations pushed Americans to examine their attitudes about racial and ethnic differences as well. Finally, many leaders of the goodwill movement were also active in international affairs, and they held up the ideal of American pluralism as an alternative to religious prejudice and hostility abroad.

While the war of words between Marshall and Anthony highlighted the limits of new interfaith understanding, the exchange also served as a catalyst for many Protestants to reflect on the nature of their attitude toward Jews. After the two men's letters were published, Isidore Singer—who remained unwavering in his endorsement of Anthony as "one of the staunchest defenders of the Amos movement"—contacted dozens of Christian and Jewish acquaintances to solicit their views on the controversy.[77] While a few respondents remained adamant that

Christian teaching demanded an effort at conversion, most correspondents adopted one of two other responses, both of which illustrated the extent to which opinions had changed.

The first reaction was to disavow any effort at converting Jews to Christianity, largely because it seemed that so little separated the two traditions. One Methodist clergyman noted that he had invited a rabbi with whom he was friendly to speak in his church and added that he had enjoyed such close and cordial friendships with his Jewish neighbors that "there hardly enters into my mind that there is in any phase a difference between myself and a Jew." Another Methodist pastor conceded the existence of "conversionist activities among Christian groups," but insisted that such efforts should be either discouraged or ignored. This clergyman, who lived in the suburbs of New York, considered it "rather tragic that Christian and Jew having so much in common, should experience difficulty in the matter of mutual appreciation." But, he added in language that reflected Singer's own values, "there is hope of a better day. Any of the prophetic teachers whom we both reverence should teach us better,—and will."[78]

While some Protestants believed that the lesson of the goodwill movement was that Christians should abandon all efforts to convert Jews, another group of Protestants believed that Jewish Americans had reached sufficient parity that members of both traditions should feel free to convert one another. They saw Judaism as little more than another Protestant denomination. Consequently, they argued, Protestants and Jews could freely seek to convert one another, not out of competition but from a desire to best meet individual religious desires. "I have among my dear friends some of the Jewish faith for whom I have both affection and respect," declared a Baptist minister. "I should like to be free to talk with them of my deepest religious convictions and to share with them any spiritual treasure that I value, and I should like them to be as free with me." Peter Ainslie adopted a similar argument: "If the Jew can show in his daily life something better than the Christian the Christian will follow him; likewise if the Christian can show in his daily life something better than the Jew the Jew will follow him."[79] From this perspective, efforts at conversion no longer represented a one-sided approach. Instead, conversion was a two-way street, by which Protestants and Jews could try to sell their beliefs to one another. To be sure, Protestants who adopted this view overlooked the inequality of their relationship with Jews in a culture still marked by considerable anti-Semitism. Nevertheless, their commitment to these views typified the favorable perspective on religious diversity that increasingly characterized American Protestant thought.

At a meeting in early 1930, the Federal Council's Committee on Goodwill held a session addressing the question of conversion, which featured a presentation from Ernest Halliday, a member of the Congregational Church's Board of Home

Missions, which was responsible for the denomination's campaign to win new adherents. While Halliday emphasized, the minutes recorded, the "right and duty of Christians to share their faith with all peoples throughout the world," he also denied that practicing Jews were in need of conversion. "The religious aims and purposes of Judaism in America are so closely akin to those of Christianity," he declared, "that Christian leaders should recognize it as worthy of fullest cooperation." On the specific question of conversion, he argued that Christians should act only in the case of Jews who were "estranged from their synagogue," and only after giving "Jewish religious leaders first opportunity to win their own people."[80] In staking this position, Halliday differed little from the position of many prominent Jews with regard to converting Christians. Central Conference of American Rabbis president Abram Simon observed the existence of "many nominal Christians" outside their "religious fold" and suggested that these "thousands of men and women, not of the Jewish faith by birth," were nevertheless "in spiritual sympathy with the principles and practices of Reform Judaism."[81]

Moreover, in a development that illustrated the significant influence of the 1920s goodwill movement, liberal Protestants' enthusiasm for pluralism expanded beyond religious diversity and into the realm of racial and ethnic difference. This represented a sharp departure from earlier years. The liberal Protestants who began to forcefully embrace religious pluralism during the late nineteenth and early twentieth centuries had a decidedly mixed record in matters of race. Lyman Abbott had provided enthusiastic support for Booker T. Washington by, among other things, commissioning *Up from Slavery* and delivering the inaugural address at the Tuskegee Institute's Bible School for African American pastors. Yet he had little tolerance for W. E. B. Du Bois, whose *The Souls of Black Folk* drew negative reviews in the *Outlook*. Likewise, while Abbott's publication stridently rebuked lynching, he offered minimal support to Ida Wells's campaign against the practice, including very nearly prohibiting her from speaking at his Plymouth Church.[82] Nor had the Federal Council of Churches made racial inclusion a priority. A decade after its founding, the organization's president noted that "there are great bodies of Negro churches which have been left pretty much to themselves." His solution was for the Federal Council to provide "moral and spiritual sympathy," not in the interest of equality, but rather so that the "colored churches" would "receive the strength of the white churches."[83]

Liberal Protestants proved little better in their attitude toward Americans of different national and ethnic backgrounds. Even during World War I, the rhetoric of religious inclusiveness among Catholics, Protestants, and Jews did not translate to an acceptance of divergent cultural practices. The very leaders of the Federal Council of Churches who advocated for an interfaith chaplaincy corps and sought to provide worship opportunities for Catholic and Jewish soldiers as well as Protestants simultaneously worked to ensure "the Americanization of foreign-born men and women," especially those "unacquainted with America's language" who therefore had "very little acquaintance with America's ideals."[84] The Federal Council's Americanization Committee sought throughout the war to eliminate any trappings of cultural difference. This distinction between religious and cultural characteristics also explains how Protestants like Henry Van Dike could distinguish between the "true Jew" who adhered to the tenets of Judaism and the "sinister figure" of the "false Jew" who embraced communism.[85]

Pioneers of the interfaith movement initially attempted to sustain the same clear distinction between religious pluralism and all other forms of racial, ethnic, and cultural difference. Alfred Williams Anthony's 1923 editorial critique of the "characteristics" he found distasteful that were "so common among Jews as to be ascribed to Jews" rested on the assumption that Jews had ethnic traits separate from their religious values.[86] But as much as liberal Protestants wanted to avoid seeing overlap among the categories of religion, race, and ethnicity, their opponents forced them to collapse the distinction. The resurgent Ku Klux Klan, one critic noted, was built on a combination of "racial and religious intolerance and hatred."[87] If liberal Protestants were to successfully proclaim their ideal of a religiously pluralistic society, they would also need to offer a favorable interpretation of ethnic and cultural difference.

As interfaith efforts spread during the 1920s, the groups initially established to foster appreciation for religious diversity increasingly looked favorably on other forms of human difference. One of the plans endorsed by Anthony's Federal Council Committee on Goodwill encouraged students to write essays that explored not only "the contribution of the Jew, the Catholic, the Protestant" but also "the negro" and "the Oriental and the Asiatic." A corollary to this project would be a "goodwill day or week" that would "utilize the folk song and folkdance and picture" and other related tools "as means of introducing the child to the richness of the tapestry of humanity."[88] The committee also encouraged participants in local interfaith exchanges, such as those of men's groups, to "bear in mind economic misunderstandings as well as religious and racial," an indication that leaders of the goodwill movement considered their mission to be more than just breaking down religious barriers. The expansion beyond differences of faith tradition was exemplified in Cleveland, where a group of "fifteen Episcopalians, fifteen Jews, fifteen Unitarians," and "fifteen colored people" arranged a series of meetings to consider topics including relations of "international neighbors" and "racial neighbors."[89]

As Americans looked abroad during the 1920s, the values of the interfaith movement were projected outward beyond the nation's borders. In 1920, several years before the formation of its Committee on Goodwill, the Federal Council of

Churches established a Committee on the Rights of Religious Minorities. The body included representative clergy of the three major religious traditions in the United States. Protestant members, including Charles Brent and Charles Macfarland, the general secretary of the Federal Council, served alongside Catholic cardinal James Gibbons and the Jewish rabbi Stephen Wise. Lay representatives included future president Herbert Hoover, former president and future Supreme Court chief justice William Howard Taft, and former ambassador Henry Morgenthau, Sr.[90] In its materials, the group boasted of its inclusive membership, stressing its nonpartisan and nonsectarian character, and noting its inclusion of "prominent men of both political parties and of varying religious affiliations, Protestant, Roman Catholic and Jewish."[91]

The committee's initial mission was to examine the state of religious life among "Protestants, Roman Catholics, Jews and Greeks" in newly independent eastern European countries including Poland, Czechoslovakia, and Yugoslavia. The committee remained active through the 1920s and 1930s, lobbying foreign governments that allowed the persecution of religious groups. In 1927, its members issued a petition to the queen of Romania asking for her personal effort to alleviate discrimination by the nation's Orthodox majority against "Baptists, Jews, Lutherans, Presbyterians, Unitarians, and Roman Catholics."[92] The committee also made public statements, particularly in opposition to anti-Semitic publications.[93] The existence of such an organization—particularly one that enjoyed the support of so many prominent citizens—indicated the degree to which the belief that Protestants, Catholics, and Jews held an equal stake in society had become a core value during the 1920s. That Americans saw fit to export such a value further signaled the extent to which it was seen as a defining aspect of national identity.

The goodwill movement of the 1920s represented the bridge that connected Americans' growing acceptance of pluralism in the years between 1870 and 1930 with the subsequent efforts to affirm pluralism in the middle decades of the twentieth century. During the 1930s, the movement shifted its focus to combatting the anti-Semitism that not only grew more virulent in Europe but also seemed significantly more prevalent in the United States. Amid such attitudes, there was less room for the optimistic spirit that had guided many of these groups during the 1920s. When Isidore Singer sought to revive the Amos Society, which had fallen on hard times amid the economic upheaval of the Great Depression, he was counseled against issuing another Christmas letter to American Christians. "There are a lot of people who will undoubtedly not like it," one correspondent declared, "especially since the attitude of a great many American non-Jews towards Jews has changed for the worse."[94] In a 1935 Passover sermon, David Philipson reflected that "the recrudescence of the anti-Jewish mediaeval barbarism" not merely in Europe but "in some unexpected quarters in our own dear country" necessitated "all the optimism of our traditional Passover hope to keep us from despair."[95]

Consequently, nearly all of the work of the National Conference of Christians and Jews during the 1930s and 1940s centered on combatting the spirit of religious intolerance, which seemed to be growing more pervasive. The organization's president, Everett Clinchy, had spent time in Germany and witnessed the widespread support for Hitler. He noted numerous similarities between the attitudes of Germans and the growing anti-Semitism in the United States, and initiated a new campaign to foster interreligious understanding. Clinchy and the National Conference organized "Tolerance Trios," consisting of a minister, priest, and rabbi who traveled around the country delivering messages about the similarity of the Protestant, Catholic, and Jewish traditions. The group also arranged an annual Brotherhood Day, which celebrated interreligious efforts. In this manner, they carried the work of the goodwill movement forward. But whereas the fight against anti-Semitism had initially been only one component of the goodwill movement's work, the widespread hostility to Jews increasingly became its sole focus.[96]

The goodwill movement as it emerged in the 1920s represented a fitting culmination to the efforts to encourage and celebrate pluralism that had emerged in U.S. society a half-century earlier. While not every organization succeeded, the groups established during the 1920s sought to bring institutional permanence to interfaith efforts that had previously been informal and improvised. And while the rise of anti-Semitism during the 1930s illustrated the limits of Americans' new attitudes, the fact that organizations already existed that could quickly respond with a message of tolerance signaled equally well just how much cultural values had changed.

EPILOGUE
Making Religious Pluralism
an American Value

In 1950, the members of Boston's Old South Church invited Elise Gordon to share recollections of her late brother-in-law, George Gordon, the minister who had led the church from 1884 to 1927. One of her memories was of a time when the Congregationalist clergyman had encountered a young man staring at the statue of the famous Boston Unitarian William Ellery Channing in the city's Public Garden. Elise Gordon recalled that after noticing the youth's interest in a religious figure, her brother-in-law asked him if he attended a church. She continued, "The boy replied, 'Yes, sir, I go to church; I'm a Catholic.' 'That's good,' said Dr. Gordon, 'Be true to your church, and learn all you can about other churches.'"[1]

It is telling that Elise Gordon chose this story as a fitting remembrance of her brother-in-law. In the 1950s, Americans sought to emphasize the nation's "Protestant-Catholic-Jewish" identity and its strong cultural commitment to a religious faith as one of its defining features. The embrace of pluralism, which had previously been limited to an elite cohort of clergy and theologians and a small number of churches in major cities, had emerged as a cornerstone cultural value in the post–World War II United States. Yet in this moment, Elise Gordon recognized the role that an earlier generation of Protestants had played in making such attitudes respectable.[2]

To be sure, the embrace of pluralism by liberal Protestants that occurred between 1870 and 1930 proved incomplete and imperfect. Most of the proponents of the new argument retained the conviction that while all forms of religion might be good, Protestant Christianity was still the best. This attitude could limit interfaith conversations or threaten them entirely, as happened with the goodwill movement of the 1920s. Nevertheless, even in its hesitant forms, this new enthusiasm for religious pluralism marked a sharp departure from the exclusivism that characterized not only Protestantism as a whole but also most individual denominations during the nineteenth century.

During the Great Depression and World War II years, certain elements of liberals' earlier embrace of pluralism proved more durable than others. The acceptance of doubt remained a widely held tenet of liberal Protestant thought, and some Protestant thinkers expanded the elements of faith that it seemed appropriate to question. By the late 1920s, the psychologist George Coe confessed his view that it was no longer "scandalous" even "to deny the existence of God." While he denied that he had become an atheist, he forcefully declared, "I reserve and claim for myself all room for thinking."[3] Ironically, the inclusive strategy that liberals had initially employed to combat outright skepticism had, it seemed, bred more skepticism. Yet this realization also pushed liberals to become even more inclusive by affirming the spiritual experiences of those who harbored even greater doubts.

Curiosity about Buddhism, Hinduism, and Islam remained, though anxieties about the effect of comparative religion on Protestantism declined in the early twentieth century. New scholarship revealed that the similarities between Christianity and other traditions were far less numerous than previously thought, and the spiritual eclecticism so in vogue in the late nineteenth century diminished after 1900. It would take the change in U.S. immigration policy in 1965 and the subsequent shift in the nature of the nation's religious demographics before Protestants once again grappled on a large scale with the relationship between their beliefs and those of Buddhists, Hindus, and Muslims.

Many of the national institutions forged during the early twentieth century proved quite resilient. The Federal Council of Churches thrived through the middle decades of the century, as did the National Conference of Christians and Jews, which after the ebb of anti-Semitism following World War II expanded its focus to broader social issues. The record for local organizations was more mixed. Some interdenominational and interfaith community groups continued to function, though others did not. In part, the Great Depression exhausted the funding available for many such groups. By the middle of the 1930s, the Maine Interdenominational Commission, which had provided the inspiration for the combined efforts among Protestant churches, was perceived "as being dead."[4]

Interaction at the local level also changed, perhaps as a result of the pulling inward that accompanied the "return to normalcy" of the 1920s. When Robert and Helen Lynd published *Middletown*, their widely read study of Muncie, Indiana, in 1929, they noted that doctrinal differences meant "relatively little" among the town's various Protestant churches, but they observed that "the interdenominational mingling of an earlier day has apparently declined somewhat." Whereas thirty-five years earlier a Catholic worker had boasted in his diary of hearing his priest address a crowd that included "lots of Protestants," by the late 1920s Protestants were "practically never seen within the doors of the one Catholic church," and even among Protestants "it is regarded as disloyal when a member of one church goes to another."[5]

Yet one legacy that remained was the sense that America's religious communities had more that united them than separated them, especially when it came to challenges from competing cultural values. In the 1930s, one Episcopal priest noted "the empty pews in the churches and in the synagogues" and lamented that "really sincere souls, both Christians and Jews," had withdrawn "to commune with philosophy, with science and with nature."[6] Even after six decades of trying, Protestants had not managed to resolve the problem of religious Americans abandoning their faith communities. But they had grown even stronger in their sense of having common purpose with Catholics and Jews because of it.

Despite their continued anxieties about declining religious commitments, Protestants nevertheless appeared confident that their embrace of pluralism had brought them significant benefits. The level of uncertainty that they expressed during the final decades of the nineteenth century was not matched during the first decades of the twentieth. When Protestants of the 1920s articulated long-standing fears about the decline of their cultural authority or the challenge of competing ideological systems like communism, they did not betray the same level of concern that had appeared in the rhetoric of a half-century earlier. This in no small measure reflected their realization that they were not alone in experiencing the encounter between religion and modern culture. Through casual discussion, small-scale cooperation, and ultimately the creation of larger institutions, Protestant Americans discovered commonality of experience across the lines of religious traditions and in so doing came to see the benefits rather than the drawbacks of religious diversity.

By the middle of the twentieth century, this emphasis on pluralism stood at the heart of mainline American Protestantism. Despite the growing challenges they faced from the fundamentalist movement and popular revivalists like Billy Graham, theological liberals remained the public face of American Protestantism through the 1960s. As they enjoyed their stature at midcentury, they made their embrace of religious diversity an even more central aspect of their identity. Protestants ultimately moved beyond the conviction that they possessed the best form of belief and practice among many, and instead evolved to a more relativistic position that treated all religions as equally true.[7] Yet this increasingly inclusive outlook represented the culmination of a project that took shape between 1870 and 1930. The desire to preserve religious commitment amid a grave crisis of faith had pressed Protestants to abandon exclusivism, and the result was a shift in views that paved the way for a culture that considered its diversity of faiths a national value.

Notes

INTRODUCTION

1. Lyman Abbott, "The Larger Love," May 2, 1897, reprinted in *Outlook* 56 (May 15, 1897): 161.
2. On Abbott, see Ira V. Brown, *Lyman Abbott, Christian Evolutionist: A Study in Religious Liberalism* (Cambridge, Mass.: Harvard University Press, 1953); Susan Curtis, *A Consuming Faith: The Social Gospel and Modern American Culture* (Columbia: University of Missouri Press, 2001), 146–56.
3. Lyman Abbott, "The Message of the Nineteenth Century to the Men of the Twentieth," June 18, 1912, reprinted in *Outlook* 102 (October 19, 1912): 354.
4. A note on terminology: in using the word "pluralism," I am following the convention of many scholars to treat the word not merely as a descriptor of the existence of diversity of beliefs, but rather as connoting a specific value, namely, that such diversity has a positive benefit for society. See Diana L. Eck, *A New Religious America: How a "Christian Country" Has Become the World's Most Religiously Diverse Nation* (San Francisco: HarperSanFrancisco, 2001), 70; Charles L. Cohen and Ronald L. Numbers, eds., *Gods in America: Religious Pluralism in the United States* (New York: Oxford University Press, 2013), 6–7.
5. Throughout this volume, I employ the term "liberal Protestants" to describe the central actors of this study. Other terminology that suggests itself includes "mainline Protestants" and "ecumenical Protestants." I favor the word "liberal," however, because it reflects a commitment to progressive religion that nearly all of the clergy and theologians considered here embraced for the entire period considered in this study. By contrast, the idea of a "mainline" set of denominations was largely a product of the interdenominationalism that I explore in chapter 4. So, too, these liberals' commitment to ecumenism as a defining feature of their religious identity emerged as a result of the forces that I explore.
6. For scholarly constructions of the Protestant establishment, see William R. Hutchison, "Protestantism as Establishment," in Hutchison, ed., *Between the Times: The Travails of the Protestant Establishment in America, 1900–1960* (New York: Cambridge University Press, 1989), esp. 3–6; Robert T. Handy, *Undermined Establishment: Church-State Relations in America, 1880–1920* (Princeton, N.J.: Princeton University Press, 1991), 7–12, 19–25.
7. On Protestant influence in the public sphere in the antebellum era, see Steven K. Green, *The Second Disestablishment: Church and State in Nineteenth-Century America* (New York: Oxford University Press, 2010), 91–95, 266–71; Robert A. Abzug, *Cosmos Crumbling: American Reform and the Antebellum Imagination* (New York: Oxford University Press, 1994), esp. chap. 2; John T. McGreevy, *Catholicism and American Freedom: A History* (New York: W. W. Norton, 2003), 38–39.
8. Green, *Second Disestablishment*, 334–41; George Frederickson, "The Coming of the Lord: The Northern Protestant Clergy and the Civil War Crisis," in Randall M. Miller, Harry S. Stout, and Charles Reagan Wilson, eds., *Religion and the American Civil War* (New York: Oxford University Press, 1998), 121–25; Tisa Wenger, "The God-in-the-Constitution Controversy: American Secularisms in Historical Perspective," in Linell E. Cady and Elizabeth Shakman Hurd, eds., *Comparative Secularisms in a Global Age* (New York: Palgrave Macmillan, 2010), 87–105.

9. Newman Smyth, "The Religious Principle in American Politics" (July 6, 1876), folder 21, box 3, series 2, Newman Smyth Papers, Yale University Library Manuscripts and Archives (New Haven, Conn.).

10. Ibid. On American reactions to the Paris Commune, see Nell Irvin Painter, *Standing at Armageddon: The United States, 1877–1919* (New York: W. W. Norton, 1987), 17–24.

11. James Henry Snowden, "The Religious Ebb-Tide" (February 12, 1899), folder 32, box 1, James Henry Snowden Papers, Pittsburgh Theological Seminary Archive (Pittsburgh, Pa.).

12. Theodore T. Munger, *The Freedom of Faith* (Boston: Houghton Mifflin, 1883), 204.

13. "An Advertisement for a New Religion by an Evolutionist," *North American Review* 127 (July 1878): 44; "Confessions of an Agnostic," *North American Review* 129 (September 1879): 276.

14. Lyman Abbott, "A Plea for Reverence," *Outlook* 57 (September 11, 1897): 124.

15. Roger Finke, "An Unsecular America," in Steve Bruce, ed., *Religion and Modernization: Sociologists and Historians Debate the Secularization Thesis* (Oxford: Clarendon Press; Oxford University Press, 1992), 148–51.

16. Jon Butler, *Awash in a Sea of Faith: Christianizing the American People* (Cambridge, Mass.: Harvard University Press, 1990), 55–63.

17. On both the role of the Second Great Awakening in shaping this generation's religious views and the seeming decline in religious enthusiasm after the Civil War, see Anne C. Rose, *Victorian America and the Civil War* (New York: Cambridge University Press, 1992), 25–26, 59–64; Christopher G. White, *Unsettled Minds: Psychology and the American Search for Spiritual Assurance, 1830–1940* (Berkeley: University of California Press, 2009), 13–19. Susan Curtis likewise identified this phenomenon of failed expectations in many Protestant leaders of the late nineteenth century, though she has subsequently questioned claims made by these Protestants in their own autobiographies; see *Consuming Faith*, xiii, 74–80.

18. Scholars have likewise identified the late nineteenth century as the time of a momentous shift in attitudes as a rejection of belief came to be seen as a respectable position. See James Turner, *Without God, without Creed: The Origins of Unbelief in America* (Baltimore: Johns Hopkins University Press, 1985); Christian D. Smith, ed., *The Secular Revolution: Power, Interests, and Conflicts in the Secularization of American Public Life* (Berkeley: University of California Press, 2003). In advancing this claim, I am assiduously avoiding taking sides in the scholarly debate over whether or not the United States has experienced a process of secularization comparable to that of western Europe. For purposes of this study, it is sufficient to note that Protestant clergy perceived that something had changed that had caused their authority to come under attack and religious faith to grow less secure. They modified their views about a range of subjects—including pluralism—accordingly.

19. Samuel L. Caldwell, "Is Christian Union to Become Organized?," *Andover Review* 6 (July 1886): 6.

20. "Christianity and Its Modern Competitors," *Andover Review* 6 (November 1886): 510.

21. John Lancaster Spalding, *Lectures and Discourses* (New York: Catholic Publication Society, 1882), 15.

22. "Editorial Notes," *Catholic World* 58 (December 1893): 451.

23. Isidore Lewinthal, "Unattached Jews," *Hebrew Standard* 30 (February 23, 1894): 1–2.

24. "Is Jewish Faith Waning?" *Hebrew Standard* 30 (June 22, 1894): 1.

25. "The Secularized Classes," *Andover Review* 11 (January 1889): 73.

26. Washington Gladden, "Church Going" (June 20, 1880), reel 16, Washington Gladden Papers (microfilm), Harvard College Library (Cambridge, Mass.; originals at Ohio Historical Society, Columbus, Ohio).

27. Washington Gladden, *Burning Questions of the Life That Now Is and That Which Is to Come* (New York: Century, 1890), 4–5.

28. On conservative Protestant thought in the late nineteenth century, see Robert Mapes Anderson, *Vision of the Disinherited: The Making of American Pentecostalism* (New York: Oxford University Press, 1979); George Marsden, *Fundamentalism and American Culture*, 2nd ed. (New York: Oxford University Press, 2006); Randall J. Stephens, *The Fire Spreads: Holiness and Pentecostalism in the American South* (Cambridge, Mass.: Harvard University Press, 2008); Grant Wacker, *Heaven Below: Early Pentecostals and American Culture* (Cambridge, Mass.: Harvard University Press, 2001).

29. On the New Theology, see Gary Dorrien, *The Making of American Liberal Theology: Imagining Progressive Religion, 1805–1900* (Louisville, Ky.: Westminster John Knox Press, 2001), 294–304; William R. Hutchison, *The Modernist Impulse in American Protestantism* (Durham, N.C.: Duke University Press, 1992), 95–105; on Protestants' reconciliation of Christianity with modern culture, see especially Curtis, *Consuming Faith*, 10–15; R. Laurence Moore, *Selling God: American Religion in the Marketplace of Culture* (New York: Oxford University Press, 1994), 205–20; on the Social Gospel, see also Ronald C. White Jr. and C. Howard Hopkins, *The Social Gospel: Religion and Reform in Changing America* (Philadelphia: Temple University Press, 1976).

30. Abbott, "The Larger Love," 161.

31. Theological liberalism did not gain meaningful traction in the southern United States until the mid-twentieth century, and even then its proponents were swimming against strong religious and cultural currents; see Gary Dorrien, *The Making of American Liberal Theology: Crisis, Irony, and Postmodernity, 1950–2005* (Louisville, Ky.: Westminster John Knox Press, 2006), 325–27.

32. Several recent histories have sought to reclaim the importance of Protestant liberalism in the twentieth-century United States. See Matthew S. Hedstrom, *The Rise of Liberal Religion: Book Culture and American Spirituality in the Twentieth Century* (New York: Oxford University Press, 2013); David A. Hollinger, *After Cloven Tongues of Fire: Protestant Liberalism in Modern American History* (Princeton, N.J.: Princeton University Press, 2013); Amy Kittselstrom, *The Religion of Democracy: Seven Liberals and the American Moral Tradition* (New York: Penguin, 2015).

33. On the broader acceptance of religious pluralism in the culture at large during and after World War II, see Hedstrom, *Rise of Liberal Religion*, 142–71; Mark Silk, *Spiritual Politics: Religion and America since World War II* (New York: Simon and Schuster, 1988), especially chap. 2; Kevin M. Schultz, *Tri-faith America: How Catholics and Jews Held Postwar America to Its Protestant Promise* (New York: Oxford University Press, 2011); Wendy L. Wall, *Inventing the "American Way": The Politics of Consensus from the New Deal to the Civil Rights Movement* (New York: Oxford University Press, 2008).

34. Historians have situated the embrace of pluralism—even among mainline liberal elites—during the middle decades of the twentieth century; see Hollinger, *After Cloven Tongues of Fire*, 18–49. One historian who did acknowledge the new embrace of religious pluralism during this era was William R. Hutchison, though his characterization of it is of a haphazard process that occurred primarily in response to the growing visibility of non-Protestant traditions in the United States. See Hutchison, *Religious Pluralism in America: The Contentious History of a Founding Ideal* (New Haven, Conn.: Yale University Press, 2003), 111–22.

35. The parallels between the strategies employed by liberal Protestants and various political reformers are striking, which is largely unsurprising given the overlap between the two groups. See Sven Beckert, *The Monied Metropolis: New York City and the Consolidation of the American Bourgeoisie, 1850–1896* (Cambridge: Cambridge University Press,

2001); Leslie Butler, *Critical Americans: Victorian Intellectuals and Transatlantic Liberal Reform* (Chapel Hill: University of North Carolina Press, 2007).

36. The classic articulation of this perspective, which has proved quite resilient in the historiography, is T. J. Jackson Lears, "From Salvation to Self-Realization: Advertising and the Therapeutic Roots of the Consumer Culture, 1880–1930," in Richard Wightman Fox and T. J. Jackson Lears, eds., *The Culture of Consumption: Critical Essays in American History, 1880–1980* (New York: Pantheon, 1983), especially 12–17. For a recent rebuttal, see Leigh E. Schmidt, "The Parameters and Problematics of American Religious Liberalism," in Leigh E. Schmidt and Sally M. Promey, eds., *American Religious Liberalism* (Bloomington: Indiana University Press, 2012), 1–3.

1. TWILIGHT FAITH

1. Washington Gladden, "The Whimsicality of Unbelief," May 30, 1880, reel 16, Washington Gladden Papers (microfilm), Harvard College Library (Cambridge, Mass.; originals at Ohio Historical Society, Columbus, Ohio).

2. On Gladden's life, see Jacob A. Dorn, *Washington Gladden: Prophet of the Social Gospel* (Columbus: Ohio State University Press, 1967), esp. chap. 1. For more limited biographical treatments, see Susan Curtis, *A Consuming Faith: The Social Gospel and Modern American Culture* (1991; repr. Columbia: University of Missouri Press, 2001), 36–44; Gary Dorrien, *The Making of American Liberal Theology: Imagining Progressive Religion, 1805–1900* (Louisville, Ky.: Westminster John Knox Press, 2001), 266–75.

3. Washington Gladden, *Recollections* (Boston: Houghton Mifflin, 1909), 89.

4. Washington Gladden, "The Limitations of Religious Thought," November 28, 1880, and "Belief and Doubt," May 8, 1881, reel 16, Gladden Papers.

5. On Gladden's role as a counsel to other ministers, see, for example, George A. Swertfager to Gladden, March 27, 1905, reel 5, Gladden Papers; on the rise of theological liberalism, see Dorrien, *Making of American Liberal Theology: Imagining Progressive Religion*, especially chap. 5; William R. Hutchison, *The Modernist Impulse in American Protestantism* (Durham, N.C.: Duke University Press, 1992), 76–87.

6. Drew Gilpin Faust, *This Republic of Suffering: Death and the American Civil War* (New York: Alfred A. Knopf, 2008), xi–xii, 6–11, 128–29.

7. On Mabie, see Edwin Wilson Morse, *The Life and Letters of Hamilton W. Mabie* (New York: Dodd, Mead, 1920), 9–10, 27–28, 152.

8. Hamilton Wright Mabie, *The Life of the Spirit* (New York: Dodd, Mead, 1899), 107; on Mabie's "saccharine morality," see Henry F. May, *The End of American Innocence: A Study of the First Years of Our Own Time, 1912–1917* (1959; repr. New York: Columbia University Press, 1992), 77; on religious interpretations of the Civil War, see Randall M. Miller, Harry S. Stout, and Charles Reagan Wilson, eds., *Religion and the American Civil War* (New York: Oxford University Press, 1998), 4–5; and Phillip Shaw Paludan, "Religion and the American Civil War," ibid., especially 23–24; Anne C. Rose, *Victorian America and the Civil War* (New York: Cambridge University Press, 1992), esp. 19–20; James H. Moorhead, *American Apocalypse: Yankee Protestants and the Civil War, 1860–1869* (New Haven, Conn.: Yale University Press, 1978); on literary criticism of the war, see Faust, *This Republic of Suffering*, 196–208.

9. Mabie, *Life of the Spirit*, 259; on the growing tendency toward humanitarianism in the antebellum period and its role in making Americans receptive to critiques of Christianity on humanitarian grounds, see James Turner, *Without God, without Creed: The Origins of Unbelief in America* (Baltimore: Johns Hopkins University Press, 1985), 142–43, 204–7.

10. Mabie, *Life of the Spirit*, 263. On the "period of trauma," see Alan Trachtenberg, *The Incorporation of America: Culture and Society in the Gilded Age*, 25th anniversary ed.

(New York: Hill and Wang, 2007), 4–7, 70–73, 86–88. See also David Montgomery, *The Fall of the House of Labor: The Workplace, the State, and American Labor Activism, 1865–1925* (Cambridge: Cambridge University Press, 1985), 130, 217–20, 230–33; Daniel T. Rodgers, *The Work Ethic in Industrial America* (Chicago: University of Chicago Press, 1978), 24–29, 50–57; Nell Irvin Painter, *Standing at Armageddon: The United States, 1877–1919* (New York: W. W. Norton, 1989), xviii, xx, 44–50.

11. Mattie B. Robinson to Robert Ingersoll, January 17, 1894, frames 32–33, reel 6, Robert Ingersoll Papers (microfilm), Harvard College Library (Cambridge, Mass.; originals at Library of Congress, Washington, D.C.). On Ingersoll's biography, see Susan Jacoby, *The Great Agnostic: Robert Ingersoll and American Freethought* (New Haven, Conn.: Yale University Press, 2012).

12. Robert G. Ingersoll, "Orthodoxy: A Lecture," in *The Works of Robert G. Ingersoll: Lectures*, vol. 2 (New York: C. P. Farrell, 1900), 342, 363.

13. O. H. French to Robert Ingersoll, June 23, 1887, frame 52, reel 18, Ingersoll Papers (microfilm); Grace D. Vanamee to Eva Ingersoll Brown, August 9, 1921, frame 76, reel 6, Ingersoll Papers (microfilm).

14. Robert Ingersoll to A.A., October 9, 1876, frames 416–22, reel 6, Ingersoll Papers (microfilm).

15. F. B. Makepeace, "Specimens of Ingersoll's Work," *The Congregationalist* 32 (May 19, 1880): 153.

16. Bertha Williams and Cora Sellers to Robert Ingersoll, March 14, 1897, frames 174–75, reel 19, Ingersoll Papers (microfilm).

17. Philip G. Wright to Robert Ingersoll, May 20, 1896, frame 3, reel 19, Ingersoll Papers (microfilm).

18. William J. Bok to Robert Ingersoll, March 19, 1887, frames 37–38, reel 18, Ingersoll Papers (microfilm).

19. On the response of American Protestants to Charles Darwin, see Jon H. Roberts, *Darwinism and the Divine in America: Protestant Intellectuals and Organic Evolution, 1859–1900* (1988; repr. Notre Dame, Ind.: University of Notre Dame Press, 2001), xiii–xiv, 117–45; see 66–67 for the response to Huxley; see also Bernard Lightman, *The Origins of Agnosticism: Victorian Unbelief and the Limits of Knowledge* (Baltimore: Johns Hopkins University Press, 1987), especially 6–13.

20. Herbert Spencer, *First Principles* (London: Williams and Norgate, 1862), 13; see also 20–21.

21. Ibid., 17.

22. Ibid., 16, 45–46. See also Lightman, *Origins of Agnosticism*, 71–76, 82–86; Roberts, *Darwinism and the Divine*, 68–69.

23. This secularization of social science was part of a larger campaign for the independence of the nation's academic institutions from the Protestant denominations with which they had historically been connected. See Christian D. Smith, "Secularizing American Higher Education: The Case of Early American Sociology," in Smith, ed., *The Secular Revolution: Power, Interests, and Conflict in the Secularization of American Public Life* (Berkeley: University of California Press, 2003). Smith argues that intellectuals like Sumner and Ward were quite committed to their antireligious views and actively sought to circumscribe the authority of the Protestant establishment. See Smith's introduction, ibid., especially 43–53, for a broader discussion of intellectuals' grievances with American Protestantism. See also Dorothy Ross, *The Origins of American Social Science* (Cambridge: Cambridge University Press, 1991), 55–56, 85–94; and Jon H. Roberts and James Turner, *The Sacred and the Secular University* (Princeton, N.J.: Princeton University Press, 2000), especially chap. 2.

24. Roberts, *Darwinism and the Divine*, 69.

25. Turner, *Without God, without Creed*, 182–83.

26. Robert G. Ingersoll, "The Gods," in *The Works of Robert G. Ingersoll: Lectures*, vol. 1 (New York: C. P. Farrell, 1900), 43–44.

27. George Harris, "Ethical Christianity and Biblical Criticism," *Andover Review* 15 (May 1891): 461. On Protestants' reconciliation of their beliefs with evolution, see Washington Gladden, *Burning Questions of the Life That Is Now and of That Which Is to Come* (New York: Century, 1890), 65–66; Newman Smyth, *Old Faiths in New Light* (New York: Charles Scribner's Sons, 1879), 143–46; see also Roberts, *Darwinism and the Divine*, 117–45.

28. Harris, "Ethical Christianity and Biblical Criticism," 461; Jurgen Herbst, *The German Historical School in American Scholarship: A Study in the Transfer of Culture* (Ithaca, N.Y.: Cornell University Press, 1965), 1–13; see also 89–97 for how study in biblical criticism affected leading American Protestants of the late nineteenth century; Daniel T. Rodgers, *Atlantic Crossings: Social Politics in a Progressive Age* (Cambridge, Mass.: Belknap Press of Harvard University Press, 1998), 84–89; Ross, *Origins of American Social Science*, 55.

29. On the argument from prophecy and dating of the Gospels, see E. Brooks Holifield, *Theology in America: Christian Thought from the Age of the Puritans to the Civil War* (New Haven, Conn.: Yale University Press, 2003), 188–89.

30. Lyman Abbott, *In Aid of Faith* (New York: E. P. Dutton, 1886), 126–27.

31. Amory Howe Bradford, *Spirit and Life: Thoughts for Today*, 2nd ed. (New York: Fords, Howard and Hurlbert, 1892), 15.

32. Ingersoll, "The Gods," 17.

33. Robert Ingersoll to H. D. J. Ingersoll, February 6, 1878, frame 199, reel 7, Ingersoll Papers (microfilm).

34. Augustine, *Confessions* (London: Penguin Books, 1961), 116–17.

35. See the confessions of William Andrews and Brother Moore's wife, excerpted in David D. Hall, ed., *Puritans in the New World* (Princeton, N.J.: Princeton University Press, 2004), 124, 126; see also Edmund S. Morgan, *Visible Saints: The History of a Puritan Idea* (1963; repr. Ithaca, N.Y.: Cornell University Press, 1965), 69–70.

36. On Unitarianism, see Holifield, *Theology in America*, 197–217.

37. Amanda Porterfield, *Conceived in Doubt: Religion and Politics in the New American Nation* (Chicago: University of Chicago Press, 2012), 5–6, 50–53.

38. Thomas Paine, *The Age of Reason, Part the Second* (1795; repr. London: R. Carlile, 1818), 12–13.

39. On the gradual evolution of an intellectual framework to sustain unbelief, see Turner, *Without God, without Creed*, especially chap. 1.

40. "The Congregational Club," *The Congregationalist* 2 (June 2, 1880): 170.

41. See Porterfield, *Conceived in Doubt*, 128–29, 142.

42. Dorrien, *Making of American Liberal Theology: Imagining Progressive Religion*, 31.

43. "The Congregational Club," 169–70; Mrs. Humphry Ward, *Robert Elsmere* (London: Smith, Elder, 1888); George A. Gordon, "Robert Elsmere," delivered November 16, 1888 (Boston: Old South Church, 1888), 3; Harold Frederic, *The Damnation of Theron Ware; or, Illumination* (New York: Stone and Kimball, 1896); on the popularity of *Theron Ware*, see Carrie Tirado Bramen, "The Americanization of Theron Ware," *Novel: A Forum on Fiction* 31 (Autumn 1997): 65.

44. Henry Ward Beecher, *Sermons* (London: J. Heaton and Son, 1864), 260.

45. Horace Bushnell, *Christ and His Salvation: In Sermons Variously Related Thereto*, 3rd ed. (New York: Charles Scribner, 1865), 40.

46. Horace Bushnell, *Sermons on Living Subjects* (New York: Scribner, Armstrong, 1872), 168; on the influence of Bushnell on mid-nineteenth-century American Protestantism, see Dorrien, *Making of American Liberal Theology: Imagining Progressive Religion*, 172–78.

47. Elizabeth Prentiss, *Stepping Heavenward* (New York: Anson D. F. Randolph, 1869).

48. James Henry Snowden, "Doubt: Its Place and How to Deal with It in Our Religious Life," November 11, 1914, folder 6, box 1, James Henry Snowden Papers, Pittsburgh Theological Seminary Archive (Pittsburgh, Pa.).

49. T. M. Post, "Transition Periods in Religious Thought," *Andover Review* 1 (January 1884): 581; see also 591–92.

50. "Foundations of Belief," *Outlook* 56 (June 26, 1897): 486.

51. Leighton Parks, "Moral Privilege," delivered December 28, 1913, reprinted in *Moral Leadership and Other Sermons* (New York: Charles Scribner's Sons, 1914), 72–73, 84–85.

52. James Henry Snowden, "The Meaning of a Touch," delivered February 26, 1893, folder 36, box 4, Snowden Papers.

53. Francis J. McConnell, *Personal Christianity: Instruments and Ends in the Kingdom of God* (New York: Fleming H. Revell, 1914), 129–30; see also 104 for a discussion of Christianizing non-Christian ideas, as McConnell did with the language of agnostics.

54. Charles H. Brent, *With God in the World: A Series of Papers* (New York: Longmans, Green, 1899), 40.

55. "The Value of Doubt," *Outlook* 56 (May 29, 1897): 245–46.

56. McConnell, *Personal Christianity*, 129, 131.

57. Bradford, *Spirit and Life*, 50–51.

58. Ibid., 98.

59. Newman Smyth, *Christian Ethics* (New York: Charles Scribner's Sons, 1892), 428–29.

60. McConnell, *Personal Christianity*, 130–31.

61. Lyman Abbott, "Letters to Unknown Friends," *Outlook* 101 (August 10, 1912): 808–9.

62. Bushnell, *Christ and His Salvation*, 67.

63. Lyman Abbott, sermon notes on Philippians 2:1–11, 3:1–12, and 2 Corinthians 5:14 (1875), folder 2, box 25, Lyman Abbott Papers, George Mitchell Special Collections, Bowdoin College Library (Brunswick, Me.).

64. Newman Smyth, untitled sermon delivered November 1, 1896, Smyth Papers, series 2, box 3, folder 13.

65. Smyth, *Christian Ethics*, 109.

66. Mabie, *Life of the Spirit*, 46–47.

67. William Adams Brown, *The Essence of Christianity: A Study in the History of Definition* (New York: Charles Scribner's Sons, 1902), 300; see also 301–2 for Brown's affirmation of Harnack's view that the early Christian church departed significantly from the teachings of Jesus. On Ritschl and Harnack more generally, see Dorrien, *The Making of American Liberal Theology: Idealism, Realism, and Modernity, 1900–1950* (Louisville, Ky.: Westminster John Knox Press, 2003), 24–28.

68. Abbott, *In Aid of Faith*, 180.

69. James Henry Snowden, "The Psychology of Religion. III. The Psychology of Conversion" (undated), folder 6, box 1, Snowden Papers; James Henry Snowden, "How to Get Strong," April 9, 1893, folder 46, box 4, Snowden Papers.

70. Washington Gladden, "[Apostolic Tests for Church Membership]," February 26, 1894, reel 25, Gladden Papers (microfilm).

71. Bradford, *Spirit and Life*, 120–21.

72. Post, "Transition Periods in Religious Thought," 578; see also 583–85.

73. Mabie, *Life of the Spirit*, 114.

74. For his exploration of these stages, see Smyth, *Christian Ethics*, 144–215.

75. Ibid., 66–67.

76. Mabie, *Life of the Spirit*, 115–16.

77. Abbott, *In Aid of Faith*, x.

78. On the popularity of recapitulation theory in America, see Gail Bederman, *Manliness and Civilization: A Cultural History of Gender and Race in the United States, 1880–1917* (Chicago: University of Chicago Press, 1995), 92, 106–10.

79. Gladden, "Limitations of Religious Thought." Proponents of progressive revelation were not merely repurposing contemporary scientific theories; they drew on distinctly Christian ideas as well. See Dorrien, *Making of American Liberal Theology: Imagining Progressive Religion*, 291–92.

80. Bruce Kuklick, *A History of Philosophy in America: 1720–2000* (New York: Oxford University Press, 2003), 123–24; Ross, *Origins of American Social Science*, 154–55.

81. Edwin Diller Starbuck, *The Psychology of Religion: An Empirical Study of the Growth of Religious Consciousness* (London: Walter Scott, 1899), 6–7.

82. Smyth, *Christian Ethics*, 8. It is statements like Smyth's that have led some scholars to argue that the Protestant establishment ceded its authority to outside experts. For a particularly thoughtful articulation of this view, see Eugene McCarraher, *Christian Critics: Religion and the Impasse in Modern American Social Thought* (Ithaca, N.Y.: Cornell University Press, 2000), 2–3, 11–20. It is worth emphasizing, though, that Smyth was not expecting psychologists to take over religious work. Rather, he saw psychology as the most recent in a series of tools available to Christians to better understand religious experience. For a compelling counterargument that liberal Protestants' embrace of psychology represented an attempt to strengthen their religious feeling rather than replace it, see Christopher G. White, *Unsettled Minds: Psychology and the American Search for Spiritual Assurance, 1830–1940* (Berkeley: University of California Press, 2009), 1–9.

83. On William James and his work in the psychology of religion, see Bruce Kuklick, *History of Philosophy in America*, especially 150–56; Louis Menand, *The Metaphysical Club* (New York: Farrar, Straus and Giroux, 2001), 75; White, *Unsettled Minds*, 59–67, 144–45.

84. William James, "The Will to Believe," in *The Will to Believe and Other Essays in Popular Philosophy* (New York: Longmans, Green, 1897), 14, 26, 28. See 12–13 for his definition of the absolutist tendency. James Turner has pointed to James's lecture as part of a more nuanced defense of Christianity that emerged in the 1890s in the wake of the collapse of older apologetics and the challenge from agnosticism. See Turner, *Without God, without Creed*, 189. While Turner is quite right in his assessment, he overlooks the degree to which James made room for doubt, which represents one of the most significant developments of the new defense of Christian tradition.

85. William James, *The Varieties of Religious Experience: A Study in Human Nature* (New York: Modern Library, 1902), 65.

86. Starbuck, *Psychology of Religion*, 24–25, 114.

87. Ibid., 242, 303.

88. On Coe's biography, see Hutchison, *Modernist Impulse in American Protestantism*, 155–58.

89. For an endorsement from the former category, see the letter from the Boston University professor of philosophy Edgar S. Brightman to George A. Coe, November 21, 1921, folder 1, box 1, George A. Coe Papers, Yale Divinity School Library (New Haven, Conn.); for examples from the latter, see A. W. Gottschall to George A. Coe, May 13, 1921, ibid.; L. Dewey Burham to George A. Coe, December 19, 1929, folder 3, box 1, Coe Papers.

90. George A. Coe, *The Spiritual Life: Studies in the Science of Religion* (New York: Eaton and Mains, 1900), 6–7, 25.

91. Coe cited Bushnell throughout his career and used Bushnell's works in courses that he taught. See, for example, the bibliography of his "Syllabus of Eight Lectures on Education in Religion and Morals," which Coe taught in Evanston, Illinois, in early 1904, folder 32, box 4, series 2, Coe Papers.

92. George A. Coe, "Religious Experience and the Scientific Movement," November 1897 (reprinted in *The Church and Christian Experience*), folder 27, box 4, series 2, Coe Papers; George A. Coe, "Religious Education as a Part of the General Education," clipping from *The Biblical World*, folder 31, box 4, series 2, Coe Papers; see also George A. Coe, *The Religion of a Mature Mind* (Chicago: Fleming H. Revell, 1902), 409–22; on Bushnell's influence on late nineteenth-century liberal Protestantism, see Dorrien, *Making of American Liberal Theology: Imagining Progressive Religion*, 398–402. Other elements of Coe's thought, especially related to education, were also influenced by liberal Protestants including Theodore Munger and Newman Smyth; see Hutchison, *Modernist Impulse in American Protestantism*, 161–62.

93. George A. Coe, "The Theoretical and the Practical," *Methodist Review* 12 (May 1896): 397–98.

94. Ibid., 398; on the generational shift between the founding generation of American social scientists of the 1860s and 1870s and the second generation, see Ross, *Origins of American Social Science*, 101–6.

95. Coe, "The Theoretical and the Practical," 402; on Coe and revivals, see Matthew Bowman, "Antirevivalism and Its Discontents: Liberal Evangelicalism, the American City, and the Sunday School, 1900–1929," *Religion and American Culture* 24 (Winter 2014): 262–90, esp. 267–69.

96. Coe, "Faith and Science," address delivered at Union Theological Seminary, January 21, 1906, folder 33, box 4, series 2, Coe Papers.

97. Coe, *Spiritual Life*, 58–59, 65.

98. Parks, "Moral Privilege," 60; similar views on doubt also took root in Britain; see Christopher Lane, *The Age of Doubt: Tracing the Roots of Our Religious Uncertainty* (New Haven, Conn.: Yale University Press, 2011).

2. CORRECTING ELIJAH'S MISTAKE

1. John Henry Barrows, ed., *The World's Parliament of Religions,* vol. 1 (Chicago: Parliament Publishing, 1893), 110.

2. Anagarika Dharmapala, "The World's Debt to Buddha," in John Henry Barrows, ed., *The World's Parliament of Religions,* vol. 2 (Chicago: Parliament Publishing, 1893): 866, 879.

3. Mohammed Webb, "The Spirit of Islam," ibid., 989, 992; on Webb, see Leigh Eric Schmidt, *Restless Souls: The Making of American Spirituality* (San Francisco: HarperSanFrancisco, 2005), 181–84.

4. Swami Vivekananda, "Hinduism," in Barrows, *World's Parliament of Religions,* 2:978.

5. Vivekananda, quoted in Barrows, *World's Parliament of Religions,* 1:170.

6. Barrows, *World's Parliament of Religions,* 1:61.

7. See John Henry Barrows, *I Believe in God the Father Almighty* (New York: Fleming H. Revell, 1892), 27–28.

8. Barrows, *World's Parliament of Religions,* 1:66–67; on Barrows, see Catherine L. Albanese, *A Republic of Mind and Spirit: A Cultural History of American Metaphysical Religion* (New Haven, Conn.: Yale University Press, 2007), 332–33.

9. Barrows, *World's Parliament of Religions,* 1:150–51.

10. Ibid., 73.

11. Washington Gladden, untitled sermon, September 10, 1893, reel 25, Washington Gladden Papers (microfilm), Harvard College Library (Cambridge, Mass.; originals at Ohio Historical Society, Columbus, Ohio).

12. Barrows, *World's Parliament of Religions,* 1:68.

13. John Henry Barrows, *Christianity the World-Religion: Lectures Delivered in India and Japan* (Chicago: A. C. McClurg, 1897), 301; for the most extensive treatment of the Parliament of Religions, see Richard Hughes Seager, *The World's Parliament of Religions: The*

East/West Encounter, Chicago, 1893 (Bloomington: Indiana University Press, 1995); see also Albanese, *Republic of Mind and Spirit*, 331–34; William R. Hutchison, *Religious Pluralism in America: The Contentious History of a Founding Ideal* (New Haven, Conn.: Yale University Press, 2003), 132–36, 171–86; on race, civilization, and the 1893 World's Fair, see Gail Bederman, *Manliness and Civilization: A Cultural History of Gender and Race in the United States, 1880–1917* (Chicago: University of Chicago Press, 1995), 31–41; Robert W. Rydell, *All the World's a Fair: Visions of Empire at American International Expositions, 1876–1916* (Chicago: University of Chicago Press, 1984), 64–66.

14. Thomas Wentworth Higginson, "The Sympathy of Religions," in Barrows, *World's Parliament of Religions*, 1:781.

15. Barrows, *World's Parliament of Religions*, 1:18.

16. "The Secularized Classes," *Andover Review* 11 (January 1889): 73; Lawrence W. Levine, *Highbrow/Lowbrow: The Emergence of Cultural Hierarchy in America* (Cambridge, Mass.: Harvard University Press, 1988), esp. 114–41.

17. See Christine M. E. Guth, *Longfellow's Tattoos: Tourism, Collecting, and Japan* (Seattle: University of Washington Press, 2004), xi, 4, 15–17.

18. See Thomas A. Tweed, *The American Encounter with Buddhism, 1844–1912: Victorian Culture and the Limits of Dissent* (Bloomington: Indiana University Press, 1992), 69–71.

19. "The Religious World," *Outlook* 56 (July 10, 1897): 659. On Asian migration to the United States in the late nineteenth century, see Madeline Y. Hsu, *Dreaming of Gold, Dreaming of Home: Transnationalism and Migration between the United States and South China, 1882–1943* (Stanford, Calif.: Stanford University Press, 2000); Erika Lee, *At America's Gates: Chinese Immigration during the Exclusion Era, 1882–1943* (Chapel Hill: University of North Carolina Press, 2003); Joshua Paddison, *American Heathens: Religion, Race, and Reconstruction in California* (Berkeley: University of California Press for the Huntington Library, 2012); Henry Yu, *Thinking Orientals: Migration, Contact, and Exoticism in Modern America* (New York: Oxford University Press, 2001).

20. Hamilton Wright Mabie, *My Study Fire* (New York: Dodd, Mead, 1890), 60–61.

21. See D. G. Hart, *The University Gets Religion: Religious Studies in American Higher Education* (Baltimore: Johns Hopkins University Press, 1999), esp. 62–66; James Turner, *Religion Enters the Academy: The Origins of the Scholarly Study of Religion in America* (Athens: University of Georgia Press, 2011).

22. Tweed, *American Encounter*, 60–61, 92–96.

23. Leighton Parks, *His Star in the East: A Study in the Early Aryan Religions* (Boston: Houghton Mifflin, 1887), 145.

24. Carl T. Jackson, *The Oriental Religions and American Thought: Nineteenth-Century Explorations* (Westport, Conn.: Greenwood Press, 1981), 143–46; Tomoko Masuzawa, *The Invention of World Religions; or, How European Universalism Was Preserved in the Language of Pluralism* (Chicago: University of Chicago Press, 2005), 138–46; Tweed, *American Encounter*, 29, 115–18; James Turner, *Without God, without Creed: The Origins of Unbelief in America* (Baltimore: Johns Hopkins University Press, 1985), 155–57.

25. John Henry Barrows, *The Christian Conquest of Asia: Studies and Personal Reflections of Oriental Religions* (New York: Charles Scribner's Sons, 1899), 31.

26. See George Washburn, "The Points of Contact and Contrast between Christianity and Mohammedanism," in Barrows, *World's Parliament of Religions*, 1:571.

27. On the popularity of meditation, see Schmidt, *Restless Souls*, 172–79.

28. Higginson, "Sympathy of Religions," 781; on Higginson and the Free Religious Association, see Schmidt, *Restless Souls*, 113–15; Leslie Butler, *Critical Americans: Victorian Intellectuals and Transatlantic Liberal Reform* (Chapel Hill: University of North Carolina Press, 2007), 20–26.

29. See the prospectus for the summer of 1897, printed in "The Religious World," *Outlook* 56 (July 3, 1897): 610.

30. Schmidt, *Restless Souls*, 136–38. On Blavatsky and Olcott, see Albanese, *Republic of Mind and Spirit*, 341–42; Jackson, *Oriental Religions*, 157–73.

31. See Emily R. Mace, "'Citizens of All the World's Temples': Cosmopolitan Religion at Bell Street Chapel," in Leigh E. Schmidt and Sally M. Promey, eds., *American Religious Liberalism* (Bloomington: Indiana University Press, 2012), 150–53.

32. James Henry Snowden, "One Body in Christ," August 13, 1893, folder 24, box 2, James Henry Snowden Papers, Pittsburgh Theological Seminary Archive (Pittsburgh, Pa.); "Following Christ," March 4, 1900, folder 29, box 1, Snowden Papers.

33. I. N. Tarbox, "The Light of Asia," *New Englander* 3 (November 1880): 711.

34. March 24, 1895, entry, folder 1: Council minutes, 1874–1895, First Congregational Church of Waucoma, Iowa, Records, Congregational Library (Boston, Mass.).

35. Horace Bushnell, *Views of Christian Nurture, and of Subjects Adjacent Thereto* (Hartford, Conn.: Edwin Hunt, 1847), 12–13.

36. James Henry Snowden, "New Theology," February 26, 1893, folder 36, box 4, Snowden Papers; see also H. Shelton Smith, *Changing Conceptions of Original Sin: A Study in American Theology since 1750* (New York: Charles Scribner's Sons, 1955), 158–63.

37. Charles Augustus Briggs, *Whither? A Theological Question for the Times* (New York: Charles Scribner's Sons, 1889), 137.

38. James Henry Snowden, "The Parliament of Religions," August 24, 1893, folder 45, box 2, Snowden Papers.

39. "Editorial—Christianity and Its Modern Competitors," *Andover Review* 7 (May 1887): 539–40; "Editorial—Aggressive Infidelity Using Its Advantage," *Andover Review* 9 (June 1888): 641. See also Gary Dorrien, *The Making of American Liberal Theology: Imagining Progressive Religion, 1805–1900* (Louisville, Ky.: Westminster John Knox Press, 2001), 135–37.

40. Washington Gladden, untitled sermon, January 21, 1900, reel 31, Gladden Papers (microfilm).

41. Gail Hamilton, *Sermons to the Clergy* (Boston: William F. Gill, 1876); for a brief biography and for various instances of Dodge reflecting on encounters with theological perspectives that were either more liberal or conservative than her own, see H. Augusta Dodge, ed., *Gail Hamilton's Life in Letters,* vol. 1 (1896; repr. Boston: Lee and Shepard, 1901), ix–xiii, 58, 257–59; see also Susan Coultrap-McQuinn, "Gail Hamilton (1833–1896)," *Legacy* 4 (Fall 1987): 53–58.

42. Gail Hamilton, "Heathendom and Christendom under Test," *North American Review (hereafter NAR)* 143 (December 1886): 542.

43. Gail Hamilton, "The American Vedas," *NAR* 144 (June 1887): 638.

44. Barrows, *Christian Conquest of Asia*, 48–49.

45. George A. Coe, "The Outlook for Personal Religion," clipping from the *Congregationalist and Christian World* (1904), folder 32, box 4, series 2, George A. Coe Papers, Yale Divinity School Library (New Haven, Conn.).

46. Parks, *His Star in the East*, 20.

47. Washington Gladden, "The Missionary Work," delivered May 26, 1899, reel 30 (box 55), Gladden Papers (microfilm).

48. Lyman Abbott, "The Larger Love," May 2, 1897; reprinted in *Outlook* 56 (May 15, 1897): 161.

49. Theodore Munger, *The Freedom of Faith* (Boston: Houghton Mifflin, 1883), 115.

50. C. W. Clapp, "The Historic Religions of India. I. Brahmanism," *New Englander* 39 (July 1880): 508.

51. Barrows, *Christian Conquest of Asia*, 54.

52. Lyman Abbott, Sermon Notes on Phil. 2:1–11, 3:1–14 and 2 Corinthians 5:14 (1875), folder 2, box 25, Lyman Abbott Papers, George Mitchell Special Collections, Bowdoin College Library (Brunswick, Me.).

53. George A. Coe, "Religious Experience and the Scientific Movement," delivered at the Methodist Episcopal Church Congress, Pittsburgh, Pa., November 1897 (reprinted in *The Church and Christian Experience*), p. 51, folder 27, box 4, series 2, Coe Papers.

54. On his relationship to Brooks, see Leighton Parks, *Moral Leadership and Other Sermons* (New York: Charles Scribner's Sons, 1914), 71.

55. Parks, *His Star in the East*, 88.

56. Leighton Parks, "A Bozu of the Monto Sect," *Century* 32 (July 1886): 481.

57. Parks, *His Star in the East*, 5, 7.

58. Ibid., 14.

59. Ibid., 55–56; on liberal Protestants' emphasis on divine immanence, see William R. Hutchison, *The Modernist Impulse in American Protestantism* (Durham, N.C.: Duke University Press, 1992), 98–105.

60. Washington Gladden, untitled sermon, January 21, 1900, reel 31, Gladden Papers; see also the subsequent sermons for February 11, February 25, March 4, March 11, and March 18, 1901, ibid.

61. Entries for March 14, 1894, and September 19, 1894, folder: Records, 1889–1906, box 1, Suffolk South Association/Conference Records, 1822–1964, Congregational Library (Boston, Mass.).

62. *Old South Record* (January 1909), Old South Church Collection, Congregational Library (Boston, Mass.).

63. Schmidt, *Restless Souls*, 167–70; Tweed, *American Encounter*, 31.

64. See the report on Amory Bradford's speech in "The Religious World," *Outlook* 56 (July 10, 1897): 659.

65. George H. Palmer, "Similarities and Contrasts of Christianity and Buddhism," *Outlook* 56 (July 19, 1897): 443–44; 449.

66. "Religious World," 133.

67. "Correspondence," *Outlook* 56 (July 10, 1897): 661.

68. In the *NAR*, see Herbert Allen Giles, "Confucianism in the Nineteenth Century," *NAR* 171 (September 1900): 359–74; T. W. Rhys Davids, "Buddhism," *NAR* 171 (October 1900): 517–27; Oskar Mann, "Mohammedanism in the Nineteenth Century," *NAR* 171 (November 1900): 754–68; A. C. Lyall, "Brahmanism," *NAR* 171 (December 1900): 920–34.

69. Arthur H. Smith, "The Message of the World's Religions. III—Confucianism," *Outlook* 56 (July 17, 1897): 689, 691.

70. Charles R. Lanman, "The Message of the World's Religion. V—Brahmanism," *Outlook* 56 (July 31, 1897): 791–92.

71. John H. Vincent, quoted in Barrows, *World's Parliament of Religions*, 1:38.

72. Washington Gladden, untitled sermon, September 10, 1893, reel 25, Gladden Papers (microfilm).

73. Barrows, *World's Parliament of Religions*, 1:75.

74. Snowden, "Parliament of Religions."

75. Parks, *Moral Leadership*, 165–66, 168.

76. George A. Gordon, *The Christ of To-day* (Boston: Houghton Mifflin, 1895), 20; see also William R. Hutchison, *Errand to the World: American Protestant Thought and Foreign Missions* (Chicago: University of Chicago Press, 1987), 91–95, 102–7.

77. John Henry Barrows, "Is Christianity Fitted to Become the World-Religion?," *American Journal of Theology* 1 (April 1897): 404–23, esp. 422.

78. See the reprinting of excerpts from Haskell's letter to University of Chicago president William Rainey Harper in Barrows, *Christianity the World-Religion*, 10–11; for his own

account of the trip, see John Henry Barrows, *A World-Pilgrimage* (Chicago: A.C. McClurg, 1897), esp. 370–82, for his discussions of Christian missions.

79. John Henry Barrows, "Conversations with Educated Hindus," *Outlook* 56 (July 17, 1897): 696.

80. Lyman Abbott, "The Message of the World's Religions. VI—Christianity," *Outlook* 56 (August 21, 1897): 991.

81. Barrows, *World's Parliament of Religions*, 1:48.

82. Benjamin W. Arnett speech, quoted in ibid., 107, 109.

83. Thomas Wentworth Higginson speech, quoted in ibid., 135.

84. Webb, "Spirit of Islam," 994–95.

85. P. C. Mozoomdar speech, quoted in Barrows, *World's Parliament of Religions*, 1:86–87; on Mozoomdar, see Schmidt, *Restless Souls*, 94–96.

86. Letter from James Gibbons, printed in Barrows, *World's Parliament of Religions*, 1:14.

87. Ibid., 16.

88. Ibid., 74.

89. Washington Gladden, untitled sermon, September 24, 1893, reel 25, Gladden Papers (microfilm).

90. Washington Gladden, untitled sermon, September 10, 1893, ibid. Gladden was not the only Protestant to leave the Parliament with this view; see Jackson, *Oriental Religions*, 254.

91. Parks, "A Bozu of the Monto Sect," 479.

92. Barrows, *Christianity the World-Religion*, 260; Barrows, "Conversations with Educated Hindus," 696.

93. Charles P. Anderson, *The Manifestation of Unity: A Charge to the Seventy-Fifth Annual Convention of the Church in the Diocese of Chicago* (Chicago: Gunthorp-Warren Printing, 1912), 16–17.

94. Leighton Parks, *The Crisis of the Churches* (New York: Charles Scribner's Sons, 1922), 17.

3. AN EXPANSIVE KINGDOM OF GOD

1. David Philipson, "Inter-religious Relationship," November 4, 1934, David Philipson Papers, folder 9, box 4, series D, Jacob Rader Marcus Center of the American Jewish Archives (Cincinnati, Ohio).

2. Ibid.

3. John W. Langdale to David Philipson, October 27, 1913, folder 11, box 1, series A, Philipson Papers; see also David Philipson, *My Life as an American Jew* (Cincinnati: John G. Kidd and Son, 1941), 158–59.

4. *The Congregationalist* 32 (November 10, 1880): 353.

5. "The Religious World," *Outlook* 55 (March 27, 1897): 849–50.

6. "The Religious World," *Outlook* 50 (October 27, 1894): 672–73.

7. Lyman Abbott, sermon notes on Philippians 2:1–11, 3:1–2, and 2 Corinthians 5:14 (1875), folder 2, box 25, Lyman Abbott Papers, George Mitchell Special Collections, Bowdoin College Library (Brunswick, Me.).

8. Lyman Abbott, *Jesus of Nazareth: His Life and His Teachings* (New York: Harper and Brothers, 1869), 242.

9. "The Religious World," *Outlook* 50 (October 27, 1894): 673.

10. On the abatement of Protestant anti-Catholicism in the early republic, see Chris Beneke, *Beyond Toleration: The Religious Origins of American Pluralism* (New York: Oxford University Press, 2006), especially 182–87.

11. On early nineteenth-century anti-Catholicism, see John T. McGreevy, *Catholicism and American Freedom: A History* (New York: W. W. Norton, 2003), 21–25; on the rise of

anti-Catholicism during the 1880s and 1890s, see John Higham, *Strangers in the Land: Patterns of American Nativism, 1860–1925*, 2nd ed. (New Brunswick, N.J.: Rutgers University Press, 1988); Donald L. Kinzer, *An Episode in Anti-Catholicism: The American Protective Association* (Seattle: University of Washington Press, 1964).

12. Theodore Roosevelt, *American in Religion* (Chicago: Blakely-Onswald, 1908).

13. Newman Smyth, *Passing Protestantism and Coming Catholicism* (New York: Charles Scribner's Sons, 1908), 103.

14. Jonathan D. Sarna, *American Judaism: A History* (New Haven, Conn.: Yale University Press, 2004), 11–12, 23–24.

15. Ibid., 133–34, 151–55; Leonard Dinnerstein, *Antisemitism in America* (New York: Oxford University Press, 1994), 11–23, 35–57.

16. Washington Gladden, *Social Facts and Forces* (New York: G. P. Putnam, 1897), 209.

17. Letter to the editor from A.I.D. of South St. Paul, Minnesota, *Outlook* 96 (November 12, 1910): 603.

18. Hamilton Wright Mabie, *My Study Fire* (New York: Dodd, Mead, 1890), 86.

19. Thomas Jefferson Jenkins, "The A.P.A. Conspirators," *Catholic World* 57 (August 1893): 691.

20. James Hoye to Washington Gladden, March 19, 1913, reel 10, Washington Gladden Papers (microfilm), Harvard College Library (Cambridge, Mass.; originals at Ohio Historical Society, Columbus, Ohio); Parley P. Womer to Gladden, November 29, 1909, reel 8, Gladden Papers (microfilm).

21. See Beneke, *Beyond Toleration*.

22. Theodore Roosevelt, "True Americanism" (1894), in *American Ideals and Other Essays, Social and Political* (New York: G. P. Putnam's Sons, 1897), 64–65.

23. James Henry Snowden, "Prejudice Removed," delivered February 7, 1897, folder 36, box 1, James Henry Snowden Papers, Pittsburgh Theological Seminary Archive (Pittsburgh, Pa.); on Catholics' service in the Civil War, see Randall M. Miller, "Catholic Religion, Irish Ethnicity, and the Civil War," in Randall M. Miller, Harry S. Stout, and Charles Reagan Wilson, eds., *Religion and the American Civil War* (New York: Oxford University Press, 1998); on Catholics' subsequent rise to the middle class, see Jay P. Dolan, *In Search of an American Catholicism: A History of Religion and Culture in Tension* (New York: Oxford University Press, 2002), 72–73.

24. William J. Onahan, "Columbian Catholic Congress at Chicago," *Catholic World* 57 (August 1893): 607; Robert T. Handy, *Undermined Establishment: Church-State Relations in America, 1880–1920* (Princeton, N.J.: Princeton University Press, 1991), 53–55; McGreevy, *Catholicism and American Freedom*, 122–24.

25. John Ireland, *The Church and Modern Society: Lectures and Addresses*, vol. 1 (1896; repr. New York: D. H. McBride, 1903), 115.

26. John Lancaster Spalding, *Education and the Higher Life* (1890; repr. Chicago: A. C. McClurg, 1900), 26.

27. Sarna, *American Judaism*, 76–88.

28. Kaufmann Kohler, "The Need of a Living Creed" (1896), in Kohler, *A Living Faith: Selected Sermons and Addresses from the Literary Remains of Dr. Kaufmann Kohler*, ed. Samuel S. Cohen (Cincinnati: Hebrew Union College Press, 1948), 3; Kohler, "Are Sunday Lectures Treason to Judaism?" ibid., especially 25–26; Sarna, *American Judaism*, 144–45, 194–95; Egal Feldman, *Dual Destinies: The Jewish Encounter with Protestant America* (Urbana: University of Illinois Press, 1990), 83–85.

29. Theodore Roosevelt, *Fear God and Take Your Part* (New York: George H. Doran, 1916), 142, 360–63.

30. Morgan M. Sheedy, "The Future of the Summer-School," *Catholic World* 56 (November 1892): 171.

31. "The New American Cardinals," *Outlook* 99 (November 11, 1911): 607–8.

32. Theodore Roosevelt to Thomas O'Gorman, March 1, 1895, frame 507, reel 5, John Ireland Papers (microfilm), Boston College Library (Chestnut Hill, Mass.; originals at Minnesota Historical Society, St. Paul, Minn.).

33. E. S. Goodrich to John Ireland, November 5, 1896, frames 663–64, reel 5, Ireland Papers (microfilm).

34. Edward C. Rich to John Ireland, October 12, 1896, frame 656, reel 5, Ireland Papers (microfilm).

35. "The American Brotherhood," *Outlook* 98 (June 10, 1911): 285.

36. See the remarks of W. D. McKinney and E. S. Lines in "The Religious World," *Outlook* 55 (March 27, 1897): 850.

37. John Lancaster Spalding, *Lectures and Discourses* (New York: Catholic Publication Society, 1882), 13.

38. John Ireland, "The Catholic Church and Civil Society," in *The Church and Modern Society*, 1:64; see also Jon Gjerde, *Catholicism and the Shaping of 19th Century America* (New York: Cambridge University Press, 2012), 76.

39. "The Catholic Church in America, 1776–1876," *Catholic World* 23 (July 1876): 448.

40. Helena T. Goessmann, "At All Sacrifices," *Catholic World* 57 (August 1893): 653–54.

41. James A. Walsh, "Indifference of Catholics," January 26, 1894, folder 3, box 3, section 2, James A. Walsh Papers, Maryknoll Mission Archive (Ossining, N.Y.).

42. "The New Protestantism of Christianity," *Catholic World* 28 (October 1879): 88.

43. Mary Catherine Chase (writing as F. M. Edselas), "Mission Lectures to Non-Catholics," *Catholic World* 57 (August 1893): 629.

44. John Ireland, "State Schools and Parish Schools," in *The Church and Modern Society*, 1:221.

45. Augustine F. Hewit, "Christian Unity in the Parliament of Religions," *Catholic World* 54 (May 1894): 163.

46. John Lancaster Spalding, *Religion, Agnosticism, and Education* (Chicago: A. C. McClurg, 1903), 184.

47. William C. Robinson, "The Attitude of the Educated Protestant Mind toward Catholic Truth," *Catholic World* 54 (February 1892): 646.

48. The Religious World," *Outlook* 58 (February 26, 1898): 545.

49. Washington Gladden, "Bishop Watterson," April 23, 1899, reel 30, Gladden Papers (microfilm).

50. George A. Gordon, "Is the Church an Incident or a Necessity?" (1920), George A. Gordon Sermons, 1896–1924, Old South Church Collection, Congregational Library (Boston, Mass.).

51. Kohler, "Need of a Living Creed," 4.

52. George Harris, "Ethical Christianity and Biblical Criticism," *Andover Review* 15 (May 1891): 461.

53. On early Unitarians, see C. Conrad Wright, *The Beginnings of Unitarianism in America* (Boston: Beacon Press, 1955); see also E. Brooks Holifield, *Theology in America: Christian Thought from the Age of the Puritans to the Civil War* (New Haven, Conn.: Yale University Press, 2003), 197–207; on the trajectory from Unitarianism to more innovative spiritual practice, see Leigh E. Schmidt, *Restless Souls: The Making of American Spirituality* (San Francisco: HarperSanFrancisco, 2005), 105–12.

54. M. Severance to Robert Ingersoll, April 23, 1888, frames 113–14, reel 18, Robert Ingersoll Papers (microfilm), Harvard College Library (Cambridge, Mass.; originals at Library of Congress, Washington, D.C.).

55. "To Liberal Ministers," *Outlook* 58 (February 5, 1898): 315.

56. "Christianity and Its Modern Competitors. I," *Andover Review* 6 (November 1886): 510.

57. George A. Coe, "The Outlook for Personal Religion," clipping from the *Congregationalist and Christian World* (1904), folder 32, box 4, series 2, George A. Coe Papers, Yale Divinity School Library (New Haven, Conn.).

58. Abram S. Isaacs, "Current Phases of American Judaism," *Andover Review* 10 (July 1888): 66; on Adler, see Benny Kraut, *From Reform Judaism to Ethical Culture: The Religious Evolution of Felix Adler* (Cincinnati: Hebrew Union College Press, 1978).

59. On the Swing trial, see Gary Dorrien, *The Making of Liberal Theology: Imagining Progressive Religion, 1805–1900* (Louisville, Ky.: Westminster John Knox Press, 2001), 275–79.

60. Washington Gladden, "(The Cases of Professors Briggs and Smith)," January 8, 1893, reel 24, Gladden Papers (microfilm); Dorrien, *Making of American Liberal Theology: Imagining Progressive Religion*, 361–65.

61. George M. Marsden, *Fundamentalism and American Culture*, 2nd ed. (New York: Oxford University Press, 2006), 27–39, 118–23; Grant Wacker, *Heaven Below: Early Pentecostals and American Culture* (Cambridge, Mass.: Harvard University Press, 2001).

62. Helen M. Sweeney, "The Catholic University," *Catholic World* 57 (April 1893): 113.

63. "The New American Cardinals," *Outlook* 99 (November 11, 1911): 607; on the condemnation of Americanism, see Dolan, *In Search of an American Catholicism*, 108–110; on the evolution debate in Catholicism, see David Mislin, "According to His Own Judgment: The American Catholic Encounter with Organic Evolution, 1875–1896," *Religion and American Culture: A Journal of Interpretation* 22 (Summer 2012): 133–62; R. Scott Appleby, *"Church and Age Unite!": The Modernist Impulse in American Catholicism* (Notre Dame, Ind.: University of Notre Dame Press, 1992), especially chap. 1.

64. Sarna, *American Judaism*, 175–84.

65. "The Week," *Outlook* 97 (January 28, 1911): 138.

66. "The Religious World," *Outlook* 50 (October 13, 1894): 595.

67. David Philipson, "The Fundamentalist Controversy," folder 6, box 4, series D, Philipson Papers.

68. On the growth of Protestant denominations, see Nathan O. Hatch, *The Democratization of American Christianity* (New Haven, Conn.: Yale University Press, 1989); Roger Finke and Rodney Stark, *The Churching of America, 1776–2005: Winners and Losers in Our Religious Economy*, 2nd ed. (New Brunswick, N.J.: Rutgers University Press, 2005), especially chapter three; Jon Butler, *Awash in a Sea of Faith: Christianizing the American People* (Cambridge, Mass.: Harvard University Press, 1990).

69. John Ireland, "Rev. Dr. R. Breed's Defense of Protestantism," frames 280–300, reel 1, Ireland Papers (microfilm).

70. Gjerde, *Catholicism*, 71; Mark A. Noll, "The Bible," in Miller, Stout, and Wilson, *Religion in the American Civil War*, 55.

71. William J. Tucker, "The Church of the Future," *Outlook* 57 (November 27, 1897): 756, 758.

72. Washington Gladden, *The Christian Pastor and the Working Church* (New York: Charles Scribner's Sons, 1898), 447.

73. Newman Smyth, untitled sermon, April 25, 1886, Smyth Papers, folder 12, box 3, series 2, Newman Smyth Papers, Yale University Library Manuscripts and Archives (New Haven, Conn.).

74. Samuel Dike, "Some Aspects of the Divorce Question," *Princeton Review* (March 1884): 182.

75. Gladden, *Christian Pastor*, 48, 101.

76. George A. Coe, "The Reason and the Functions of General Religions Education," in *Proceedings of the World's Congress of Arts and Sciences* (1904), folder 32, box 4, series 2, Coe Papers.

77. George Hodges, *Faith and Social Service: Eight Lectures Delivered before the Lowell Institute,* 4th ed. (New York: Thomas Whittaker, 1896), 8; "Christianity and Its Modern Competitors," *Andover Review* 6 (November 1886): 652.

78. On the Protestant Social Gospel, see Ronald C. White Jr. and C. Howard Hopkins, *The Social Gospel: Religion and Reform in Changing America* (Philadelphia: Temple University Press, 1976); Susan Curtis, *A Consuming Faith: The Social Gospel and Modern American Culture* (1991; repr. Columbia: University of Missouri Press, 2001); Dorrien, *Making of American Liberal Theology: Imagining Progressive Religion,* 308–12.

79. Theodore T. Munger, *The Freedom of Faith* (Boston: Houghton Mifflin, 1883), 32.

80. On language of the Kingdom of God in Rauschenbusch and the Social Gospel movement, see Gary Dorrien, *The Making of American Liberal Theology: Idealism, Realism, and Modernity, 1900–1950* (Louisville, Ky.: Westminster John Knox Press, 2003), 109–17; on Rauschenbusch, see Christopher Hodge Evans, *The Kingdom Is Always But Coming: A Life of Walter Rauschenbusch* (Grand Rapids, Mich.: William B. Eerdmans, 2004).

81. Walter Rauschenbusch, *A Theology for the Social Gospel* (New York: Macmillan, 1917), 12–14, 107.

82. Augustine F. Hewit, "Ignis Aeternus," *Catholic World* 57 (April 1893): 16.

83. Ireland, *The Church and Modern Society,* 1:xix; on *Rerum,* see McGreevy, *Catholicism and American Freedom,* 126–38.

84. Ireland, *The Church and Modern Society,* 1:xxi.

85. Augustine F. Hewit, "The Lesson of the 'White City,' Second Part," *Catholic World* 60 (October 1894): 82.

86. "Talk about New Books," *Catholic World* 57 (August 1893): 722; Washington Gladden, *Tools and the Man: Property and Industry under the Christian Law* (Boston: Houghton Mifflin, 1893).

87. (The Letter and the Spirit)," 1893, reel 25, Gladden Papers (microfilm); James Henry Snowden, "Children of Light," February 13, 1898, folder 34, box 1, Snowden Papers.

88. Kohler, "Are Sunday Lectures Treason to Judaism?," 26; on the problem of progressive revelation for Protestant-Jewish relations, see Feldman, *Dual Destinies,* 146–49.

89. "Stick to the Bible," *Outlook* 99 (October 28, 1911): 451.

90. Ibid., 452.

91. David Philipson, "The Humanist Movement" (1929), folder 8, box 4, series D, Philipson Papers.

92. "The Unity of the Faith," *Outlook* 95 (June 18, 1910): 336–37.

93. Horace Bushnell, *Sermons on Living Subjects* (New York: Scribner, Armstrong, 1872), 66–67.

94. Lyman Abbott, *America in the Making* (New Haven, Conn.: Yale University Press, 1911), 30.

95. Gail Hamilton, "Why I Am a Congregationalist," *North American Review* 144 (April 1887): 331.

96. James Henry Snowden, "Christian Life," delivered January 13, 1900, folder 30, box 1, Snowden Papers.

97. "The Religious World," *Outlook* 50 (November 24, 1894): 863.

98. James A. Walsh, untitled sermon, 1895, folder 4, box 3, section 2, Walsh Papers; Lyman Abbott, *The Christian Ministry* (Boston: Houghton Mifflin, 1905), 177, 188–89.

99. Untitled document on the Seminar on the Relations of Roman Catholics and Jews, folder 13, box 2, series B, Philipson Papers.

100. Kaufmann Kohler, *Jewish Theology: Systematically and Historically Considered* (New York: Macmillan, 1918), 17.

101. Thomas O'Gorman, "Where God and Man Meet," *Catholic World* 58 (November 1893): 208.

102. Ireland, *The Church and Modern Society*, 1:74.

103. Washington Gladden, *Burning Questions of the Life That Now Is and of That Which Is to Come* (New York: Century, 1890), 232–33.

4. DRAWING TOGETHER

1. *Circular of Information: The Interdenominational Commission of Maine* (Lewiston: Maine Interdenominational Commission, 1913), 4.

2. Charles Augustus Briggs, *Whither? A Theological Question for the Times* (New York: Charles Scribner's Sons, 1889), 42; on the wave of business consolidation, see Oliver Zunz, *Making America Corporate, 1870–1920* (Chicago: University of Chicago Press, 1990), especially chap. 1; Alan Trachtenberg, *The Incorporation of America: Culture and Society in the Gilded Age*, 25th anniversary ed. (New York: Hill and Wang, 2007), 83–86.

3. On Anthony, see his entry in G. A. Burgess and J. T. Ward, *Free Baptist Cyclopaedia* (Chicago: Free Baptist Cyclopedia, 1889), and "Alfred W. Anthony: Biographical Sketch by His Daughter Elisabeth A. Dexter, 1954," box 4, series 5, Alfred Williams Anthony Papers, Edmund S. Muskie Archives and Special Collections Library, Bates College (Lewiston, Me.).

4. *Circular of Information*, 4, 7.

5. Alfred Williams Anthony to the Interdenominational Commission of Maine, February 22, 1916, correspondence 1910–1919, 1935–1937 folder, box 3, Anthony Papers.

6. Charles W. Shields, "The Social Problem of Church Unity," *Century* 40 (September 1890): 687, 695; George Coe, "Notes on the Recent Census of Religious Bodies," *American Journal of Sociology* 15 (May 1910): 808–9.

7. "The Interdenominational Conference at Madison," December 5–7, 1910, clipping in Articles and News Clippings 1900–1915 folder, box 3, Anthony Papers; "Constitution of the Massachusetts Federation of Churches," folder 4, box 4, subseries 3, series 1, Massachusetts Council of Churches Records, Congregational Library (Boston, Mass.).

8. William C. Doane, "Family Life," in Elias B. Sanford, ed., *Church Federation: Interchurch Conference on Federation* (New York: Fleming H. Revell, 1906), 241; on the creation of the Federal Council, see also Samuel McCrea Cavert, *The American Churches in the Ecumenical Movement, 1900–1968* (New York: Association Press, 1968).

9. "City Federations of Churches in the United States" (1913), folder 13, box 11, Federal Council of the Churches of Christ in America (FCC) Records, Presbyterian Historical Society (Philadelphia, Pa.).

10. Statement of the Federal Council of Churches Commission on Federated Movements (February 11, 1914), folder 7, box 75, FCC Records; Minutes of the Committee of Direction of the Commission on Inter-church Federations of the Federal Council of the Churches of Christ in America, October 23, 1918, folder 9, box 75, FCC Records.

11. "Suggestions concerning 'The Church and Community Conference'" (1920), p. 3, folder 9, box 75, FCC Records.

12. James Henry Snowden, "One Hundred Years in Washington," October 2, 1910, folder 10, box 1, James Henry Snowden Papers, Pittsburgh Theological Seminary Archive (Pittsburgh, Pa.).

13. *Directory of State and Local Federations in the United States, 1914*, pp. 23–24, folder 8, box 75, FCC Records.

14. James Turner, *Without God, without Creed: The Origins of Unbelief in America* (Baltimore: Johns Hopkins University Press, 1985), 23–25.

15. Roger Finke and Rodney Stark, *The Churching of America, 1776–2005: Winners and Losers in Our Religious Economy*, 2nd ed. (New Brunswick, N.J.: Rutgers University Press, 2005), 60–61, 197–98; Nathan O. Hatch, *The Democratization of American Christianity* (New Haven, Conn.: Yale University Press, 1989), 3–4, 65–65; Jon Butler, *Awash in a Sea of Faith: Christianizing the American People* (Cambridge, Mass.: Harvard University Press, 1990), 273–74.

16. E. Brooks Holifield, *Theology in America: Christian Thought from the Age of the Puritans to the Civil War* (New Haven, Conn.: Yale University Press, 2003).

17. Chris Beneke, *Beyond Toleration: The Religious Origins of American Pluralism* (Oxford: Oxford University Press, 2006), 73–75, 81–87; on reform in the early nineteenth century, see Robert Abzug, *Cosmos Crumbling: Antebellum Reform and the Religious Imagination* (New York: Oxford University Press, 1994); on the YMCA, see Cliff Putney, *Muscular Christianity: Manhood and Sports in Protestant America, 1880–1920* (Cambridge, Mass.: Harvard University Press, 2001), 64–72.

18. Henry Ward Beecher, "The Partialness of Christian Knowledge," in *Sermons* (London: J. Heaton and Son, 1864), 272; Horace Bushnell, *Christ and His Salvation: In Sermons Variously Related Thereto*, 3rd ed. (New York: Charles Scribner, 1865), 24; see also Samuel S. Hill, "Religion and the Results of the Civil War," in Randall M. Miller, Harry S. Stout, and Charles Reagan Wilson, eds., *Religion and the American Civil War* (New York: Oxford University Press, 1998), 372–74.

19. On the American Missionary Association and its connection to many leading Protestants of the late nineteenth century, see Ralph E. Luker, *The Social Gospel in Black and White: American Racial Reform, 1885–1914* (Chapel Hill: University of North Carolina Press, 1991), 12–14.

20. The classic text on the American response to immigration in this period remains John Higham, *Strangers in the Land: Patterns of American Nativism, 1860–1925*, 2nd ed. (New York: Rutgers University Press, 1968), especially 158–60; for precise statistics, see Stephan Thernstrom, ed., *Harvard Encyclopedia of American Ethnic Groups* (Cambridge, Mass.: Belknap Press of Harvard University Press, 1980), 147–49.

21. On the emergence of the industrial economy and subsequent shifts in labor practices, see David Montgomery, *The Fall of the House of Labor: The Workplace, the State, and American Labor Activism, 1865–1925* (Cambridge: Cambridge University Press, 1985), 130, 217–20, 230–33; Daniel T. Rodgers, *The Work Ethic in Industrial America, 1850–1920* (Chicago: University of Chicago Press, 1978), 24–29, 50–57; Nell Irvin Painter, *Standing at Armageddon: The United States, 1877–1919* (New York: W. W. Norton, 1987), xx, xviii, 44–50.

22. Newman Smyth, "Social Caeasarism," May 30, 1886, folder 21, box 3, series 2, group 623, Newman Smyth Papers, Yale University Library Manuscripts and Archives (New Haven, Conn.).

23. On the 1886 strikes and Haymarket riot, see Painter, *Standing at Armageddon*, 44–50; for the religious response to Haymarket, see Thekla Ellen Joiner, *Sin in the City: Chicago and Revivalism, 1880–1920* (Columbia: University of Missouri Press, 2007), 47–49; for treatment of these issues more broadly, see Henry F. May, *The Protestant Churches and Industrial America* (New York: Harper, 1959), especially chap. 2.

24. William W. Adams, "The Spiritual Problem of the Manufacturing Town. I," *Andover Review* 5 (February 1886): 129–30.

25. John Bodnar, *The Transplanted: A History of Immigrants in Urban America* (Bloomington: Indiana University Press, 1985), 104–5; see also Lizabeth Cohen, *Making a New Deal: Industrial Workers in Chicago, 1919–1939* (Cambridge: Cambridge University Press, 1990), 13, 21–30, 83–94.

26. "The Problem at Hope Chapel: Some Impressions," *Old South Record* (December 1910), Old South Church Collection, Congregational Library (Boston, Mass.).

27. Paul S. Boyer, *Urban Masses and Moral Order in America, 1820–1920* (Cambridge, Mass.: Harvard University Press, 1978), 137–39; and May, *Protestant Churches and Industrial America*, 201, 228.

28. Washington Gladden, *The Christian Pastor and the Working Church* (New York: Charles Scribner's Sons, 1898), 429.

29. Briggs, *Whither?*, 40.

30. William W. Adams, "The Spiritual Problem of the Manufacturing Town," *Andover Review* 5 (July 1886): 612; see also 624–25.

31. Ibid., 628–29.

32. Gladden, *Christian Pastor*, 431.

33. Report of the Annual Meeting of the First Congregational Church of Freeport, Maine, December 28, 1898, Church Record Book, 1887–1928, First Congregational Church of Freeport Collection, Congregational Library (Boston, Mass.).

34. Samuel W. Dike, "The Religious Problem of the Country Town," *Andover Review* 2 (August 1884): 123–24.

35. Ibid., 123.

36. Coe, "Notes on the Recent Census," 808–9.

37. Gladden, "Problems of Evangelization—II. The Country Towns," May 15, 1881, reel 16, Washington Gladden Papers (microfilm), Harvard College Library (Cambridge, Mass.; originals at Ohio Historical Society, Columbus, Ohio).

38. First Congregational Church of Waucoma, Iowa, council minutes, especially entries for December 24, 1893, January 5, 1894, January 13, 1920, January 11, 1922, and January 16, 1923, First Congregational Church of Waucoma Collection, Congregational Library (Boston, Mass.).

39. William DeWitt Hyde, "Church Federation in Maine," clipping from *Christian Work: An Illustrated Family Newspaper* (February 1900), Articles and News Clippings, 1900–1915 folder, box 3, Anthony Papers.

40. Gladden, "Problems of Evangelization—II."

41. Dike, "Religious Problem of the Country Town," 127.

42. Washington Gladden, "St. Louis Council," November 21, 1880, reel 16, Gladden Papers (microfilm).

43. James Henry Snowden, "What Is That to Thee?," March 18, 1900, folder 29, box 1, Snowden Papers.

44. Charles P. Anderson, *The Manifestation of Unity: A Charge to the Seventy-Fifth Annual Convention of the Church in the Diocese of Chicago* (Chicago: Gunthorp-Warren Printing, 1912), 19–21.

45. Henry Van Dyke, "Christian Unity the Basis of Church Union," December 31, 1911, folder 12, box 3, Henry Van Dyke Papers, Presbyterian Historical Society (Philadelphia, Pa.).

46. Washington Gladden, "The Christian League of Connecticut," *Century* 25 (November 1882): 55.

47. Ray Stannard Baker to Gladden, October 7, 1907, reel 8, Gladden Papers (microfilm).

48. Alfred Williams Anthony, "The New Interdenominationalism," *American Journal of Theology* 20 (October 1916): 495–96.

49. Gladden, "Christian League," 55.

50. The issues at stake were well articulated in a letter from Alfred Williams Anthony to C. M. Clark, April 29, 1916, Correspondence 1910–1919, 1935–1937 folder, box 3, series 3, Anthony Papers.

51. "Editorial Matter," *Outlook* 50 (October 6, 1894): 536.

52. Lyman Abbott, "The Test of Character," *Outlook* 56 (August 14, 1897): 940.

53. James Henry Snowden, "The Religious Ebb-Tide," February 12, 1899, folder 32, box 1, Snowden Papers.

54. Raymond Calkins, "Place of the Creed in the Life of the Church," in Newman Smyth and Williston Walker, eds., *Approaches toward Church Unity* (New Haven, Conn.: Yale University Press, 1919), 91.

55. Sanford, *Church Federation*, 35–36.

56. "Do We Wish It?" (undated), folder 8, box 75, FCC Records.

57. Semi-annual Report of the Executive Secretary of the Commission on the Federated Movements of the Federal Council of the Churches of Christ in America, June 26, 1916, folder 7, box 75, FCC Records.

58. Ibid.

59. Van Dyke, "Christian Unity."

60. See April 3, 1923 entry, booklet: Diary 1923, box 3, Charles H. Brent Papers, Library of Congress (Washington, D.C.).

61. "The War-Time Tasks of Every Church and Community: A Practical Manual of Work for All Churches during the War" (1917), p. 37, folder 10, box 75, FCC Records.

62. Minutes of the meeting of the General Committee on Army and Navy Chaplains, July 19, 1917, folder 8, box 70, FCC Records.

63. Minutes of the meeting of the General War-Time Commission of the Churches, September 20, 1917, folder 9, box 70, FCC Records; on the activities of the Federal Council of Churches during the war, see also John Piper, *The American Churches in World War I* (Athens: Ohio University Press, 1985).

64. "War-Time Tasks of Every Church and Community."

65. Minutes of the meeting of the Committee on Camp Neighborhoods, November 28, 1917, folder 8, box 70, FCC Records.

66. Minutes of the Committee on the Coordination of the Work about the Training Camps, August 17, 1917, folder 9, box 70, FCC Records.

67. Robert E. Speer, opening address of the meeting of the General War-Time Commission, February 22, 1918, p. 5, folder 1, box 70, FCC Records.

68. Theodore Roosevelt, *Fear God and Take Your Own Part* (New York: George H. Doran, 1916), 18–19.

69. Alfred Williams Anthony, *Kinds and Kindliness of Co-operation: Interdenominational Problems* (Lewiston: Interdenominational Commission of Maine, 1915), 5–6.

70. Ibid., 9.

71. Alfred Williams Anthony to Frederick Palladino, September 2, 1915, correspondence folder, box 3, Anthony Papers.

72. Alfred Williams Anthony, "Statement to the Maine Interdenominational Commission" (ca. 1916), Statement to the Commission by Its Secretary folder, box 3, Anthony Papers.

73. Francis J. McConnell, *Personal Christianity: Instruments and Ends in the Kingdom of God* (New York: Fleming H. Revell, 1914), 89.

74. Lyman Abbott, "Many Members One Body" (undated), folder 7, box 28, Lyman Abbott Papers, George Mitchell Special Collections, Bowdoin College Library (Brunswick, Me.).

75. Lyman Abbott, "A Reasonable Hope," delivered February 23, 1890, folder 3, box 26, Abbott Papers.

76. See Sanford, *Church Federation*, 64.

77. McConnell, *Personal Christianity*, 89–90.

78. George A. Gordon, "Is the Church an Incident or a Necessity?" (1920), George A. Gordon Sermons, 1896–1924, Old South Church Collection, Congregational Library (Boston, Mass.).

79. *Old South Record* 8 (April 1916), box 1, Old South Church Collection; George A. Gordon, "Contemporaries," in *Our Contemporaries*, Old South Ministers: George A. Gordon box, Old South Church Collection. For more on the relationship between religion and consumer culture, see R. Laurence Moore, *Selling God: American Religion in the Marketplace of Culture* (New York: Oxford University Press, 1994), especially 206–20; John M. Giggie and Diane Winston, "Hidden in Plain Sight: Religion and Urban Commercial Culture in Modern America," in Giggie and Winston, eds., *Faith in the Market: Religion and the Rise of Urban Commercial Culture* (New Brunswick, N.J.: Rutgers University Press, 2002), especially 1–5; and David Morgan, "Protestant Visual Culture and the Challenges of Urban America during the Progressive Era," ibid., especially 37–40.

80. "Notes and Queries," *Outlook* 58 (January 22, 1898): 247.

81. Suffolk South Association/Conference Records, 1822–1964; see entries for November 12, 1879, September 8, 1880, March 14, 1894, December 3, 1905, and January 10, 1906, Suffolk South Association Records, Congregational Library (Boston, Mass.).

82. "A Problem in Church Fellowship," *Outlook* 58 (January 1, 1898): 11–12.

83. Mark Benbow, *Leading Them to the Promised Land: Woodrow Wilson, Covenant Theology, and the Mexican Revolution, 1913–1915* (Kent, Ohio: Kent State University Press, 2010), 7; Andrew Preston, *Sword of the Spirit, Shield of the Faith: Religion in American War and Diplomacy* (New York: Alfred A. Knopf, 2012); on the religious experiences of soldiers, see Jonathan H. Ebel, *Faith in the Fight: Religion and the American Soldier in the Great War* (Princeton, N.J.: Princeton University Press, 2010).

84. Speer, opening address of the meeting of the General War-Time Commission; on anxieties about morality in the war zone more broadly, see Christopher Capozzola, *Uncle Sam Wants You: World War I and the Making of the Modern American Citizen* (New York: Oxford University Press, 2008), 117–43.

85. Minutes of the meeting of the Executive Committee of the General War-Time Commission, June 5, 1918, folder 10, box 70, FCC Records.

86. James Henry Snowden, "One Body in Christ," delivered August 13, 1893, folder 45, box 2, Snowden Papers.

87. John Henry Barrows, ed., *The World's Parliament of Religions*, vol. 1 (Chicago: Parliament Publishing, 1893), 11.

88. *The National Divorce Reform League—An Abstract of Its Annual Reports, October 1885* (Boston: National Divorce Reform League, 1885), 1; see also David Mislin, "'Against the Foes That Destroy the Family, Protestants and Catholics Can Stand Together': Divorce and Christian Ecumenism," in Andrew Preston, Bruce J. Schulman, and Julian E. Zelizer, eds., *Faithful Republic: Religion and Politics in Modern America* (Philadelphia: University of Pennsylvania Press, 2015).

89. John Ireland, *Intemperance and Law: Bishop Ireland in Buffalo*, frame 496, reel 3, John Ireland Papers (microfilm), Boston College Library (Chestnut Hill, Mass.; originals at Minnesota Historical Society, St. Paul, Minn.).

90. Ibid., frame 502. On Putnam, see J. N. Larned, *A History of Buffalo, Delineating the Evolution of the City*, vol. 2 (New York: Progress of the Empire State Company, 1911), 143.

91. Deirdre M. Moloney, *American Catholic Lay Groups and Transatlantic Social Reform in the Progressive Era* (Chapel Hill: University of North Carolina Press, 2002), 57, 66–67; John F. Quinn, *Father Mathew's Crusade: Temperance in Nineteenth-Century Ireland and Irish America* (Amherst: University of Massachusetts Press, 2002).

92. Frances E. Willard, *Woman and Temperance; or, The Work and Workers of the Woman's Christian Temperance Union* (Hartford, Conn.: Park Publishing, 1893), 396, 456.

93. "Strikes at Wall of Church Bigotry," clipping from the *Worcester Daily Telegram* (March 3, 1919), folder 19, box 10, FCC Records.

94. Theodore Roosevelt to Thomas O'Gorman, March 1, 1895, frame 507, reel 1, Ireland Papers (microfilm); John Ireland, *The Church and Modern Society: Lectures and Addresses* (1896; repr. Chicago: D. H. McBride, 1903), xxi.

95. On the history of Catholic schools and the tension between Catholics and public education, see Jay P. Dolan, *In Search of an American Catholicism: A History of Religion and Culture in Tension* (New York: Oxford University Press, 2002), 59–60; John T. McGreevy, *Catholicism and American Freedom: A History* (New York: W. W. Norton, 2003), 37–42.

96. On Protestant support, see Francis B. Wheeler to John Ireland, June 18, 1890, frames 193–94, reel 4, Ireland Papers (microfilm); see also McGreevy, *Catholicism and American Freedom*, 120–21.

97. George A. Coe, "The Reasons and the Functions of General Religious Education," in *Proceedings of the World's Congress of Arts and Sciences* (1904), folder 32, box 4, Coe Papers; Coe, "Religious Education as a Part of General Education," clipping from the *Proceedings of the Religious Education Association* (1903), folder 31, box 4, Coe Papers; on religion in late nineteenth century education, see Kraig Beyerlein, "Educational Elites and the Movement to Secularize Public Education: The Case of the National Education Association," in Christian D. Smith, ed., *The Secular Revolution: Power, Interests, and Conflicts in the Secularization of American Public Life* (Berkeley: University of California Press, 2003), especially 160–62, 166–67, 186–94; Warren Nord, *Religion and American Education* (Chapel Hill: University of North Carolina Press, 1995), 67–83.

98. Gladden, *Christian Pastor*, 467–70, 472.

99. "Strikes at Wall of Church Bigotry."

100. Charles Stelzle, "Proposals with Regard to the Labor Temple" (1911), folder 6, box 1, Labor Temple Records, Presbyterian Historical Society (Philadelphia, Pa.).

101. Description of the Work of the Labor Temple (undated), folder 4, box 1, Labor Temple Records; Henry Sloane Coffin to Jesse F. Forbes, December 13, 1920, folder 7, box 1, Labor Temple Records.

102. Worth M. Tippy, "Joint Committee on War Production Communities: Report on the Logging Camps of the Pacific Northwest, with Recommendations," folder 14, box 22, FCC Records.

103. "Social and Religious Conditions in Centers of Wartime Industries, Suggested Outline for Study and Organization," addendum to minutes of the meeting of the Special Workers for Centers of War-Time Industries, April 24, 1918, folder 14, box 22, FCC Records.

104. Report of the Joint Committee on War Production Communities to the Home Missions Council, January 14, 1919, p. 2, folder 14, box 22, FCC Records.

105. Minutes of a meeting of the Executive Committee of the G[eneral] W[ar-Time] C[ommission], November 21, 1917, folder 9, box 70, FCC Records.

106. Samuel Bushnell to Newman Smyth, December 20, 1917, folder 1, box 1, series 1, group 623, Smyth Papers.

107. William A. R. Goodwin to Charles H. Brent, December 1, 1917, December 1917 correspondence folder, box 14, Brent Papers. For more on wartime interfaith efforts, especially among chaplains in Europe, see Lee J. Levinger, *A Jewish Chaplain in France* (New York: Macmillan, 1922), 103–4, 137–38.

108. "The Church and the War," *Outlook* 118 (April 24, 1918): 664.

109. Minutes of the meeting of the Executive Committee of the General War-Time Commission of the Churches, March 6, 1918, folder 10, box 70, FCC Records.

110. On the Committee of Six's origins, see Raymond B. Fosdick to John J. Burke, November 3, 1917, folder 5, box 5, National Catholic War Council Records, Catholic University of America Archives (Washington, D.C.).

111. John J. Burke to Newton D. Baker, August 13, 1918, folder 3, box 5, National Catholic War Council Records.

112. Charles H. Brent to Newman Smyth, April 14, 1919, folder 7, box 1, series 1, Smyth Papers.

113. Charles H. Brent, "Unity," 1919 Sermon Notebook, box 27, Brent Papers.

114. Roy B. Guild to Ira G. McCormack, January 26, 1920, folder 13, box 75, FCC Records.

115. Robert E. Speer, *The War and the Religious Outlook* (New York: Association Press, 1919), 20.

116. William Adams Brown, "The Church of the Future: The Final Report of the Committee on the War and the Religious Outlook," p. 19, folder 11, box 22, Federal Council Records.

5. A LARGER VISION

1. Newman Smyth, "The Religious Principle in American Politics," July 2, 1876, folder 21, box 3, series 2, Newman Smyth Papers, Yale University Library Manuscripts and Archives (New Haven, Conn.).

2. Newman Smyth, "Extempore Speech concerning His Religious Experience" (1882), folder 18, box 3, series 2, Smyth Papers; on Smyth, see Gary Dorrien, *The Making of American Liberal Theology: Imagining Progressive Religion, 1805–1900* (Louisville, Ky.: Westminster John Knox Press, 2001), 282–90; William R. Hutchison, *The Modernist Impulse in American Protestantism* (Durham, N.C.: Duke University Press, 1992), 174–84; Peter G. Gowing, "Newman Smyth: New England Ecumenist" (ThD thesis, Boston University, 1960).

3. Newman Smyth, "Social Caesarism," May 30, 1886, folder 3, box 21, series 2, Smyth Papers.

4. Newman Smyth, *Passing Protestantism and Coming Catholicism* (New York: Charles Scribner's Sons, 1908), 33.

5. Newman Smyth to Charles H. Brent, December 20, 1921, folder 10, box 1, series 1, Smyth Papers.

6. Gail Hamilton, "Why I Am a Congregationalist," *North American Review* 144 (April 1887): 331.

7. Charles W. Shields, "The Social Problem of Church Unity," *Century* 40 (September 1890): 688; on the various meanings of the words, see William R. Hutchison, *The Modernist Impulse in American Protestantism*, 177–78.

8. Charles Augustus Briggs, *Whither? A Theological Question for the Times* (New York: Charles Scribner's Sons, 1889), 42, 269.

9. On Briggs's own religious evolution, see Mark S. Massa, "'Mediating Modernism': Charles Briggs, Catholic Modernism, and an Ecumenical 'Plot,'" *Harvard Theological Review* 81 (October 1988): 413–30.

10. Briggs, *Whither?*, 269.

11. Newman Smyth, *Passing Protestantism and Coming Catholicism*, 17–18.

12. John Ireland, *The Church and Modern Society*, vol. 1 (1896; repr. Chicago: D. H. McBride, 1903), 56, 74, 81–82.

13. W. C. Robinson, "The Attitude of the Educated Protestant Mind toward Catholic Truth," *Catholic World* 54 (February 1892): 646; on his participation in the Connecticut event, see "Editorial Notes," *Outlook* 50 (October 27, 1894): 659.

14. Washington Gladden, *Burning Questions of the Life That Now Is and of That Which Is to Come* (New York: Century, 1890), 232–33.

15. For various treatments of this moment in American Catholic history, see Robert D. Cross, *The Emergence of Liberal Catholicism in America* (Cambridge, Mass.: Harvard Uni-

versity Press, 1959); R. Scott Appleby, *"Church and Age Unite!": The Modernist Impulse in American Catholicism* (Notre Dame, Ind.: University of Notre Dame Press, 1992); Jay P. Dolan, *In Search of an American Catholicism: A History of Religion and Culture in Tension* (New York: Oxford University Press, 2002), 99–107.

16. Smyth, *Passing Protestantism and Coming Catholicism,* 190.

17. On the steps leading up to the condemnation of Americanism, see Dolan, *In Search of an American Catholicism,* 105–10; on John Ireland's views after the papal condemnation, see Neil T. Storch, "John Ireland's Americanism after 1899: The Argument from History," *Church History* 51 (December 1882): 434–44.

18. John Lancaster Spalding, *Religion, Agnosticism, and Education* (Chicago: A. C. McClurg, 1903), 204.

19. Roderick MacEachen to George A. Coe, Easter 1928, folder 3, box 1, George A. Coe Papers, Yale Divinity School Library (New Haven, Conn.). Though this letter is from two decades later, MacEachen was active during the time of the modernist controversy. Throughout his correspondence with Coe, which lasted throughout the 1920s, he repeatedly endorsed views of progressive religion. On Catholic modernists, see Appleby, *"Church and Age Unite!,"* 3–5.

20. Smyth, *Passing Protestantism and Coming Catholicism,* 40.

21. Charles Augustus Briggs, *Church Unity: Studies of Its Most Important Problems* (New York: Charles Scribner's Sons, 1909), 12, 438, 440.

22. MacEachen to Coe, Easter 1928.

23. Ibid., 12.

24. Briggs, *Church Unity,* 202.

25. Ibid., 174.

26. John Ireland, "Is the Papacy an Obstacle to the Reunion of Christendom?" *North American Review* 184 (April 1907): 708–9.

27. Newman Smyth to C. P. Anderson, November 28, 1917, folder 5, box 1, series 1, Smyth Papers.

28. John H. Barrows, ed., *The World's Parliament of Religions,* vol. 1 (Chicago: Parliament Publishing, 1893), 50; on Ainslie, see W. E. Garrison, "In Memoriam: Peter Ainslie," *Church History* 3 (June 1934): 154.

29. Charles P. Anderson, *The Work of the Church on Behalf of Unity: The Hale Memorial Sermon, 1917* (Milwaukee: Young Churchman, 1917), 19.

30. Chauncey Brewster to Newman Smyth, November 13, 1915, folder 11, box 1, series 1, Smyth Papers.

31. "The Lambeth Quadrilateral," reprinted in Newman Smyth and Williston Walker, eds., *Approaches toward Church Unity* (New Haven, Conn.: Yale University Press, 1919), 147.

32. Samuel McCrea Cavert, *The Christian Churches in the Ecumenical Movement, 1900–1968* (New York: Association Press, 1968), 28.

33. See Elias B. Sanford, ed., *Church Federation: Inter-church Conference on Federation* (New York: Fleming H. Revell, 1906), 46.

34. James Henry Snowden, "The New Theology," February 8, 1886, folder 102, box 4, James Henry Snowden Papers, Pittsburgh Theological Seminary Archive (Pittsburgh, Pa.).

35. See Philip Benedict, *Christ's Churches Purely Reformed: A Social History of Calvinism* (New Haven, Conn.: Yale University Press, 2002), 87–88.

36. For the initial proposal, see the letter from Arthur J. Gammack and Leon D. Bliss to Thomas F. Davis and the Commission on Church Unity of the Congregational Church of the United States, December 12, 1914, folder 18, box 1, series 1, Smyth Papers; "The Lenox Proposals," folder 29, box 4, series 2, Smyth Papers. On the trajectory of the proposal, see Thomas F. Davis to Newman Smyth, February 26, 1915, folder 18, box 1, series 1,

Smyth Papers; Smyth to C. P. Anderson, November 14, 1915, and November 26, 1915, folder 4, box 1, series 1, Smyth Papers; Raymond Calkins to Smyth, November 27, 1917, folder 16, box 1, series 1, Smyth Papers; see also Peter G. Gowing, "Newman Smyth and the Congregational-Episcopal Concordat," *Church History* 33 (June 1964): 178–79.

37. Newman Smyth to C. P. Anderson, November 14, 1915, and November 26, 1915, folder 4, box 1, series 1, Smyth Papers; on Trinity Church as a center of High Church Anglicanism, see E. Brooks Holifield, *Theology in America: Christian Thought from the Age of the Puritans to the Civil War* (New Haven, Conn.: Yale University Press, 2003), 234–38.

38. Robert W. Speer, Opening address at the meeting of the General War-Time Commission, February 22, 1918, p. 5, folder 10, box 70, Federal Council of the Churches of Christ in America (FCC) Records, Presbyterian Historical Society (Philadelphia, Pa.).

39. Peter Ainslie, *Towards Christian Unity* (Baltimore: Association for the Promotion of Christian Unity, 1918), 98.

40. See Smyth's proposal, quoted in Gowing, "Newman Smyth and the Congregational-Episcopal Concordat," 179.

41. Newman Smyth to Washington Gladden, December 3, 1917, reel 14, Washington Gladden Papers (microfilm), Harvard College Library (Cambridge, Mass.; originals at Ohio Historical Society, Columbus, Ohio).

42. George Gordon to Newman Smyth, December 4, 1917, folder 23, box 1, series 1, Smyth Papers.

43. Raymond Calkins to Newman Smyth, November 27, 1917, folder 16, box 1, series 1, Smyth Papers.

44. Charles P. Anderson, *The Manifestation of Unity* (Gardiner, Me.: Joint Commission for a World Conference on Faith and Order, 1913), 3; Anderson to Newman Smyth, January 18, 1918, folder 5, box 1, series 1, Smyth Papers.

45. Alfred Williams Anthony to Peter Ainslie, December 17, 1917, folder 1, box 1, series 1, Smyth Papers.

46. Clyde Armitage to Newman Smyth, January 16, 1918, folder 7, box 1, series 1, Smyth Papers.

47. Raymond Calkins to Newman Smyth, December 27, 1917, folder 16, box 1, series 1, Smyth Papers.

48. Brent conceded that this was something he was not able to do if he was under the authority of church leaders who did not share this view; Charles H. Brent to W. A. R. Goodwin, February 7, 1918, February 1918 folder, box 14, Charles Henry Brent Papers, Library of Congress (Washington, D.C.).

49. Charles H. Brent to Mrs. Monks, December 22, 1918, 1922 folder, box 16, Brent Papers.

50. Charles H. Brent to Newman Smyth, April 14, 1919, folder 10, box 1, series 1, Smyth Papers.

51. "Minutes of the Informal Conference with Chaplain Brent at the Office of the Federal Council," February 14, 1919, folder 12, box 70, FCC Records.

52. Charles H. Brent to Cameron J. Davis, August 10, 1918, August 1918 folder, box 15, Brent Papers.

53. Committee on the War and the Religious Outlook, *The Local Church after the War* (New York: Association Press, 1920), 9–10.

54. Ainslie, *Towards Christian Unity*, 89–90.

55. Charles H. Brent to Charles Fiske, October 23, 1925, 1925 folder, box 16, Brent Papers.

56. Preliminary outline, "The Message and Method of the Christian Church for the New Era; or, An Adequate Message and Method for Inter-church Cooperation in the New Era," folder 9, box 75, FCC Records.

57. Charles H. Brent to Newman Smyth, April 14, 1919, folder 10, box 1, series 1, Smyth Papers.

58. William Adams Brown, "The Church Facing the Future: The Final Report of the Committee on the War and the Religious Outlook," p. 19, folder 11, box 22, FCC Records.

59. Barrows, *World's Parliament of Religions,* 1:5–6.

60. Henry Van Dyke, "Christian Unity the Basis of Church Union," December 31, 1911, folder 12, box 3, Henry Van Dyke Papers, Presbyterian Historical Society (Philadelphia, Pa.).

61. Charles H. Brent, sermon on Genesis 1:2–3 (1919), sermon notes 1918, box 27, Brent Papers.

62. Charles H. Brent, address on the USS *George Washington,* May 2, 1919, sermon notes 1919, box 27, Brent Papers.

63. Robert H. Gardiner to Charles H. Brent, November 15, 1918, November 1918 folder, box 16, Brent Papers.

64. Ainslie, *Towards Christian Unity,* 98.

65. "The Message and Method of the Christian Church."

66. Charles H. Brent to Unknown, January 21, 1918, January 1918 folder, box 14, Brent Papers.

67. "Proposals for an Approach toward Unity by a Conference of Episcopalians and Congregationalists," reprinted in Smyth and Walker, *Approaches toward Church Unity,* 158.

68. For the full text, see ibid., 163–65.

69. Newman Smyth to Charles H. Brent, November 23, 1923, folder 10, box 1, series 1, Smyth Papers.

70. Diary of Charles H. Brent, entry for May 20, 1923, box 3, Brent Papers.

71. Nehemiah Boynton, "The Lausanne Conference," December 18, 1926, folder 13, box 12, FCC Records.

72. Charles H. Brent to Arthur C. A. Hall, August 30, 1927, July–September 1927 folder, box 17, Brent Papers; see also Benny Kraut, "A Wary Collaboration: Jews, Catholics, and the Protestant Goodwill Movement," in William R. Hutchison, ed., *Between the Times: The Travails of the Protestant Establishment in America, 1900–1960* (Cambridge: Cambridge University Press, 1989), 215.

73. James Henry Snowden, "One Body in Christ," August 13, 1893, folder 45, box 2, Snowden Papers.

74. William L. Mudge to George Frederick Wells, May 2, 1911, folder 12, box 11, FCC Records.

75. Briggs, *Christian Unity,* 16.

76. Briggs, *Whither?,* 251; Newman Smyth, "Vital Principles of Church Development," in Smyth and Walker, *Approaches toward Church Unity,* 48–49.

77. Minutes of a conference of the Committee on the War and the Religious Outlook's Sub-committee on Principles of Christian Unity, July 12–13, 1920, p. 4, folder 10, box 22, FCC Records.

78. Snowden, "One Body in Christ."

79. Ibid.

80. Lyman Abbott, "The Spirit in the Message," October 20, 1889, folder 2, box 26, Lyman Abbott Papers, George Mitchell Special Collections, Bowdoin College Library (Brunswick, Me.); Lyman Abbott, "Mr. Rockefeller's Contribution to Christian Union," *Outlook* 117 (December 19, 1917): 636.

81. George A. Gordon, "Is the Church an Incident or a Necessity?" (1920), George A. Gordon Sermons, 1896–1924, Old South Church Collection, Congregational Library (Boston, Mass.).

82. Snowden, "One Body in Christ."
83. Brown, "The Church Facing the Future," 19.
84. Ainslie, Towards Christian Unity, 80.

6. PROCLAIMING COMMON GROUND

1. "Keynote of Dinner Is Religious Amity," *New York Times* (February 24, 1926): 19; "Statement from the committee's founding documents," quoted in "Committee on Goodwill between Jews and Christians, Federal Council of the Churches of Christ in America," October 26, 1928, folder 18, box 10, Federal Council of the Churches of Christ in America (FCC) Records, Presbyterian Historical Society (Philadelphia, Pa.); on Cadman's chaplaincy, see Cliff Putney, *Muscular Christianity: Manhood and Sports in Protestant America, 1880–1920* (Cambridge, Mass.: Harvard University Press, 2001), 185.

2. Alfred Williams Anthony, "The Jewish Problem," clipping from the *Christian Work* (October 4, 1924), box 6, Alfred Williams Anthony Papers, Edmund S. Muskie Archives and Special Collections Library, Bates College (Lewiston, Me.).

3. William McKibbin to David Philipson, November 25, 1907, and Philipson to McKibbin, November 28, 1907, folder 11, box 1, series D, David Philipson Papers, Jacob Rader Marcus Center of the American Jewish Archives (Cincinnati, Ohio).

4. "Program of the Algonquin Club," November 17, 1927, R. H. Stafford box, Old South Church Collection, Congregational Library (Boston, Mass.).

5. Abram Simon, "Jew and Christian! Can They Understand Each Other?" delivered November 19, 1922, folder 2, box 1, Abram Simon Papers, Jacob Rader Marcus Center of the American Jewish Archives (Cincinnati, Ohio); on pulpit exchanges between Protestants and Jews, see also Lawrence G. Charap, "Imperceptibly We Convert Another: Jewish-Protestant Dialogue in America, 1883–1915" (PhD diss., Brown University, 2000).

6. Jonathan C. Day, "A Better Fraternalism," *Hebrew Standard* 72 (July 5, 1918): 9.

7. A number of excellent studies of the goodwill movement have already been written, though most fail to connect it to a desire among Protestants to embrace pluralism that predated the 1920s; see Benny Kraut, "A Wary Collaboration: Jews, Catholics, and the Protestant Goodwill Movement," in William R. Hutchison, ed., *Between the Times: The Travail of the Protestant Establishment in America, 1900–1960* (Cambridge: Cambridge University Press, 1989), 193–230; Benny Kraut, "Towards the Establishment of the National Conference of Christians and Jews: The Tenuous Road to Religious Goodwill in the 1920s," *American Jewish History* 77 (1988): 388–412; see also Kevin M. Schultz, *Tri-faith America: How Catholics and Jews Held Postwar America to Its Protestant Promise* (New York: Oxford University Press, 2011), 29–31.

8. *Tolerance* (KKK pamphlet), folder 9, box 12, FCC Records; for various accounts of anti-Semitism in the 1920s, see Egal Feldman, *Dual Destinies: The Jewish Encounter with Protestant America* (Urbana: University of Illinois Press, 1990), 178–84; Jonathan D. Sarna, *American Judaism: A History* (New Haven, Conn.: Yale University Press, 2004), 214–22; Leonard Dinnerstein, *Antisemitism in America* (New York: Oxford University Press, 1994), especially chap. 5.

9. Abram Simon, "Let Us Understand Each Other," clipping from the *Congressional Record* (1924), Simon folder 2, box 1, Simon Papers.

10. Leighton Parks, *The Crisis of the Churches* (New York: Charles Scribner's Sons, 1922), 255; on the linking of Jews and Bolshevism, see Dinnerstein, *Antisemitism in America*, 79–80.

11. Henry Van Dyke, "The World Needs Christmas," December 24, 1922, folder 15, box 3, Henry Van Dyke Papers, Presbyterian Historical Society (Philadelphia, Pa.).

12. See "The Religious Issues," *Christian Century* 45 (October 18, 1928): 1252. See also Elesha J. Coffman, *The Christian Century and the Rise of the Protestant Mainline* (New York: Oxford University Press, 2013), 80–87.

13. Day, "Better Fraternalism," 9.

14. Charles H. Brent to Mrs. John Markoe, February 9, 1920, folder: 1920, box 16, Charles Henry Brent Papers, Library of Congress (Washington, D.C.).

15. Alfred Williams Anthony, "The Cultivation of Good Will," clipping from the *Jewish Tribune* (October 5, 1923), scrapbooks collection, box 6, series 6, Anthony Papers.

16. Henry Van Dyke, "In Defense of Religious Liberty" (1928), folder 14, box 3, Van Dyke Papers.

17. "Ku Klux Klan Disowned by the Churches," resolution adopted September 29, 1922, folder 9, box 12, FCC Records.

18. Joseph Silverman to Samuel McCrea Cavert, January 11, 1923, and Cavert to Silverman, January 15, 1923, folder 9, box 12, FCC Records.

19. Samuel McCrea Cavert to Howard Agnew Johnson, September 15, 1922, folder 9, box 12, FCC Records.

20. For earlier interpretations of these organizations, see Kraut, "Wary Collaboration," 193–230; and Kraut, "Towards the Establishment of the National Conference of Christians and Jews," 388–412.

21. Anthony, "Cultivation of Good Will."

22. Abram Simon, "The Function of the Liberal Movement," March 25, 1923, folder 1, box 1, Simon Papers.

23. Henry Van Dyke, untitled address, May 25, 1919, folder 15, box 3, Van Dyke Papers.

24. Abram Simon, "Fellowship of Faiths: Judaism on Peace and Brotherhood" (undated), box 1, folder 1, Simon Papers.

25. David Philipson, "Humanity's Melting Pot," broadcast June 7, 1926, folder 8, box 4, series D, Philipson Papers.

26. Vivian G. Simmons, "The Jewish Soldier's Religion," Hebrew Standard 72 (December 6, 1918): 12.

27. Lee J. Levinger, *A Jewish Chaplain in France* (New York: Macmillan, 1922), 137.

28. See "The Goodwill Movement Tested," press release, June 7, 1929, folder 18, box 14, series A, Central Conference of American Rabbis Records (CCAR), Jacob Rader Marcus Center of the American Jewish Archives (Cincinnati, Ohio). See also Kraut, "Wary Collaboration," 204.

29. "Committee on Goodwill between Jews and Christians, Federal Council of the Churches of Christ in America."

30. See the reprinting of the original "setup and plans of the Committee," reprinted in ibid.

31. The minutes of the first meeting of the joint committee appeared as an addendum to "The Goodwill Movement Tested."

32. "Committee on Goodwill between Jews and Christians" (October 26, 1928).

33. See the untitled document on the founding of the National Conference of Jews and Christians, folder 13, box 2, series B, Philipson Papers.

34. Abram Simon, "Message of the President, Central Conference of American Rabbis," October 20, 1925, folder 1, box 1, Simon Papers.

35. Minutes of the Committee on Goodwill between Christians and Jews, June 8, 1925, folder 13, box 2, series B, Philipson Papers.

36. Agenda for the meeting of the Committee on Goodwill between Jews and Christians, January 27, 1926, folder 18, box 10, FCC Records.

37. "Committee on Goodwill between Jews and Christians" (October 26, 1928).

38. Ibid.

39. Simon, "Message of the President" (1925).

40. "Tentative Program, Federal Council's Committee on Goodwill between Jews and Christians," September 1928, folder 13, box 2, series B, Philipson Papers.

41. "Agenda for the Meeting of the Committee on Goodwill," January 27, 1926.

42. See attachment to O. D. Foster to David Philipson, December 3, 1926, folder 5, box 1, series A, Philipson Papers.

43. "[Suggestions on] the American Association on Religion in Universities and Colleges," enclosure with Foster to Philipson, December 3, 1926.

44. Ibid.

45. Ibid.

46. See the eventual letterhead, such as it appeared on O. D. Foster's letter to David Philipson, October 23, 1928, folder 5, box 1, series A, Philipson Papers; on Catholic participation, see Abram Simon to David Philipson, May 12, 1927, folder 19, box 1, series A, Philipson Papers.

47. "[Suggestions on] the American Association on Religion."

48. These goals appeared in the minutes of the gathering of the representatives of various religious communities in Des Moines, held May 12, 1925, and were enclosed with Eugene Mannheimer to David Philipson, August 18, 1926, folder 13, box 1, series A, Philipson Papers.

49. O. D. Foster to David Philipson, July 15, 1926, folder 5, box 1, series A, Philipson Papers; on the School of Religion, see also D. G. Hart, *The University Gets Religion: Religious Studies in American Higher Education* (Baltimore: Johns Hopkins University Press, 1999), 84–87.

50. Mannheimer to Philipson, May 25, 1925.

51. Memoranda on visits to universities, spring 1927, attached to American Association on Religion in Colleges and Universities agenda, May 11, 1927, meeting, folder 7, box 2, series B, Philipson Papers.

52. Isidore Singer, "National and Prophetic Judaism at the Bar of Jewish Public Opinion," June 23, 1927, folder 2, box 1, Isidore Singer Papers, Jacob Rader Marcus Center of the American Jewish Archives (Cincinnati, Ohio).

53. Isidore Singer, "A Plea for the Creation of a Federation of Synagogues and a School of the Prophets," April 4, 1930, folder 2, box 1, Singer Papers.

54. Isidore Singer, *A Religion of Truth, Justice and Peace: A Challenge to Church and Synagogue to Lead in the Realization of the Social and Peace Gospel of the Hebrew Prophets* (New York: Amos Society, 1924), 120.

55. Isidore Singer, "The Pittsburgh Amos Message," March 28, 1928, in "Theology at the Crossroads: A Few Outspoken Messages on the Present Religious Crisis Addressed to Church and Synagogue," folder 2, box 1, Singer Papers.

56. Singer, *Religion of Truth, Justice and Peace*, 113–15.

57. Newman Smyth, *Christian Ethics* (New York: Charles Scribner's Sons, 1892), 9.

58. Walter Rauschenbusch, *Christianity and the Social Crisis* (New York: Macmillan, 1907), 3.

59. Francis J. McConnell, *Personal Christianity: Instruments and Ends in the Kingdom of God* (New York: Fleming H. Revell, 1914), 63–64; McConnell, *The Increase of Faith: Some Present-Day Aids to Belief* (New York: Eaton and Mains, 1912), 185–86.

60. Isidore Singer, "A Jewish Christmas Message to the Gentiles," December 22, 1926, folder 2, box 1, Singer Papers.

61. Isidore Singer, "A Jewish Christmas Message to the Gentiles," December 21, 1927, folder 2, box 1, Singer Papers.

62. Alfred Williams Anthony commentary on Singer's Christmas Message, printed in Singer, *Theology at the Crossroads*.

63. Peter Ainslie to Isidore Singer, February 3, 1923, folder 1, box 1, Singer Papers; Singer, *Religion of Truth, Justice and Peace*, 289, 298; the names of various academic leaders appeared on the Amos Society letterhead.

64. Abram Simon, "Message of the President, Central Conference of American Rabbis," October 20, 1925, folder 1, box 1, Simon Papers.

65. Everett R. Clinchy to Boris D. Bogen, January 6, 1929, folder 13, box 2, series B, Philipson Papers.

66. Minutes of the Executive Board of the National Conference of Christians and Jews, January 1, 1928, folder 11, box 15, FCC Records.

67. Enclosure in Max J. Kohler to H. G. Enelow, January 14, 1929, folder 13, box 14, series A, CCAR Papers.

68. Thomas B. Appleget to O. D. Foster, July 15, 1926 (attached to O. D. Foster to David Philipson, July 21, 1926), folder 5, box 1, series A, Philipson Papers.

69. W. Douglas Mackenzie's commentary on Singer's Christmas Message, printed in Singer, *Theology at the Crossroads*; Simon, "Message of the President, Central Conference of American Rabbis" (1925).

70. Kraut, "Wary Collaboration," 209.

71. Anthony, "Cultivation of Good Will."

72. See Clifton Harby Levy, "A Reply to Dr. Anthony," *Jewish Tribune* (October 5, 1923), clipping in box 6, Anthony Papers; "Bulletin of the Information Service of the Department of Research and Education of the Federal Council," no. 5 (May 8, 1926), folder 18, box 10, FCC Records.

73. Louis Marshall to Alfred Williams Anthony, June 10, 1929, reprinted in "The Goodwill Movement Tested," folder 18, box 14, series A, CCAR Papers.

74. Alfred Williams Anthony to Louis Marshall, June 17, 1929, ibid.

75. Louis Marshall to H. G. Enelow, June 20, 1929, folder 18, box 14, series A, CCAR Papers.

76. John Milton Moore to Isidore Singer, September 20, 1929, folder 4, box 1, Singer Papers.

77. Isidore Singer to various, September 10, 1929, folder 1, box 1, Singer Papers.

78. J. Alexander Bays to Isidore Singer, September 26, 1929, and Wallace H. Finch to Singer, September 22, 1929, folder 3, box 1, Singer Papers.

79. Robert A. Ashworth to Isidore Singer, September 29, 1929, folder 2, box 1, Singer Papers; Peter Ainslie to Singer, September 21, 1929, folder 4, box 1, Singer Papers.

80. Minutes of the meeting of the Committee on Goodwill between Jews and Christians, February 21, 1930, folder 18, box 10, FCC Records.

81. Abram Simon, "American Judaism in the Making," January 18, 1924, folder 1, box 1, Simon Papers.

82. Ralph Luker, *The Social Gospel in Black and White: American Racial Reform, 1885–1914* (Chapel Hill: University of North Carolina Press, 1991), 74–78, 108–14, 134–40, 240.

83. Charles S. Macfarland, "The Federal Council, Its Plans, Purposes, and Field of Service," folder 3, box 13, FCC Records.

84. "Suggestions for an Americanization Campaign through the Churches," folder 15, box 3, FCC Records.

85. Van Dyke, "World Needs Christmas."

86. Anthony, "Cultivation of Good Will."

87. Henry P. Fry to Samuel McCrea Cavert, April 27, 1923, folder 9, box 12, FCC Records.

88. Agenda for the meeting of the Committee on Goodwill, January 7, 1926.

89. Ibid.

90. Minutes of the meeting of the Special Committee for the Protection of the Rights of Religious Minorities, April 7, 1920, folder 18, box 18, FCC Records.

91. Minutes of the American Committee on Religious Rights and Minorities, June 7, 1929, ibid.

92. Minutes of the meeting of the American Committee on the Rights of Religious Minorities, January 27, 1927, folder 18, box 18, FCC Records.

93. American Committee on the Rights of Religious Minorities, June 7, 1929.

94. Harry Schneiderman to Isidore Singer, December 23, 1934, folder 3, box 2, Singer Papers.

95. David Philipson, "The Jewish Never Say Die Spirit," April 18, 1935, folder 10, box 4, series D, Philipson Papers.

96. Schultz, *Tri-faith America*, 32–33, 35–41.

EPILOGUE

1. Elise D. Gordon, "Some Recollections of Dr. Gordon," April 2, 1950, George A. Gordon box, Old South Church Collection, Congregational Library (Boston, Mass.).

2. The classic articulation of the new understanding of pluralism in the 1950s was Will Herberg, *Protestant-Catholic-Jew: An Essay in American Religious Sociology* (Garden City, N.Y.: Doubleday, 1955); see also Mark Silk, *Spiritual Politics: Religion and America since World War II* (New York: Simon and Schuster, 1988), especially chap. 2; Kevin M. Schultz, *Tri-faith America: How Catholics and Jews Held Postwar America to Its Protestant Promise* (New York: Oxford University Press, 2011).

3. George A. Coe to Dr. Kilgore, June 14, 1927, folder 1, box 1, series 1, George A. Coe Papers, Yale Divinity School Library (New Haven, Conn.).

4. Willard S. Bass to Alfred Williams Anthony, April 20, 1935, Correspondence 1935–1937 folder, box 3, Alfred William Anthony Papers, Edmund S. Muskie Archives and Special Collections Library, Bates College (Lewiston, Me.).

5. Robert S. Lynd and Helen Merrell Lynd, *Middletown: A Study in Contemporary Culture* (New York: Harcourt, Brace, 1929), 333–34.

6. Walter W. Reid to Isidore Singer, May 1, 1933, folder 7, box 1, Isidore Singer Papers, Jacob Rader Marcus Center of the American Jewish Archives (Cincinnati, Ohio).

7. See David A. Hollinger, *After Cloven Tongues of Fire: Protestant Liberalism in Modern American History* (Princeton, N.J.: Princeton University Press, 2013), 20–49.

Selected Bibliography

Note: Full citations for articles in periodicals listed under "Primary Source Periodicals" are given in the notes only.

MANUSCRIPT COLLECTIONS

Boston, Massachusetts

THE CONGREGATIONAL LIBRARY AND ARCHIVES
    First Congregational Church of Freeport, Maine, Records
    First Congregational Church of Waucoma, Iowa, Records
    Massachusetts Council of Churches Records
    Old South Church Collection
    Suffolk South Association Records

Brunswick, Maine

GEORGE MITCHELL SPECIAL COLLECTIONS, BOWDOIN COLLEGE LIBRARY
    Lyman Abbott Papers

Cambridge, Massachusetts

HARVARD COLLEGE LIBRARY
    Robert Ingersoll Papers (microfilm; originals at the Library of Congress, Washington, D.C.)
    Washington Gladden Papers (microfilm; originals at Ohio Historical Society, Columbus, Ohio)

Chestnut Hill, Massachusetts

BOSTON COLLEGE LIBRARY
    John Ireland Papers (microfilm; originals at Minnesota Historical Society, St. Paul, Minn.)

Cincinnati, Ohio

THE JACOB RADER MARCUS CENTER OF THE AMERICAN JEWISH ARCHIVES
    Abram Simon Papers
    Central Conference of American Rabbis Records
    David Philipson Papers
    Isidore Singer Papers

Lewiston, Maine

EDMUND S. MUSKIE ARCHIVES AND SPECIAL COLLECTIONS LIBRARY, BATES COLLEGE
    Alfred Williams Anthony Papers

New Haven, Connecticut
YALE DIVINITY SCHOOL LIBRARY
    George A. Coe Papers

YALE UNIVERSITY LIBRARY MANUSCRIPTS AND ARCHIVES
    Newman Smyth Papers

Ossining, New York
MARYKNOLL MISSION ARCHIVE
    James A. Walsh Papers

Philadelphia, Pennsylvania
PRESBYTERIAN HISTORICAL SOCIETY
    Federal Council of the Churches of Christ in America Records
    Henry Van Dyke Papers
    Labor Temple Records

Pittsburgh, Pennsylvania
PITTSBURGH THEOLOGICAL SEMINARY ARCHIVE
    James Henry Snowden Papers

Washington, D.C.
CATHOLIC UNIVERSITY OF AMERICA ARCHIVES
    National Catholic War Council Records

LIBRARY OF CONGRESS
    Charles Henry Brent Papers

PRIMARY SOURCE PERIODICALS

American Journal of Sociology
American Journal of Theology
Andover Review
Catholic World
Century
The Congregationalist
Hebrew Standard
Methodist Review
The New Englander
New York Times
North American Review
Outlook
The Princeton Review

PUBLISHED PRIMARY SOURCES

Abbott, Lyman. *America in the Making*. New Haven, Conn.: Yale University Press, 1911.
———. *The Christian Ministry*. Boston: Houghton Mifflin, 1905.
———. *In Aid of Faith*. New York: E. P. Dutton, 1886.
———. *Jesus of Nazareth: His Life and His Teachings*. New York: Harper and Brothers, 1869.

Ainslie, Peter. *Towards a Christian Unity*. Baltimore: Association for the Promotion of Christian Unity, 1918.

Anderson, Charles P. *The Manifestation of Unity*. Gardiner, ME: Joint Commission for a World Conference on Faith and Order, 1913.

———. *The Manifestation of Unity: A Charge to the Seventy-Fifth Annual Convention of the Church in the Diocese of Chicago*. Chicago: Gunthorp-Warren Printing, 1912.

———. *The Work of the Church on Behalf of Unity: The Hale Memorial Sermon, 1917*. Milwaukee: Young Churchman, 1917.

Anthony, Alfred Williams. *Kinds and Kindliness of Co-operation: Interdenominational Problems*. Lewiston: Interdenominational Commission of Maine, 1915.

Augustine. *Confessions*. London: Penguin Books, 1961.

Barrows, John Henry. *The Christian Conquest of Asia: Studies and Personal Reflections of Oriental Religions*. New York: Charles Scribner's Sons, 1899.

———. *Christianity the World-Religion: Lectures Delivered in India and Japan*. Chicago: A. C. McClurg, 1897.

———. *I Believe in God the Father Almighty*. New York: Fleming H. Revell, 1892.

———. *A World-Pilgrimage*. Chicago: A. C. McClurg, 1897.

———, ed. *The World's Parliament of Religions*. 2 vols. Chicago: Parliament Publishing, 1893.

Beecher, Henry Ward. *Sermons*. London: J. Heaton and Son, 1864.

Bradford, Amory Howe. *Spirit and Life: Thoughts for Today*. 2nd ed. New York: Fords, Howard and Hurlbert, 1892.

Brent, Charles H. *With God in the World: A Series of Papers*. New York: Longmans, Green, 1899.

Briggs, Charles Augustus. *Church Unity: Studies of Its Most Important Problems*. New York: Charles Scribner's Sons, 1909.

———. *Whither? A Theological Question for the Times*. New York: Charles Scribner's Sons, 1889.

Brown, William Adams. *The Essence of Christianity: A Study in the History of Definition*. New York: Charles Scribner's Sons, 1902.

Burgess, G. A., and J. T. Ward. *Free Baptist Cyclopaedia*. Chicago: Free Baptist Cyclopaedia, 1889.

Bushnell, Horace. *Christ and His Salvation: In Sermons Variously Related Thereto*. 3rd ed. New York: Charles Scribner, 1865.

———. *Sermons on Living Subjects*. New York: Scribner, Armstrong, 1872.

———. *Views of Christian Nurture, and of Subjects Adjacent Thereto*. Hartford, Conn.: Edwin Hunt, 1847.

Circular of Information: The Interdenominational Commission of Maine. Lewiston: Maine Interdenominational Commission, 1913.

Coe, George A. *The Religion of a Mature Mind*. Chicago: Fleming H. Revell, 1902.

———. *The Spiritual Life: Studies in the Science of Religion*. New York: Eaton and Mains, 1900.

Committee on the War and the Religious Outlook. *The Local Church After the War*. New York: Association Press, 1920.

Dodge, H. Augusta, ed. *Gail Hamilton's Life in Letters*. Vol. 1. 1896. Reprint, Boston: Lee and Shepard, 1901.

Frederic, Harold. *The Damnation of Theron Ware; or, Illumination*. New York: Stone and Kimball, 1896.

Gladden, Washington. *Burning Questions of the Life That Now Is and That Which Is to Come*. New York: Century, 1890.

———. *The Christian Pastor and the Working Church*. New York: Charles Scribner's Sons, 1898.

——. *Recollections*. Boston: Houghton Mifflin, 1909.
——. *Social Facts and Forces*. New York: G. P. Putnam, 1897.
——. *Tools and the Man: Property and Industry under the Christian Law*. Boston: Houghton Mifflin, 1893.
Gordon, George A. *The Christ of To-day*. Boston: Houghton Mifflin, 1895.
——. "Robert Elsmere." Boston: Old South Church, 1888.
Hamilton, Gail. *Sermons to the Clergy*. Boston: William F. Gill, 1876.
Herberg, Will. *Protestant-Catholic-Jew: An Essay in American Religious Sociology*. Garden City, N.Y.: Doubleday, 1955.
Hodges, George. *Faith and Social Service: Eight Lectures Delivered before the Lowell Institute*. 4th ed. New York: Thomas Whittaker, 1896.
Ingersoll, Robert G. *The Works of Robert G. Ingersoll:Lectures*. New York: C. P. Farrell, 1900.
Ireland, John. *The Church and Modern Society: Lectures and Addresses*. 1896. Reprint, Chicago: D. H. McBride, 1903.
James, William. *The Varieties of Religious Experience: A Study in Human Nature*. New York: Modern Library, 1902.
——. *The Will to Believe and Other Essays in Popular Philosophy*. New York: Longmans, Green, 1897.
Kohler, Kaufmann. *Jewish Theology: Systematically and Historically Considered*. New York: Macmillan, 1918.
——. *A Living Faith: Selected Sermons and Addresses from the Literary Remains of Dr. Kaufmann Kolher*. Edited by Samuel S. Cohen. Cincinnati: Hebrew Union College Press, 1948.
Larned, J. N. *A History of Buffalo, Delineating the Evolution of the City*. Vol. 2. New York: Progress of the Empire State, 1911.
Levinger, Lee J. *A Jewish Chaplain in France*. New York: Macmillan, 1922.
Lynd, Robert S., and Helen Merrell Lynd. *Middletown: A Study in Contemporary Culture*. New York: Harcourt, Brace, 1929.
Mabie, Hamilton Wright. *The Life of the Spirit*. New York: Dodd, Mead, 1899.
——. *My Study Fire*. New York: Dodd, Mead, 1890.
McConnell, Francis J. *The Increase of Faith: Some Present-Day Aids to Belief*. New York: Eaton and Mains, 1912.
——. *Personal Christianity: Instruments and Ends in the Kingdom of God*. New York: Fleming H. Revell, 1914.
Munger, Theodore T. *The Freedom of Faith*. Boston: Houghton Mifflin, 1883.
The National Divorce Reform League—An Abstract of Its Annual Reports, October 1885. Boston: National Divorce Reform League, 1885.
Paine, Thomas. *The Age of Reason, Part the Second*. 1795. Reprint, London: R. Carlile, 1818.
Parks, Leighton. *The Crisis of the Churches*. New York: Charles Scribner's Sons, 1922.
——. *His Star in the East: A Study in the Early Aryan Religions*. Boston: Houghton Mifflin, 1887.
——. *Moral Leadership and Other Sermons*. New York: Charles Scribner's Sons, 1914.
Philipson, David. *My Life as an American Jew*. Cincinnati: John G. Kidd and Son, 1941.
Prentiss, Elizabeth. *Stepping Heavenward*. New York: Anson D. F. Randolph, 1869.
Rauschenbusch, Walter. *Christianity and the Social Crisis*. New York: Macmillan, 1907.
——. *A Theology for the Social Gospel*. New York: Macmillan, 1917.
Roosevelt, Theodore. *American Ideals and Other Essays, Social and Political*. New York: G. P Putnam's Sons, 1897.
——. *American in Religion*. Chicago: Blakely-Onswald, 1908.

———. *Fear God and Take Your Own Part*. New York: George H. Doran, 1916.
Sanford, Elias B., ed. *Church Federation: Inter-church Conference on Federation*. New York: Fleming H. Revell, 1906.
Singer, Isidore. *A Religion of Truth, Justice and Peace: A Challenge to Church and Synagogue to Lead in the Realization of the Social and Peace Gospel of the Hebrew Prophets*. New York: Amos Society, 1924.
Smyth, Newman. *Christian Ethics*. New York: Charles Scribner's Sons, 1892.
———. *Old Faiths in New Life*. New York: Charles Scribner's Sons, 1879.
———. *Passing Protestantism and Coming Catholicism*. New York: Charles Scribner's Sons, 1908.
Smyth, Newman, and Williston Walker, eds. *Approaches toward Church Unity*. New Haven, Conn.: Yale University Press, 1919.
Spalding, John Lancaster. *Education and the Higher Life*. 1890. Reprint, Chicago: A. C. McClurg, 1900.
———. *Lectures and Discourses*. New York: Catholic Publication Society, 1882.
———. *Religion, Agnosticism, and Education*. Chicago: A. C. McClurg, 1903.
Speer, Robert E. *The War and the Religious Outlook*. New York: Association Press, 1919.
Spencer, Herbert. *First Principles*. London: Williams and Norgate, 1862.
Starbuck, Edwin Diller. *The Psychology of Religion: An Empirical Study of the Growth of Religious Consciousness*. London: Walter Scott, 1899.
Ward, Mrs. Humphry. *Robert Elsmere*. London: Smith, Elder, 1888.
Willard, Frances E. *Woman and Temperance; or, The Work and Workers of the Woman's Christian Temperance Union*. Hartford, Conn.: Park Publishing, 1893.

SECONDARY SOURCES

Abzug, Robert A. *Cosmos Crumbling: American Reform and the Antebellum Imagination*. New York: Oxford University Press, 1994.
Albanese, Catherine L. *A Republic of Mind and Spirit: A Cultural History of American Metaphysical Religion*. New Haven, Conn.: Yale University Press, 2007.
Anderson, Robert Mapes. *Vision of the Disinherited: The Making of American Pentecostalism*. New York: Oxford University Press, 1979.
Appleby, R. Scott. *"Church and Age Unite!": The Modernist Impulse in American Catholicism*. Notre Dame, Ind.: University of Notre Dame Press, 1992.
Beckert, Sven. *The Monied Metropolis: New York City and the Consolidation of the American Bourgeoisie, 1850–1896*. Cambridge: Cambridge University Press, 2001.
Bederman, Gail. *Manliness and Civilization: A Cultural History of Gender and Race in the United States, 1880–1917*. Chicago: University of Chicago Press, 1995.
Benbow, Mark. *Leading Them to the Promised Land: Woodrow Wilson, Covenant Theology, and the Mexican Revolution, 1913–1915*. Kent, Ohio: Kent State University Press, 2010.
Benedict, Philip. *Christ's Churches Purely Reformed: A Social History of Calvinism*. New Haven, Conn.: Yale University Press, 2002.
Beneke, Chris. *Beyond Toleration: The Religious Origins of American Pluralism*. New York: Oxford University Press, 2006.
Bodnar, John. *The Transplanted: A History of Immigrants in Urban America*. Bloomington: Indiana University Press, 1985.
Bowman, Matthew. "Antirevivalism and Its Discontents: Liberal Evangelicalism, the American City, and the Sunday School, 1900–1929." *Religion and American Culture* 24 (2014): 262–90.
Boyer, Paul S. *Urban Masses and Moral Order in America, 1820–1920*. Cambridge, Mass.: Harvard University Press, 1978.

SELECTED BIBLIOGRAPHY

Bramen, Carrie Tirado. "The Americanization of Theron Ware." *Novel: A Forum on Fiction* 31 (1997): 83–86.
Brown, Ira V. *Lyman Abbott, Christian Evolutionist: A Study in Religious Liberalism*. Cambridge, Mass.: Harvard University Press, 1953.
Bruce, Steve, ed. *Religion and Modernization: Sociologists and Historians Debate the Secularization Thesis*. Oxford: Clarendon Press; Oxford University Press, 1992.
Butler, Jon. *Awash in a Sea of Faith: Christianizing the American People*. Cambridge, Mass.: Harvard University Press, 1990.
Butler, Leslie. *Critical Americans: Victorian Intellectuals and Transatlantic Liberal Reform*. Chapel Hill: University of North Carolina Press, 2007.
Cady, Linell E., and Elizabeth Shakman Hurd, eds. *Comparative Secularisms in a Global Age*. New York: Palgrave Macmillan, 2010.
Capozzola, Christopher. *Uncle Sam Wants You: World War I and the Making of the Modern American Citizen*. New York: Oxford University Press, 2008.
Cavert, Samuel McCrea. *The American Churches in the Ecumenical Movement, 1900–1968*. New York: Association Press, 1968.
Charap, Lawrence G. "Imperceptibly We Convert Each Other: Jewish-Protestant Dialogue in America, 1883–1915." PhD diss., Brown University, 2000.
Coffman, Elesha J. *The Christian Century and the Rise of the Protestant Mainline*. New York: Oxford University Press, 2013.
Cohen, Charles L., and Ronald L. Numbers, eds. *Gods in America: Religious Pluralism in the United States*. New York: Oxford University Press, 2013.
Cohen, Lizabeth. *Making a New Deal: Industrial Workers in Chicago, 1919–1939*. Cambridge: Cambridge University Press, 1990.
Coultrap-McQuinn, Susan. "Gail Hamilton (1833–1896)." *Legacy* 4 (1987): 53–58.
Cross, Robert D. *The Emergence of Liberal Catholicism in America*. Cambridge, Mass.: Harvard University Press, 1959.
Curtis, Susan. *A Consuming Faith: The Social Gospel and Modern American Culture*. Baltimore: Johns Hopkins University Press, 1991. Reprint, Columbia: University of Missouri Press, 2001.
Dinnerstein, Leonard. *Antisemitism in America*. New York: Oxford University Press, 1994.
Dolan, Jay P. *In Search of an American Catholicism: A History of Religion and Culture in Tension*. New York: Oxford University Press, 2002.
Dorn, Jacob A. *Washington Gladden: Prophet of the Social Gospel*. Columbus: Ohio State University Press, 1967.
Dorrien, Gary. *The Making of American Liberal Theology: Crisis, Irony, and Postmodernity, 1950–2005*. Louisville, Ky.: Westminster John Knox Press, 2006.
———. *The Making of American Liberal Theology: Idealism, Realism, and Modernity, 1900–1950*. Louisville, Ky.: Westminster John Knox Press, 2003.
———. *The Making of American Liberal Theology: Imagining Progressive Religion, 1805–1900*. Louisville, Ky.: Westminster John Knox Press, 2001.
Ebel, Jonathan H. *Faith in the Fight: Religion and the American Soldier in the Great War*. Princeton, N.J.: Princeton University Press, 2010.
Eck, Diana L. *A New Religious America: How a "Christian Country" Has Become the World's Most Religiously Diverse Nation*. San Francisco: HarperSanFrancisco, 2001.
Evans, Christopher Hodge. *The Kingdom Is Always But Coming: A Life of Walter Rauschenbusch*. Grand Rapids, Mich.: William B. Eerdmans, 2004.
Faust, Drew Gilpin. *This Republic of Suffering: Death and the American Civil War*. New York: Alfred A. Knopf, 2008.
Feldman, Egal. *Dual Destinies: The Jewish Encounter with Protestant America*. Urbana: University of Illinois Press, 1990.

Finke, Roger, and Rodney Stark. *The Churching of America, 1776–2005: Winners and Losers in Our Religious Economy*. 2nd ed. New Brunswick, N.J.: Rutgers University Press, 2005.
Fox, Richard Wightman, and T. J. Jackson Lears, eds. *The Culture of Consumption: Critical Essays in American History, 1880–1980*. New York: Pantheon, 1983.
Giggie, John M., and Diane Winston, eds. *Faith in the Market: Religion and the Rise of Urban Commercial Culture*. New Brunswick, N.J.: Rutgers University Press, 2002.
Gjerde, John. *Catholicism and the Shaping of 19th Century America*. New York: Cambridge University Press, 2012.
Gowing, Peter G. "Newman Smyth and the Congregational-Episcopal Concordat." *Church History* 33 (1964): 175–91.
———. "Newman Smyth: New England Ecumenist." ThD thesis, Boston University, 1960.
Green, Steven K. *The Second Disestablishment: Church and State in Nineteenth-Century America*. New York: Oxford University Press, 2010.
Guth, Christine M. E. *Longfellow's Tattoos: Tourism, Collecting, and Japan*. Seattle: University of Washington Press, 2004.
Hall, David D., ed. *Puritans in the New World*. Princeton, N.J.: Princeton University Press, 2004.
Handy, Robert T. *Undermined Establishment: Church-State Relations in America, 1880–1920*. Princeton, N.J.: Princeton University Press, 1991.
Hart, D. G. *The University Gets Religion: Religious Studies in American Higher Education*. Baltimore: Johns Hopkins University Press, 1999.
Hatch, Nathan O. *The Democratization of American Christianity*. New Haven, Conn.: Yale University Press, 1989.
Hedstrom, Matthew S. *The Rise of Liberal Religion: Book Culture and American Spirituality in the Twentieth Century*. New York: Oxford University Press, 2013.
Herbst, Jurgen. *The German Historical School in American Scholarship: A Study in the Transfer of Culture*. Ithaca, N.Y.: Cornell University Press, 1965.
Higham, John. *Strangers in the Land: Patterns of American Nativism, 1860–1925*. 2nd ed. New Brunswick, N.J.: Rutgers University Press, 1988.
Holifield, E. Brooks. *Theology in America: Christian Thought from the Age of the Puritans to the Civil War*. New Haven, Conn.: Yale University Press, 2003.
Hollinger, David A. *After Cloven Tongues of Fire: Protestant Liberalism in Modern American History*. Princeton, N.J.: Princeton University Press, 2013.
Hsu, Madeline Y. *Dreaming of Gold, Dreaming of Home: Transnationalism and Migration between the United States and South China, 1882–1943*. Stanford, Calif.: Stanford University Press, 2000.
Hutchison, William R. *Errand to the World: American Protestant Thought and Foreign Missions*. Chicago: University of Chicago Press, 1987.
———, ed. *Between the Times: The Travails of the Protestant Establishment in America, 1900–1960*. New York: Cambridge University Press, 1989.
———. *The Modernist Impulse in American Protestantism*. Durham, N.C.: Duke University Press, 1992.
———. *Religious Pluralism in America: The Contentious History of a Founding Ideal*. New Haven, Conn.: Yale University Press, 2003.
Jackson, Carl T. *The Oriental Religions and American Thought: Nineteenth-Century Explorations*. Westport, Conn.: Greenwood Press, 1981.
Jacoby, Susan. *The Great Agnostic: Robert Ingersoll and American Freethought*. New Haven, Conn.: Yale University Press, 2012.
Joiner, Thekla Ellen. *Sin in the City: Chicago and Revivalism, 1880–1920*. Columbia: University of Missouri Press, 2007.

Kinzer, Donald L. *An Episode in Anti-Catholicism: The American Protective Association.* Seattle: University of Washington Press, 1964.
Kittelstrom, Amy. *The Religion of Democracy: Seven Liberals and the American Moral Tradition.* New York: Penguin, 2015.
Kraut, Benny. *From Reform Judaism to Ethical Culture: The Religious Evolution of Felix Adler.* Cincinnati: Hebrew Union College Press, 1978.
———. "Towards the Establishment of the National Conference of Christians and Jews: The Tenuous Road to Religious Goodwill in the 1920s." *American Jewish History* 77 (1988): 388–412.
Kuklick, Bruce. *A History of Philosophy in America: 1720–2000.* New York: Oxford University Press, 2003.
Lane, Christopher. *The Age of Doubt: Tracing the Roots of Our Religious Uncertainty.* New Haven, Conn.: Yale University Press, 2011.
Lee, Erika. *At America's Gates: Chinese Immigration during the Exclusion Era, 1882–1943.* Chapel Hill: University of North Carolina Press, 2003.
Levine, Lawrence W. *Highbrow/Lowbrow: The Emergence of Cultural Hierarchy in America.* Cambridge, Mass.: Harvard University Press, 1988.
Lightman, Bernard. *The Origins of Agnosticism: Victorian Unbelief and the Limits of Knowledge.* Baltimore: Johns Hopkins University Press, 1987.
Luker, Ralph E. *The Social Gospel in Black and White: American Racial Reform, 1885–1914.* Chapel Hill: University of North Carolina Press, 1991.
Marsden, George M. *Fundamentalism and American Culture.* 2nd ed. New York: Oxford University Press, 2006.
Massa, Mark S. "'Mediating Modernism': Charles Briggs, Catholic Modernism, and an Ecumenical 'Plot.'" *Harvard Theological Review* 81 (1988): 413–30.
Masuzawa, Tomoko. *The Invention of World Religions; or, How European Universalism Was Preserved in the Language of Pluralism.* Chicago: University of Chicago Press, 2005.
May, Henry F. *The End of American Innocence: A Study of the First Years of Our Own Time, 1912–1917.* 1959. Reprint, New York: Columbia University Press, 1992.
———. *The Protestant Churches and Industrial America.* New York: Harper, 1959.
McCarraher, Eugene. *Christian Critics: Religion and the Impasse in Modern American Social Thought.* Ithaca, N.Y.: Cornell University Press, 2000.
McGreevy, John T. *Catholicism and American Freedom: A History.* New York: W. W. Norton, 2003.
Menand, Louis. *The Metaphysical Club.* New York: Farrar, Straus and Giroux, 2001.
Miller, Randall M., Harry S. Stout, and Charles Reagan Wilson, eds. *Religion and the American Civil War.* New York: Oxford University Press, 1998.
Mislin, David. "'According to His Own Judgment': The American Catholic Encounter with Organic Evolution, 1875–1896." *Religion and American Culture* 22 (Summer 2012): 133–62.
Moloney, Deirdre M. *American Catholic Lay Groups and Transatlantic Social Reform in the Progressive Era.* Chapel Hill: University of North Carolina Press, 2002.
Montgomery, David. *The Fall of the House of Labor: The Workplace, the State, and American Labor Activism, 1865–1925.* Cambridge: Cambridge University Press, 1985.
Moore, R. Laurence. *Selling God: American Religion in the Marketplace of Culture.* New York: Oxford University Press, 1994.
Moorhead, James H. *American Apocalypse: Yankee Protestants and the Civil War, 1860–1869.* New Haven, Conn.: Yale University Press, 1978.
Morgan, Edmund S. *Visible Saints: The History of a Puritan Idea.* Ithaca, N.Y.: Cornell University Press, 1965.

Morse, Edwin Wilson. *The Life and Letters of Hamilton W. Mabie.* New York: Dodd, Mead, 1920.

Nord, Warren. *Religion and American Education.* Chapel Hill: University of North Carolina Press, 1995.

Paddison, Joshua. *American Heathens: Religion, Race, and Reconstruction in California.* Berkeley: University of California Press for the Huntington Library, 2012.

Painter, Nell Irvin. *Standing at Armageddon: The United States, 1877–1919.* New York: W. W. Norton, 1987.

Piper, John. *The American Churches in World War I.* Athens: Ohio University Press, 1985.

Porterfield, Amanda. *Conceived in Doubt: Religion and Politics in the New American Nation.* Chicago: University of Chicago Press, 2012.

Preston, Andrew. *Sword of the Spirit, Shield of Faith: Religion in American War and Diplomacy.* New York: Alfred A. Knopf, 2012.

Preston, Andrew, Bruce J. Schulman, and Julian E. Zelizer, eds. *Faithful Republic: Religion and Politics in Modern America.* Philadelphia: University of Pennsylvania Press, 2015.

Putney, Cliff. *Muscular Christianity: Manhood and Sports in Protestant America, 1880–1920.* Cambridge, Mass.: Harvard University Press, 2001.

Quinn, John F. *Father Mathew's Crusade: Temperance in Nineteenth-Century Ireland and Irish America.* Amherst: University of Massachusetts Press, 2002.

Roberts, Jon H. *Darwinism and the Divine in America: Protestant Intellectuals and Organic Evolution, 1859–1900.* Madison: University of Wisconsin Press, 1988. Reprint, Notre Dame, Ind.: University of Notre Dame Press, 2001.

Roberts, Jon H. and James Turner. *The Sacred and the Secular University.* Princeton, N.J.: Princeton University Press, 2000.

Rodgers, Daniel T. *Atlantic Crossing: Social Politics in a Progressive Age.* Cambridge, Mass.: Belknap Press of Harvard University Press, 1998.

———. *The Work Ethic in Industrial America.* Chicago: University of Chicago Press, 1978.

Rose, Anne C. *Victorian America and the Civil War.* New York: Cambridge University Press, 1992.

Ross, Dorothy. *The Origins of American Social Science.* Cambridge: Cambridge University Press, 1991.

Rydell, Robert W. *All the World's a Fair: Visions of Empire at American International Expositions, 1876–1916.* Chicago: University of Chicago Press, 1984.

Sarna, Jonathan D. *American Judaism: A History.* New Haven, Conn.: Yale University Press, 2004.

Schmidt, Leigh Eric. *Restless Souls: The Making of American Spirituality.* San Francisco: HarperSanFrancisco, 2005.

Schmidt, Leigh E., and Sally M. Promey, eds. *American Religious Liberalism.* Bloomington: Indiana University Press, 2012.

Schultz, Kevin M. *Tri-faith America: How Catholics and Jews Held Postwar America to Its Protestant Promise.* New York: Oxford University Press, 2011.

Seager, Richard Hughes. *The World's Parliament of Religions: The East/West Encounter, Chicago, 1893.* Bloomington: Indiana University Press, 1995.

Silk, Mark. *Spiritual Politics: Religion and America since World War II.* New York: Simon and Schuster, 1988.

Smith, Christian D., ed. *The Secular Revolution: Power, Interests, and Conflicts in the Secularization of American Public Life.* Berkeley: University of California Press, 2003.

Smith, H. Shelton. *Changing Conceptions of Original Sin: A Study in American Theology since 1750.* New York: Charles Scribner's Sons, 1955.

Stephens, Randall J. *The Fire Spreads: Holiness and Pentecostalism in the American South*. Cambridge, Mass.: Harvard University Press, 2008.
Storch, Neil T. "John Ireland's Americanism after 1899: The Argument from History." *Church History* 51 (1985): 434–44.
Thernstrom, Stephan, ed. *Harvard Encyclopedia of American Ethnic Groups*. Cambridge, Mass.: Belknap Press of Harvard University Press, 1980.
Trachtenberg, Alan. *The Incorporation of America: Culture and Society in the Gilded Age*. 25th anniversary ed. New York: Hill and Wang, 2007.
Turner, James. *Religion Enters the Academy: The Origins of the Scholarly Study of Religion in America*. Athens: University of Georgia Press, 2011.
——. *Without God, without Creed: The Origins of Unbelief in America*. Baltimore: Johns Hopkins University Press, 1985.
Tweed, Thomas A. *The American Encounter with Buddhism, 1844–1912: Victorian Culture and the Limits of Dissent*. Bloomington: Indiana University Press, 1992.
Wacker, Grant. *Heaven Below: Early Pentecostals and American Culture*. Cambridge, Mass.: Harvard University Press, 2001.
Wall, Wendy L. *Inventing the "American Way": The Politics of Consensus from the New Deal to the Civil Rights Movement*. New York: Oxford University Press, 2008.
White, Christopher G. *Unsettled Minds: Psychology and the American Search for Spiritual Assurance, 1830–1940*. Berkeley: University of California Press, 2009.
White, Ronald C., Jr., and C. Howard Hopkins. *The Social Gospel: Religion and Reform in Changing America*. Philadelphia: Temple University Press, 1976.
Wright, C. Conrad. *The Beginnings of Unitarianism in America*. Boston: Beacon Press, 1955.
Yu, Henry. *Thinking Orientals: Migration, Contact, and Exoticism in Modern America*. New York: Oxford University Press, 2001.
Zunz, Oliver. *Making America Corporate, 1870–1920*. Chicago: University of Chicago Press, 1990.

Acknowledgments

I am deeply grateful to Jon H. Roberts at Boston University for his tireless mentorship throughout the writing of this book. Brooke L. Blower, Charles Capper, Barbara Diefendorf, Louis Ferleger, and Bruce Schulman, also at Boston University, commented on the manuscript at various stages of development. Through the generosity of the American Political History Institute, I had the privilege of spending five months at Cambridge University during a critical period in this book's development. While there, Anthony J. Badger, Michael O'Brien, and Andrew Preston provided helpful and thoughtful guidance.

Many other friends and colleagues have offered feedback on various chapters. I am grateful to David Atkinson, Christine Axen, Andrew Ballou, Margaret Bendroth, Kathryn Cramer Brownell, Chris Beneke, Charlotte Carrington-Farmer, Healan Gaston, Sara Georgini, Rachel Gordan, Matthew Hedstrom, Katherine Rye Jewell, Andrew Jewett, Hillary Kaell, Aaron Lecklider, Ronald Numbers, Kip Richardson, Mark Silk, Kevin Schultz, Randall Stephens, and Gene Zubovich. The members of the North American Religion Colloquium at Harvard University and the Boston Historians of American Religion offered valuable advice on this project at various stages of development.

The research for this project benefited enormously from the assistance of numerous librarians and archivists. I am deeply appreciative of the staff members at the Congregational Library, the Pittsburgh Theological Seminary, the Presbyterian Historical Society, the American Jewish Archives, the Library of Congress, the Catholic University of America, the libraries of Bowdoin College and Bates College, and the manuscript collections at Yale's Sterling Library and the Yale Divinity School library. Michael McGandy at Cornell University Press was instrumental in shepherding the manuscript from submission to completion.

I am grateful to the Boston University history department and the American Studies department at the University of Massachusetts–Boston for providing me employment opportunities as I completed this book. The excellent work of Alexis Buckley made it possible for me to focus on the completion of the manuscript. Most recently, I am grateful for the community provided by my current academic home in the Intellectual Heritage program at Temple University, and particularly to Doug Greenfield, Natasha Rossi, and Joseph Schwartz.

Finally, and most important, I offer my heartfelt thanks to family and friends. My mother, Kim Mislin, has offered unwavering love, support, and encouragement through this entire process. John and Susan Russell offered me the use of their guest room for a few weeks in the fall of 2012. They got more than they bargained for over the next two years, but I am extraordinarily grateful for their generosity, which made it possible to bring this project to completion. Carol Bragg, Bill Cran, Jerry Elmer, and Anita, Joshua, and Rebecca Kestin provided thoughtful comments and constant support. Sylvia Ferrell-Jones offered frequent encouragement, as well as needed reminders of the relevance of this project. Last but certainly not least, my husband, Jonathan Elmer, has been constant in his support and encouragement. Words cannot express my gratitude for the hours spent proofreading, the meals prepared, the prodding needed to meet my writing quota for the day, and, most importantly, reminders to step away from the computer screen.

Index

Abbott, Lyman, 4, 29, 31–32, 103; on Catholicism, 64, 70, 74, 78; on Puritans, 87; on racial equality, 159; on religious pluralism, 1–2, 8, 53–56, 59, 107, 109, 138; retirement of, 104; on skepticism, 26, 65
Adams, Henry, 45
Adler, Cyrus, 140, 151
Adler, Felix, 75, 83
African Americans, 17, 159; Ku Klux Klan and, 143, 146, 159, 160; at Parliament of Religions, 59–60. *See also* race
African Methodist Episcopal Church, 59–60
agnosticism, 20–23, 38–39, 79, 104; atheism and, 4, 20, 34, 152, 164; Ingersoll on, 75; James on, 34, 174n84; Kohler on, 74; McConnell on, 26–29; Singer on, 152; Snowden on, 26–27. *See also* skepticism
Ainslie, Peter, 133, 154; on Federal Council of Churches, 139; on Jewish conversion, 158; on Joint Commission on Unity, 127; on World War I, 130, 135
American Association on Religion in Colleges and Universities, 142, 148, 150–52
American Missionary Association, 96
American (Know-Nothing) Party, 66, 112
American Protective Association (APA), 66, 68, 143
Americanist Catholics, 69–71, 77, 114; Leo XIII on, 78, 124
Americanization Committee of Federal Council of Churches, 159–60
Amos Society, 142, 148, 152–55, 157, 161
Anderson, Charles P., 100–101, 127, 131
Andover Seminary, 41
Anglo-Saxonism, 8, 42, 59–61, 143. *See also* race
Anthony, Alfred Williams, 101–2, 141, 146; on anti-Semitism, 145, 160; Federal Council of Churches and, 91, 92, 148–49; on interdenominationalism, 91, 106–7, 122, 131; on Jewish-Christian understanding, 154, 156–57; National Conference of Christians and Jews and, 155
anti-Catholicism, 3, 65–69, 71, 88, 114; Democratic Party and, 69, 145–46; Know-Nothing Party and, 112; Ku Klux Klan and, 143. *See also* Catholicism
anti-Semitism, 66–67, 71, 88, 115, 142–45, 161; Christian groups against, 148–49; of Henry Ford, 143, 145, 149; World War II and, 143, 164. *See also* Judaism
Arnett, Benjamin, 59–60
Arnold, Edwin, 47
atheism, 4; Coe on, 164; Huxley on, 20; James on, 34; Singer on, 152. *See also* agnosticism
Augustine's *Confessions,* 23

Baha'ism, 48
Baker, Newton D., 117
Baker, Ray Stannard, 101
baptism, 83, 111, 128
Barrows, John Henry, 41–44; on denominationalism, 62; on Islam, 47, 52, 53; on religious pluralism, 58–61
Beecher, Henry Ward, 2, 64; on Ingersoll, 19; on interdenominationalism, 96; on skepticism, 25
Benedict XV (pope), 135
Bigelow, William Sturgis, 45
Blaine, James, 66
Blavatsky, Helena, 49
blue laws, 67, 156
Bonney, Charles Carroll, 42
Bradford, Amory, 28, 31, 56
Brent, Charles H., 28, 117, 151, 161; on Christian unity, 131–32, 134, 137, 139, 147; on communism, 133, 145; on internationalism, 134, 135, 147; National Conference of Christians and Jews and, 155; photograph of, 133; World Conference on Faith and Order and, 136
Briggs, Charles Augustus, 90; on children's salvation, 50–51; on Christian unity, 121–23, 125, 126, 137; death of, 126; heresy trial of, 76; on papacy, 126
Brooks, Phillips, 54
Brown, William Adams, 30, 115, 117, 118; on Christian unity, 134, 139
Brownson, Orestes, 80

211

INDEX

Buddhism, 6, 40–44, 49–62, 164; Islam versus, 47–48; Theosophy and, 49; Unitarians and, 75
Bushnell, Horace, 30, 36; on children's salvation, 50; on denominationalism, 96; on skepticism, 25–26

Cadman, S. Parkes, 140, 154
Catholicism, 44, 52, 55, 61–89; Americanist, 69–71, 77, 78, 114, 124; democracy and, 66, 70, 145–46; immigrants and, 5–6, 65–67, 69, 96–97, 143; individualism and, 79–80; interdenominational cooperation with, 93–95, 112, 121, 165; modernist, 125–26; Republican Party and, 69; secularization of, 71–76, 79; social philosophy of, 83–84; temperance movement and, 112–13. *See also* anti-Catholicism
Cavert, Samuel McCrea, 146
Channing, William Ellery, 25, 74, 75, 163
Chase, Mary Catherine, 73
Child, Lydia Maria, 48
Citizens' Reform Association, 112
Civil War, 3, 4, 17, 69, 80
Clinchy, Everett, 162
Coe, George Albert, 33, 35–38, 75; on atheism, 164; on denominationalism, 91–92, 99; on religious pluralism, 53, 54; on secular education, 114; on Social Gospel movement, 81
Columbian Exposition (Chicago 1893), 40–43
Commission on International Justice and Goodwill, 148
communion. *See* Lord's Supper
communism, 105, 115, 160; Jewish supporters of, 143–45; labor unrest and, 97–98, 114, 116; Red Scare of 1919 and, 133, 144, 145
comparative religions, 42, 45–62, 91, 164
Comte, Auguste, 47
Concordat, Congregational-Episcopal, 135, 138, 192n36
Confucianism, 48, 53, 55, 57, 58
Copeland, Royal S., 143
Cosmic Club of Cincinnati, 63
Council of Church Boards of Education, 150–51
creeds, 102–3, 122, 128, 138, 149

Darwin, Charles, 19–20. *See also* evolutionary theory
Day, Jonathan C., 115, 141–42, 145
democracy, 40–41; Catholicism and, 66, 69, 70, 145–46
Dharmapala, Anagarika, 40, 56
divorce, 112

Dodge, Mary Abigail, 52, 87, 121
Du Bois, W. E. B., 159

Elijah (prophet), 51
Emerson, Ralph Waldo, 48
Ethical Culture movement, 75
Evangelical Alliance, 96
evolutionary theory, 2, 5, 19–21; Leo XIII on, 78, 124; New Theology and, 82; Spencer on, 5, 6, 20, 21, 24, 32

Farmer, Sarah, 48, 49, 56
Federal Council of Churches, 11–12, 94, 102–4, 110, 140, 164; Ainslie on, 139; Americanization Committee of, 159–60; Anthony and, 141; on Christian unity, 120–22, 131, 134, 137; Commission on International Justice and Goodwill of, 148; Committee on Goodwill between Jews and Christians of, 142, 148–50, 155–62, 164; Committee on the Rights of Religious Minorities of, 161; creedal statement of, 128; Guild on, 113; as Ku Klux Klan opponent, 146; on League of Nations, 135; during World War I, 105–6, 116, 118, 131
Ford, Henry, 143, 145, 149
Foster, Ora Delmer, 151, 155
Frederic, Harold, 25
Free Religious Association, 48, 56, 57, 75
French Revolution, 3

General War-Time Commission of the Churches, 105–6, 110, 111, 116, 129–30
Gibbons, James, 61, 161; as Americanist Catholic, 69, 77, 78; at Parliament of Religions, 124
Gladden, Washington, 14–16, 26, 31, 104; on Catholicism, 67, 68, 123; on denominationalism, 61–62, 88, 98–100; on faith, 32–33; on individualism, 81; on interdenominationalism, 101–2, 115, 121; on Judaism, 85; Parliament of Religions and, 42, 57; on religious pluralism, 51–53, 55, 74, 77, 130; social philosophy of, 84
goodwill movement between Protestants and Jews, 12, 69–70, 140–42, 148–50, 155–62, 164
Gordon, Elise, 163
Gordon, George, 58; on denominationalism, 108–9, 130, 138; interfaith views of, 74, 163; successor of, 141
Graham, Billy, 165
Great Awakening, Second, 4, 50, 168n17
Great Depression, 161, 164

Greek Orthodox Church, 30, 138, 161
Guild, Roy B., 113, 118

Halliday, Ernest, 158–59
Hamilton, Gail. *See* Dodge, Mary Abigail
Harnack, Adolf von, 30
Harris, George, 21
Haskell, Caroline, 58–59
Haymarket Square riot, 97
heresy trials (Presbyterian), 76–77
Hewit, Augustine, 73, 83, 84
Higginson, Thomas Wentworth, 49, 60; Free Religious Association and, 48, 57, 75
Higher Criticism, 21–22, 30
Hinduism, 6, 41–44, 48, 51–62, 164; pantheism of, 82; Theosophy and, 49; Unitarians and, 75
Hirsch, Emil, 61
Holiness movement, 77
Hoover, Herbert, 133, 144
Hughes, Charles Evan, 140
Huxley, Thomas, 19–20
Hyde, William DeWitt, 91, 92, 100

immigrants, 99, 159–60, 164; Catholic, 5–6, 65–67, 69, 96–97, 143; Jewish, 5–6, 67, 69–70, 96–97, 143
Indiana University, 152
individualism, 79–81, 83, 95
Ingersoll, Robert Green, 18–19, 21, 22, 24; on materialism, 43; skepticism of, 83, 133
Inter-Church Council (Ames, Iowa), 93
internationalism, 134–35, 147
International Workers of the World (IWW), 116
Iowa, University of, 151–52
Ireland, John, 61, 122; as Americanist Catholic, 69–71, 77, 78, 114; evangelism of, 88; on organized labor, 114; on papacy, 126; on progressive revelation, 124, 125; Roosevelt on, 71, 114; on sectarianism, 80; on secularization, 72, 73; social philosophy of, 83–84; on temperance movement, 112–13
Islam, 6, 43, 51–59, 61, 164; Buddhism versus, 47–48; democracy and, 40–41

Jainism, 61
James, William, 33–34
Jesus Christ, 53–54; Buddha and, 47; person of, 29–31, 36, 38, 107–8
Jewish Theological Seminary, 78, 140
Joint Commission on Unity, 127–29
Judaism, 41, 44, 55, 57, 61–89; dietary restrictions in, 70; immigrants and, 5–6, 67, 69–70, 96–97, 143; interdenominational cooperation with, 93–95, 112; Protestant goodwill movement with, 12, 69–70, 140–42, 148–50, 155–62, 164; secularization of, 71–76, 79. *See also* anti-Semitism
juvenile delinquency, 104

Keane, John J., 61, 124; as Americanist Catholic, 69, 70, 77, 78
King James Bible, 3, 114
Know-Nothing Party, 66, 112
Kohler, Kaufmann, 61, 70, 75, 78; on agnosticism, 74; on Christianity, 85, 88
Kohut, Alexander, 78
Ku Klux Klan, 143, 146, 159, 160

Labor Temple (New York City), 115, 141, 145
labor unrest, 97–98, 113–14, 116; Haymarket Square riot, 97; Pullman Strike, 113; during World War I, 105, 115
LaFarge, John, 45
Lambeth Quadrilateral, 128
Lanman, Charles Rockwell, 57
Lausanne Conference, 136
League of Nations, 134, 135, 147
Leeser, Isaac, 69–70
Leo XIII (pope), 83, 84, 127; on Americanist Catholics, 78, 124; on evolution, 78, 124
Lord's Supper, 83, 102, 110, 111, 128, 132
Low, Seth, 121
Lynd, Robert and Helen, 164–65

Mabie, Hamilton Wright, 17–18, 30–32, 45–46, 109, 130
MacEachen, Roderick, 125, 126
Macfarland, Charles, 161
Maha Bodhi society, 56
Maine Interdenominational Commission, 90–92, 100, 102, 103, 107, 141; end of, 164
Manning, William T., 129
marriage, 112
Marshall, Louis, 156, 157
McConnell, Francis, 26–29, 107, 153; on denominationalism, 108; in National Conference of Christians and Jews, 155
McCormick, Theological Seminary (Chicago), 154
McKinley, William, 69, 71
missionaries, 58, 59, 62
Moody, Dwight L., 1, 77
Morganthau, Henry, 161
Morrison, Charles Clayton, 145, 146
Mozoomdar, Protap Chunder, 60
Munger, Theodore, 82

INDEX

National Conference on Christians and Jews, 12, 155, 162, 164
National Divorce Reform League, 112
natural theology, 21
New Theology, 7, 82, 119
New York Federation of Churches, 93
Norton, Andrews, 74

O'Gorman, Thomas, 88
Olcott, Henry Steel, 49
Omar Khayyam, 49
Oregon, University of, 152
"organic unity," 120–22, 137, 139

Paine, Thomas, 23–25
Paley, William, 54
Palmer, A. Mitchell, 144, 145
Palmer, George H., 56
Panic of 1893, 18
papal infallibility, 66, 124, 126
Paris Commune (1871), 3
Parks, Leighton, 26, 27, 38; on missionaries, 58, 62; on pantheism, 82; on religious relativism, 47, 53–55, 62; on Russian Revolution, 144
Parliament of Religions. *See* World's Parliament of Religions
Pershing, John J., 132, 133
Philipson, David, 75, 151; on anti-Semitism, 161–62; Federal Council of Churches and, 148; interfaith views of, 63–64, 78–79, 85–86; on internationalism, 147
Pius X (pope), 126, 127
Potter, Henry, 121
Prentiss, Elizabeth, 26
progressive revelation, 52–53, 57, 103, 124–25
prostitution, 96, 110
Protocols of the Elders of Zion, 143, 145. *See also* anti-Semitism
psychology of religion, 33–35, 174n82
Pullman Strike (1894), 113
Puritans, 4, 23, 87
Putnam, James O., 112

Quakerism, 55

race, 142–44; Anglo-Saxonism and, 8, 42, 59–61, 143; Ku Klux Klan and, 143, 146, 159, 160. *See also* African Americans
Rauschenbusch, Walter, 82–83, 104, 153
Red Scare (1919), 133, 144, 145. *See also* communism
revelation, progressive, 52–53, 57, 103, 124–25
Ritschl, Albrecht, 30

Robinson, William C., 73–74, 123
Rockefeller family, 151, 155
Roosevelt, Franklin D., 155
Roosevelt, Theodore, 2, 66; on discrimination, 68; on inclusiveness, 70, 106; on John Ireland, 71, 114
Russian Revolution (1917), 105, 133, 144–45
Ryan, John A., 155

sacraments, 128
School of Religion at the University of Iowa, 152
Second Great Awakening, 4, 50, 168n17
Sermon on the Mount, 122
Seventh-day Adventists, 101
Simon, Abram, 141, 143, 146–47, 151; on Amos Society, 154; on interfaith efforts, 159; photograph of, 144
Singer, Isidore, 152–57, 161
skepticism, 20–26, 38–39, 79, 91, 164; Abbott on, 26, 65; Beecher on, 25; individualism and, 80–81; Ingersoll on, 75, 83, 133; Kohler on, 74; McConnell on, 26–29. *See also* agnosticism
Smith, Al, 145–46
Smith, Arthur Henderson, 57
Smith, Christian D., 171n23
Smyth, Newman, 3–4, 28–29, 33; anti-Catholicism of, 66, 120; on Christian unity, 120, 122–23, 125–30, 135–39; on individualism, 81; on psychology of religion, 174n82; on socialism, 97; theology of, 30–32, 119, 153
Snedeker, Charles, 63
Snowden, James Henry, 31, 103; on agnosticism, 26–27; on children's salvation, 51; on creeds, 128, 138; on interdenominationalism, 87, 93, 100, 110, 136; on religious pluralism, 49, 69, 85, 87
Social Gospel movement, 7, 81–85, 153
socialism, 97–98, 114. *See also* communism
Spalding, John Lancaster, 122; as Americanist Catholic, 69, 70, 77, 78; on progressive revelation, 124–25; on secularization, 72, 73
Spalding, Martin, 80
Speer, Robert E., 106, 118, 129–30
Spencer, Herbert, 5, 6, 20, 21, 24, 32. *See also* evolutionary theory
spiritualism, 49
St. Joseph's Seminary (New York City), 125
Stafford, Russell, 141
Stanford University, 152
Starbuck, Edwin Diller, 33, 35, 38
Stelzle, Charles, 115

Stoicism, 55
Strong, Josiah, 66, 96
Sumner, William Graham, 20, 37
Sunday, Billy, 77
Sweeney, Helen, 78
Swing, David, 76

Taft, William Howard, 66, 161
temperance movement, 66, 96, 104, 112–13
Tennyson, Alfred, 14
Theosophical Society, 48–49
Tucker, William J., 80
Turner, James, 174n84
Tuskegee Institute, 159

Union Theological Seminary (New York City), 15, 35, 76, 134, 139
Unitarianism, 55, 57, 101; interfaith beliefs of, 74–75, 118
University of California at Los Angeles (UCLA), 152

Van Dyke, Henry, 101, 104; on communism, 145, 160; on internationalism, 134, 147
Vivekananda, Swami, 41
Voltaire, 25

Walker, James J., 140
Ward, Lester Frank, 20, 37
Ward, Mary, 25
Washington, Booker T., 159
Webb, Mohammed Alexander, 40–41, 43, 45, 60
Wells, Ida B., 159
Wheaton College, 77
Willard, Frances, 113
Wilson, Woodrow, 109, 135
Wise, Stephen, 161
World Conference on Faith and Order, 136
World War I, 104–5, 109–10, 115–16; anti-Semitism after, 142–44; Christian unity movement and, 129–36; labor unrest during, 105, 115; papal negotiations during, 135
World War II, 116, 143, 162, 164
World's Parliament of Religions, 40–44, 55–62, 134, 142

Youmans, Edward, 20
Young Men's Christian Association (YMCA), 96

Zahm, John, 78, 124
Zoroastrianism, 41, 58, 61